PRAISE FOR *FROM BACKROOM TO BOARDROOM*

"It's been noted that more than 80 percent of companies are in the midst of their digital transformation, and more than 90 percent are running into major obstacles and roadblocks throughout the process. In her newest book, Dr. Debbie Qaqish has written the manual for marketing operations (MO) leaders and marketing executives to lead the charge in driving successful change with technology, data, process and high-performing teams. In a world where marketers are increasingly accountable for driving revenue and better enterprise-wide decision-making, she clearly lays out where to focus your energy and the pitfalls to avoid. The feedback and quotes from industry professionals throughout the book are great reassurances that we are all fighting the good fight together on this journey."

—DAVID ALEXANDER
vice president of marketing, F5

"Modern marketing leaders are driven by the complex, dynamic and interconnected digital customer. The next-generation performance marketers are now responsible for revenue operations, customer experiences, talent management and a brand's emotional quotient. Dr. Qaqish's book wonderfully explores these elements and more to help you accelerate through the barriers necessary to gain that seat at the table."

—ANAND THAKER
strategic executive advisor and MarTech industry insider

"Dr. Qaqish's engaging, thought-provoking second book is an absolute must-read for marketers and business leaders—from CMOs and marketing execs to marketing operations leaders, both today and aspiring, and all business leaders looking to gain competitive advantage through their marketing function. The role and expectations of marketing organizations have fundamentally changed over the past decade. Marketing leaders that adapt agile, connected and revenue-driven practices are the ones that will succeed in our future economy, but this can only be achieved through a powerful foundation of operational excellence. By diving into the ways marketing operations can help achieve business objectives and overcome challenges faced by today's CMOs while also charting the evolution of marketing technology and the rise of marketing operations, Qaqish presents a clear case for why status quo is no longer an option. The book delivers a fresh perspective and definitive playbook on the critical need and road map to success for creating a best-in-class marketing operations organization. Extensive interviews and commentary by innovative marketing leaders help anchor her perspective and provide a real-world lens on the recommendations. Not to be missed, especially as marketing leaders struggle to adapt to rapid change in their organizations and prove their seat at the executive table."

—JULIA STEAD
chief marketing officer, Allocadia

"Looking for a competitive advantage? Stop passing leads, start passing intelligence. You'll close bigger deals, faster and more efficiently. Look to marketing ops leadership to connect marketing to revenue growth.

For decades, marketing has been passing leads and sales has been rejecting those leads as viable opportunities. It's time to change this age-old process. Lead conversion to opportunity is too low and the cost of selling is too high. A dramatically different approach is required, and the time for transformation is now. It's the role of strategic marketing operations to enable sales and marketing to separate the lead volume noise from the ready-to-buy signal. The noise is slowing us down and wasting resources. The signal reveals late-stage opportunities where our resources are best spent. The solution is to intercept interest through digital signals and convert that intelligence to revenue. This puts marketing operations squarely in the transformation driver's seat. It'll be a bit of a journey, so take this book along for the ride as your road map to deliver value."

—PATTY FOLEY-REID
senior program director, marketing investments and analytics

"This book is a goldmine for B2B marketing executives. The perfect blend of high-level strategy, and the exact tactical blueprint you need to put a marketing operations organization in place. The world of marketing has changed dramatically in recent years. Today's marketing leaders need to be focused on driving revenue. This book provides the framework you need to build a high-performing, modern marketing organization."

—NOREEN ALLEN
chief marketing officer, Bandwidth, Inc.

FROM BACKROOM TO BOARDROOM

THE PEDOWITZ GROUP
DR. DEBBIE QAQISH

EARN **YOUR SEAT** WITH
STRATEGIC MARKETING OPERATIONS

ForbesBooks

Copyright © 2021 by Dr. Debbie Qaqish.

All rights reserved. No part of this book may be used or reproduced in any manner whatsoever without prior written consent of the author, except as provided by the United States of America copyright law.

Published by ForbesBooks, Charleston, South Carolina.
Member of Advantage Media Group.

ForbesBooks is a registered trademark, and the ForbesBooks colophon is a trademark of Forbes Media, LLC.

Printed in the United States of America.

10 9 8 7 6 5 4 3 2 1

ISBN: 978-1-950863-68-6
LCCN: 2021905025

Cover design by David Taylor.
Layout design by Megan Elger.

This custom publication is intended to provide accurate information and the opinions of the author in regard to the subject matter covered. It is sold with the understanding that the publisher, Advantage|ForbesBooks, is not engaged in rendering legal, financial, or professional services of any kind. If legal advice or other expert assistance is required, the reader is advised to seek the services of a competent professional.

Advantage Media Group is proud to be a part of the Tree Neutral® program. Tree Neutral offsets the number of trees consumed in the production and printing of this book by taking proactive steps such as planting trees in direct proportion to the number of trees used to print books. To learn more about Tree Neutral, please visit **www.treeneutral.com**.

Since 1917, Forbes has remained steadfast in its mission to serve as the defining voice of entrepreneurial capitalism. ForbesBooks, launched in 2016 through a partnership with Advantage Media Group, furthers that aim by helping business and thought leaders bring their stories, passion, and knowledge to the forefront in custom books. Opinions expressed by ForbesBooks authors are their own. To be considered for publication, please visit **www.forbesbooks.com**.

CONTENTS

FOREWORD xiii

INTRODUCTION 1

CHAPTER 1 5
PROFILE OF A STRATEGIC MARKETING OPERATIONS LEADER

CHAPTER 2 29
THE CMO CONNECTION

CHAPTER 3 59
THE MARKETING OPERATIONS MATURITY MODEL (MOM)

CHAPTER 4 79
THE EFFICIENT/EFFECTIVE STAGE

CHAPTER 5 .113
THE GET REVENUE STAGE

CHAPTER 6 139
THE CUSTOMER CENTRIC STAGE

CHAPTER 7 173
THE NEXT GENERATION STAGE

CHAPTER 8 195
GET, KEEP AND GROW TALENT

CHAPTER 9 233
THE VALUE OF STRATEGIC MO TO KEY STAKEHOLDERS

CHAPTER 10 251
SETTING IT IN MOTION: NEXT STEPS TO BUILDING A STRATEGIC MO FUNCTION

APPENDIX 269

ENDNOTES 287

FOREWORD

"The island of misfit toys."

That phrase is burned into my memory. Years ago, I remember sitting in the front row at a conference for marketing operations executives. I was jet lagged and undercaffeinated. The speaker on stage, a VP from a major analyst company, was talking about ... to be honest, I don't recall. But then he spoke those words:

"Let's face it: marketing operations has been the island of misfit toys."

The audience, which until then must have been as jet lagged and undercaffeinated as I was in their silence, suddenly burst to life in murmurs and motion—not because they disagreed with that charge but because they felt that way too.

For years, marketing operations was a potpourri of unglamorous tasks that nobody else in the department considered "real marketing." Spreadsheets. Databases. Reports. Gantt charts and org charts. Endless stacks of digital assets that were like the government warehouse scene at the end of *Raiders of the Lost Ark*.

All were necessary for marketing to function. But no one in marketing operations was winning Clio Awards or getting red-carpet treatment at the Cannes Lions festival. Heck, even recognition from senior leadership at one's own company was rare.

But then the world changed.

Over the past decade, there have been two tectonic shifts in marketing as we know it, both the results of the world becoming more digital.

First, the role of technology in marketing went from peripheral to pivotal. Every touch point with prospects and customers is now either delivered through or supported by software. Data is no longer an aggregated afterthought, piles of paper readouts that cause executives' eyes to glaze over. It's the fuel powering the machinery of modern marketing, from the front stage to the backstage, and everything in between.

Managing marketing's technology "stack" and the data flowing through it has become a critical function that now receives C-level executive attention.

Second, the scope of marketing expanded from brand/demand generation to a holistic view of customer experience, from the first touch point through lifetime loyalty. Marketing mechanisms and feedback loops are embedded throughout sales and customer support—and even the product or service being delivered. All of that requires marketing operations and technology to span multiple domains, integrate with multiple systems and coordinate with multiple teams across every corner of the organization.

Marketing is now so much more than the marketing department. We've collided into Peter Drucker's famous quote: "Business has only two functions—marketing and innovation."

Marketing operations is no longer the island of misfit toys. At the best companies, it is now the Pangaea supercontinent, populated by superheroes.

Marketing operations has gone from straggling to strategic. Or, more accurately, marketing operations now has the opportunity to be strategic. To rise, as Dr. Debbie Qaqish eloquently puts it, "from the backroom to the boardroom." But you must seize the moment. You must "earn your seat."

This book is your guide, and Dr. Qaqish is your coach.

You couldn't ask for a better resource on your journey. Dr. Qaqish has spent years leading strategic marketing operations projects and programs for many of the world's best brands. In this book, you'll learn directly from the practices of Microsoft, AMEX, SAP, McKesson, Thomson Reuters and more.

We're entering the golden age of marketing operations and technology.

Embrace it. Shape it. Lead the way. This book will show you how.

SCOTT BRINKER

editor, ChiefMarTec.com
author, *Hacking Marketing*

INTRODUCTION

As a professional marketer, aren't you tired of the "backroom" stigma and being treated as a second-class citizen? Do you believe you are ready and deserve to move up and claim an elevated voice and more strategic role? Then read on, because I wrote these pages for you.

I put this book together because I wanted a tool that could provide inspiration to frustrated and underappreciated marketers. In the chapters that follow, you'll find a vision of what can be and a chance to reimagine, redefine and reinvent the role of B2B marketing. In short, it is a key to a bigger and better future for marketing propelled by what I call "*strategic* marketing operations."

But it's more than just a dream or a lofty thought. Drawing from my years of practical experience and academic research, I've put together a path you can follow to make this new approach a tangible reality in your organization. The method involves understanding the fast-rising role of strategic marketing operations and how this function enables CMOs to drive revenue, harness customer centricity, and lead digital transformation. The path also encompasses recognizing where you currently stand and how to move forward with the right mindset, skill set and tool set.

Of particular importance along this path is a model I've shared time and again with marketing operations that are ready and eager to be more than button pushers. You'll find the model, called the Marketing Operations Maturity (MOM) model, presented in careful detail throughout this book. Think of it as your road map and your guide to earning and keeping that boardroom seat.

Don't just take my word for it. In the book, you'll hear from more than twenty marketing leaders and business executives who have successfully implemented new strategies and up-leveled their organizations. These individuals have not only walked the path, but they also have loaned their time to graciously share their experiences, their achievements and the lessons they've learned along the way.

I spoke with these marketing front-runners while writing this book, and my conversations with them, together with their in-depth insights, are interwoven throughout the chapters. Before beginning, I want to extend heartfelt gratitude to these contributors. Collectively, they are a think tank for our profession. Individually, they are pioneers and change agents for their organizations. Their generosity in sharing their journeys, as well as the good, the bad and the ugly along the way, served to take this book to the next level. They inspired me, and I am confident they will inspire you as well.

A most sincere thank-you to the following contributors: Meaghan Amato, Claudine Bianchi, Scott Brinker, Dan Brown, Heather Cole, Latane Conant, Rachel Cruz, Tom DelMonte, Mitch Diamond, Danny Essner, Stephanie Ferguson, Ashleigh Ford, Brandon Jensen, Jim Lefevere, Kira Mondrus-Moyal, Rohit Prabhakar, Ken Robinson, Abby Ryan, Beki Scarbrough, Alex Simoes, Aron Sweeney, Randy Taylor, Reuben Varella, Kevin Young and Brian Vass.

PROFILE OF A STRATEGIC MARKETING OPERATIONS LEADER

I'll never forget the first time I used the term "button pusher" to describe how some people view the value of marketing operations (MO). It was during a presentation I gave at MarTech West in 2018. As I looked through the bright lights and into the faces of my audience, I could see their immediate and almost visceral response to my comment: *they didn't like it*. Yet for many of those in attendance, that was exactly how their MO group was perceived. Being the button-pusher organization was their reality.

After the presentation, I had multiple conversations with audience members who voiced their irritation and frustration with this perception of their organization. Many expressed how they believed they could do so much more and be so much more, especially in terms of affecting business and driving value. Emotions ran high in these discussions, and I almost felt like a therapist.

During these conversations, I heard the following common thread: MO is an underused and underrealized capability that could have a big impact on revenue, growth, customer centricity and digital transformation. In reality, this concept is widespread, reaching beyond the walls of that 2018 conference. Over the years, I have found it to be prevalent in too many MO organizations.

My story doesn't end there, though. As I reflected on my experiences of talking to and working with marketing executives, I began to analyze and categorize this issue. By doing so, I found the solution to change this perception of MO as "button pushers." I developed a way, in fact, for MO to be a widely used and valued capability that does indeed have a big impact on revenue, growth, customer centricity and digital transformation.

The solution to shift into this bigger role lies in leadership. I bet you thought I was going to say something related to technology. Certainly, technical acumen and access is required. However, the essence of this leap from button pusher to strategic partner is leadership. Think about that for a moment. At its core, leadership is the secret ingredient that can turn MO into a strategic player—and leave its image of button pushers in the past.

THE TIME IS NOW

More importantly, and of particular relevance for this book, is that now is the perfect time for MO to transition into a strategic leader. Marketing—as a discipline, as a practice, as a function, as a competency, and as a capability—is changing. In part, the evolution of marketing correlates to the advancements in technology. At the same time, it is also tied to market shifts and societal upsets such as the pandemic. In this mass of upheaval and confusion, MO can and should be an accelerator, an enabler, and a guide for harnessing change. The shifting atmosphere provides a gateway for MO to evolve and be viewed as a strategic asset for an organization.

When I spoke with Stephanie Ferguson, a corporate vice president at Microsoft, during an interview for this book, she expressed the shift clearly. "When I started, my job was to do digital and experiential marketing," she said. "I was a brand manager. I had to recruit talent. I had to enable sellers, and that was a great job."

Fast-forward to today. "With technology and the need for operations, marketing leadership requirements have evolved," Stephanie explained. Naturally, given those developments, her day-to-day duties now look radically different than they did five years ago. "I am more than a sales enabler," she said. "I'm a business owner. I have accountability."

She's also moved beyond that start as a digital and experiential marketer. "I am actually a customer experience advocate and fan builder," Stephanie told me during our discussion. "I am not a talent recruiter. I am a talent developer because marketing operations talent is hard to get."

More importantly, Stephanie's role as a strategic leader continued to expand. "Before I wasn't a growth innovator. Now I can look at ways to actually grow the business. I have moved from a marketing leader to a marketing transformation leader, and I love that."

Stephanie's description of her role today as a marketing leader is a far cry from the four *P*s (product, price, place and promotion) taught in college marketing

> **Before I wasn't a growth innovator. Now I can look at ways to actually grow the business. I have moved from a marketing leader to a marketing transformation leader, and I love that.**

curricula. Indeed, today's new demands require different skills than in the past. They also create opportunities for MO to move up and take on more of a leadership role.

Moreover, Stephanie's experience reflects a consistent conversation I have every time I speak with an executive. In fact, while carrying out many one-on-one conversations with marketing and MO leaders for this book, two distinct leadership themes became apparent. They are as follows:

- The role of MO leadership is the differentiating factor between a button-pusher organization and one that is viewed and used as a strategic asset for growth.
- The success of the CMO (chief marketing officer) and marketing is highly dependent on the leadership in MO.

The combination of empowering technologies and MO leadership is, for the first time, making it possible to move marketing from the backroom to the boardroom. For this reason, it is an exciting time and is full of opportunities.

> Marketing operations really does give me, as the CMO, incremental credibility. It gives me a stronger narrative to tell what's working, what's not working, where our investments are actually providing returns and how we're thinking about channel optimization. I think about MO as helping me, as a leader, get to that next level and deliver my message with incremental credibility and validity.
>
> **—KEN ROBINSON,** chief marketing officer at Net Documents

In this book, you'll learn what kind of leadership in marketing and MO is required for this new game. You'll see, step by step, how to take marketing from the backroom to the boardroom. The transition involves an evolution of sorts, consisting of the right leadership behaviors, a recognition of the challenges that leaders face today, a gathering of the needed talent and a journey of growth within an organization.

To get started, this chapter focuses on understanding the behaviors of a strategic MO leader. Notice I use the term "behaviors." Traits and characteristics are static constructs. In other words, just because you have them, it doesn't mean you use them. In contrast, I believe leadership is an active role. Leadership is not about your qualifications or what you say you will do. Rather, it is about what you do every day.

PROFILE OF A STRATEGIC MARKETING OPERATIONS LEADER

What sort of career path is needed to become an MO leader today? As I researched this question, I came across an intriguing answer. A large percentage of the strategic MO leaders I interviewed for this book and know through my work did not take a traditional marketing or IT-oriented career path. In addition to having a variety of degrees, the interviewees had diverse work experiences. They had spent time not only in marketing but also in sales, consulting, technology, operations, finance and science. Surprisingly, one interviewee, who is now a marketing leader, began her career with a degree in English. Another interviewee, now a well-respected business leader, first spent four years in book publishing.

Many attributed their career success to the variety in their backgrounds. For more information on their degrees and areas of expertise, see Figure 11:1 ("Interviewees with Advanced Degrees"); Figure 11.2 ("Degrees Held by Interviewees"); Figure 11.3 ("Business Expertise by Degree"); and Figure 11.4 ("Areas of Work Experience") in the appendix. Interestingly, among the leaders I interviewed for this book, 48 percent worked in public companies, 22 percent worked in companies with five hundred or fewer employees, and 30 percent worked in companies with five hundred to one thousand employees. These statistics indicate the importance of a strategic MO organization in companies of all sizes.

While there isn't necessarily a cookie-cutter career path that needs to be taken to become an MO leader, there are certain behaviors common across strategic MO leaders. I discovered these behaviors during my many conversations with the interviewees for this book and also through my own experience working with and developing MO teams and leaders. Based on this research, I formed a profile that outlines six behaviors for the successful strategic MO leader. These behaviors are outlined in Figure 1.1, "Six Behaviors for the Successful Strategic MO Leader":

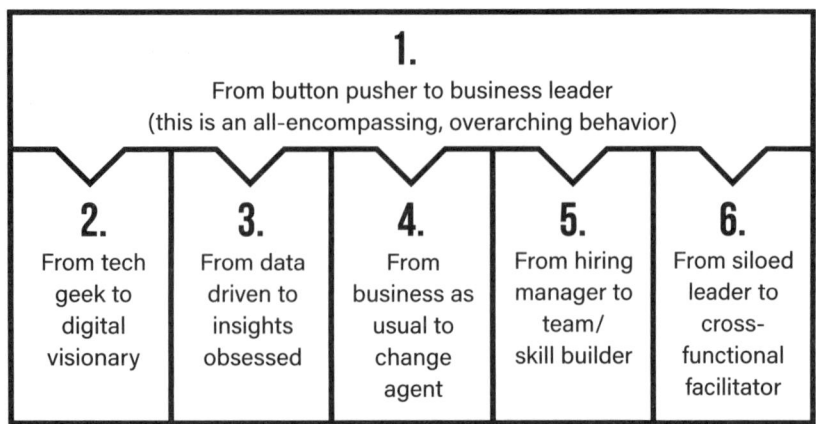

FIGURE 1.1

In the following sections, I'll share a closer look at each of these behaviors. By putting them together, you'll gain a full picture of how to be a strategic MO leader today. And for all the CMOs reading this book, these are the people you will want to hire.

FROM BUTTON PUSHER TO BUSINESS LEADER

If you're still reeling from the "button-pusher" story I shared at the beginning of this chapter, I have good news. I'm going to shatter that misconception, and it starts with the first behavior on my list: being a business leader. Let's first clarify the difference between a manager and a leader. Then I'll discuss the specifics of business leadership for MO.

A manager has people working for them. A leader, however, has people following them. Notice the difference? The first action is required, while the second action is voluntary. To step up as a leader means you provide vision, focus, motivation, inspiration, a collective identity and an environment for achievement. You are transparent, passionate, and committed and an excellent communicator. You have people who believe in you as a leader. Without followers, a leader cannot exist.

A business leader has an extensive understanding of the business as a whole. She recognizes the role her organization plays in achieving high-level goals. Her organization is part of the strategic planning process and has a respected voice in shaping, tweaking, and driving strategy. The MO leader as a business leader is proactive in thinking about the business and bringing new solutions to the table.

In an interview, Brandon Jensen, director of marketing at Juniper Networks, shared, "We have evolved from button pushers to thinking about how we should run the business and how we should think about the business."

The business-oriented MO leader lets the world know that they are much more than button pushers. They engineer marketing performance and the attainment of business goals through their combined business acumen, technology and data expertise. Outside of marketing, they are connected to and understand how the company works. They know how to create partnerships. Taking all together, they have the ability to create business insights that can better inform product decisions, funding decisions, new strategies and sales pursuits.

> **We have evolved from button pushers to thinking about how we should run the business and how we should think about the business.**

Having a business mindset produces valuable results. The process, however, doesn't occur overnight. When I spoke with Brandon Jensen of Plex Systems, he discussed this evolvement. "It takes some maturity to get to the point where others look to you for advice," he said. "In the past, I told my team, 'I don't want you to be task monkeys. You need to be strategic in the way you approach the business, so that we can be a value to the organization. We should be able to say no to things and give reasons why, such as it doesn't move the business forward as efficiently or in a direction of the goals that we have.'"

Over time, as Brandon led his team with this approach, others took notice. He told me, "Now, people come to us for advice a lot more rather than just asking, 'Can you give me this report?' or 'Can you build this campaign in your marketing automation platform?'"

Today's changing marketing needs make now the ideal time to shift into a business-minded leader. While exciting, being a business leader is a complex undertaking. In the next sections, I'll break down the five sub-behaviors that fall under this overarching behavior. Together, they will help you form a clear picture of how to be a strategic MO leader in action.

FROM TECH GEEK TO DIGITAL VISIONARY

I've worked in the technology space for most of my career. During that time, I've had the pleasure of meeting more than one digital visionary. All the digital visionaries I've crossed paths with have a few abilities in common. They understand both current and future technology. They can see its potential to transform a business, to build competitive advantage and to win in the digital age. They all know how to practically apply technology to build a better business. In fact, more and more companies are hiring digital transformation officers to do precisely this.

> With the latest technologies, marketing operations can actually see which strategies are creating business ... and this insight should certainly be going to the C-suite.
>
> —CLAUDINE BIANCHI, chief marketing officer at Zoovu

Acting as a digital visionary is a vital role played by the MO leader. Having this behavior is also necessary to up-level to a strategic MO organization. Now is an optimal time for the MO leader to take on this strategic responsibility. Digital transformation in marketing and across organizations is considered a matter of business survival. In 2020, 97 percent of business leaders stated COVID-19 had sped up their digital transformation efforts.[1] Moreover, 79 percent said COVID-19 increased the budget for digital transformation.[2]

These trends create the perfect opportunity for the MO leader. Companies are hungry for both knowledge and leadership to compete more effectively. MO leaders can step forward to harness technology and data to pursue business goals. They can shed the tech geek persona, which is transactional and reactionary. They can replace it with a leadership style that is proactive, change oriented and highly strategic. These attributes lead to both a seat and a voice at the table.

DUAL ROLE IN DIGITAL TRANSFORMATION

The strategic MO leader plays a dual role in digital transformation. First, this type of leader works closely with the CMO to create, sell and execute digital transformation in marketing. A hallmark of their success is to move marketing from a cost center to a revenue and growth center. Therefore, a strategic MO executive blends a deep understanding of current and future technologies, a passion for culling insights from data, a focus on the end-to-end customer journey and a business approach to drive digital transformation within marketing.

Second, the strategic MO leader often works with a cross-functional team on the digital transformation of the wider business. In some situations, marketing transforms before the rest of the company. When this happens, marketing has an incredible opportunity to provide unique knowledge, experience and leadership in business transformation.

I spoke with Heather Cole, vice president of enterprise marketing products and solutions at AMEX, about her experiences with driving broadscale transformation. To do so, she advised setting a clear strategic vision you can easily articulate. She also discussed bringing in others early. "When I stepped in to lead this function, it was a collection of multiple teams from across the company that had been brought together into a center of excellence, but each team was at a different level of MO maturity," she said. "We set out on an ambitious transformation road map to make our MO function significantly more unified, efficient and customer centric. To be successful, you cannot underestimate the importance of having a common vision, sharing that vision often and ensuring buy-in to that vision."

Also keep in mind that transformation takes time and is a journey, not a destination. "When it comes to transformation, it doesn't mean everything all at once," Stephanie shared. "It's a journey that you've probably never been on, but I think the key thing to do is to look at it and ask, 'Where can I bite something off and show results?' Then you show some early results and look for the next place where you can show more results."

> **To be successful, you cannot underestimate the importance of having a common vision, sharing that vision often and ensuring buy-in to that vision.**

FROM DATA DRIVEN TO INSIGHTS OBSESSED

For years marketers have heard the refrain, "It's all about data." Actually, this statement is not true. Actionable insight is what allows any part of the business to take immediate and appropriate action. The strategic MO leader is charged with making this a reality. Given the customer-driven and digital world we live in, it is a powerful deliverable that can immediately up-level MO and marketing in the business.

> When I took over as the leader of MO for SAP, the first thing my boss, the head of North America marketing, said to me was, "You know, if you could do one thing, get better at insights."
>
> **—TOM DELMONTE,** head of North America marketing operations at SAP

Being insights obsessed begins with a basic data foundation of quality, cleanliness, relevance, governance, network and normalization. Creating this set of actions is often a huge hurdle for a marketing organization and one they must overcome. A strategic MO leader takes this foundation of good data and elevates it to a platform that generates actionable insights. As a result, marketing becomes a repeatable, predictable and scalable (RPS) revenue machine. It also allows other parts of the company to make data-driven decisions in ways they could not before.

The strategic MO leader's first action (after cleaning data) is to instill the data/insight obsession. They then implement it into all parts of the marketing organization. They work with the entire marketing team to help them embrace, use and take responsibility for the quality and analysis of the data available to the marketing team. They work to democratize data by helping the marketing team see the power and the possibilities derived from making data-driven decisions. They work with marketing to help them turn data into insights to improve the performance of marketing. "It's been a little bit painful for people, but the data tells the story," Brandon Jensen of Plex Systems told me. "It just helps us get better at the business, and pivot faster than we otherwise would have."

Beyond the marketing team, today's CMO cannot do their job without a strategic MO leader who is providing both data and business insights. The CMO is on the hot seat in executive and board meetings. I've seen these board presentations change radically as the CMO shares data and data-derived insights rather than guesses. The result is a game changer for marketing, as it builds validity and credibility with executives.

I sat down and talked with Abby Ryan, global director of marketing operations at SAP Concur, about data-derived insights. Part of the validity and credibility for MO comes from how the data and insights are sourced, she noted. "I think there is a tendency for people to show the best-looking data that they can, especially when money is involved," Abby explained. "Within the marketing ops function, because we're not the ones creating the programs, nor are we beholden to pipeline targets, we're able to just tell it like it is. That's really powerful, because it's actionable data."

CUSTOMER DATA IS KING

Chief among all kinds of data is customer data. As more companies pivot to being customer focused, marketing is sitting on a gold mine of data waiting for someone to arrive with an excavator. Powerful data is essential to inform working knowledge of the customer, including digital body language and demographic data kept within marketing systems. Having the right data aids the creation of personas, segments, messaging and actions. Moreover, it updates your knowledge of the end-to-end customer journey and key actions required along the way for all customer-facing parts of the company.

I have been in countless organizations that talk about being customer focused, yet they rarely look at the behavioral data of prospects and customers at their fingertips. Being insights obsessed is like being a miner: you find the data, process the data and create insights that are of value to the company.

> I'm not asking for dashboards. I'm asking for actionable insights.
>
> —ROHIT PRABHAKAR, vice president of digital marketing at Thomson Reuters

Data will continue to be a challenge for the strategic MO leader. I have never seen a company at which this was not true, and I don't expect to anytime soon. Many of the MO leaders I interviewed advised ensuring that you have a strong data analysis capability on your team. You need this strategic capability, and it isn't possible to borrow from another function.

FROM SINGLE-TRICK PONY TO A PROCESS ENGINEER

One of the most exciting aspects of the strategic MO leader is their role as a process engineer. MO has a unique view and a data-driven approach that allows them to link and optimize processes in marketing and across other functional areas such as sales and customer success. The best example I can think of for this is the lead management process.

For years, both marketing and sales have been frustrated by their inability to get on the same page in terms of lead flow and lead processing. Marketing works hard to produce high-quality leads that are often dismissed by sales. You know the story.

In contrast, there is something almost magical when the strategic MO leader takes over reengineering this core process. First, MO brings immediate credibility into any conversation with sales. Using data rather than gut intuition, they can make a case for change and demonstrate the benefit to sales. Second, the MO leader takes a project management approach, minus all the drama and emotion, in figuring out what is wrong and what they need to do to fix it. The net result is that the lead management process—a core element to the revenue engine—becomes repeatable, scalable and predictable (RPS). I consider this one of the strategic MO leader's most critical successes.

Lead management is only one process that I've seen MO take on, get buy-in to the changes and drive more value from the business. Other core processes include the buyer journey, personas and customer centricity. As more and more companies make the pivot to become customer centric, this is a big opportunity for the strategic MO leader. (More about this later in the book.)

Process is key above all: that's the point Danny Essner, vice president of revenue marketing at Sisense, Inc., made when I spoke with him. "A pitfall for many marketers is they fall into the 'This is really cool technology' trap," he explained. "There is a lot of bright, shiny stuff, and I understand the lure. It is easy to get overwhelmed. I say don't let the technology get ahead of process. Sit back, offline, with pen and paper and find out what your business processes are, and then determine which technology will best optimize that process." Taking this step can be done in partnership with sales. "Then let the technology mold to support these policies rather than have the technology drive processes," Danny said.

FROM BUSINESS AS USUAL TO CHANGE AGENT

Change and the acceleration of change are the only constants in our world today, and nowhere is this truer than in the technology sector. The implementation of any single piece of technology introduces a modification—either in a process or in how someone does their job. Layer on big data, more technology, more stakeholders, and more complexity in business and the number one job of any leader now becomes to manage change. For the strategic MO leader, she is often leading the charge and helping multifunctional stakeholders adopt the change.

I don't use the term *change agent* casually, although it is often glossed over or downplayed as a critical activity. Let's look at the definition of a change agent to see what is involved.

First, a change agent can be someone from inside or outside the company. For the MO organization, I most often see the MO leader in this role. Next, being a change agent goes well beyond normal reporting structures. She is a catalyst who influences change through vision and inspiration. A change agent is constantly promoting the *why* of the change and enabling the change down to an individual level. Essentially, she shows how to make things better.

While technology and process are parts of the change, a change agent also focuses on the people aspect. Employees have to internalize and adopt the change. Working at an individual level, the change agent must identify and address prevalent attitudes and behaviors that could hinder change. She must also be aware of the organizational culture that could get in the way. As Peter Drucker said, "Culture eats strategy for breakfast."

The strategic MO leader is perfectly positioned to be a change agent. She has diversified knowledge of the company, leads the reengineering of processes, owns the technology and the data and is results-driven. "I would say the role of marketing ops for me is as much being my partner as being a change agent for the marketing team," said Latane Conant, chief marketing officer at 6sense, during an interview for this book.

THE BEST CHANGE MANAGEMENT TOOL: COMMUNICATION

One critical element to any change management is communication. Over the last ten years, I have seen the need for this skill skyrocket. Marketing has left the ivory tower and now works in a cross-functional, collaborative environment knit together by technology, data and process. Furthermore, COVID-19 led to an increase in virtual working environments, which further heightens the need for improved communications.

To be a successful change agent, the strategic MO leader must communicate at a master level. The communication must also be tailored for each "persona" or key stakeholder group the leader is trying to influence. I often counsel any change leader to act like a politician with a platform and a stump speech. They need to deliver that speech as many times as possible, to as many people as possible, in whatever venue is possible. Many clients I work with actually create a persona-based communication plan and strategy to ensure everyone is aligned.

> I have passion for looking at that broader picture, driving change management and then figuring out, "How do we smartly, operationally do this?"
>
> **—STEPHANIE FERGUSON,** corporate vice president at Microsoft

FROM HIRING MANAGER TO TEAM/SKILL BUILDER

The essential differences between being a hiring manager and being a team and skill builder consist of vision and time horizon. As a hiring manager, you live in a world that is well ordered. Job descriptions are in place. Roles are defined and have specific places on the team. In contrast, a team/skill builder works with a vision of the future, and things are not so clear. New job descriptions may need to be written, and roles and responsibilities might be more fluid. Flexibility, agility and outside-the-box thinking are required to meet the ever-changing needs of the business. Hiring managers deliver for the current requirements. Team/skill builders are delivering for the future.

Team and skill building are important both for the success of MO and for marketing overall. They are so vital, in fact, that an entire chapter (see page 195) is dedicated to this topic. From finding, getting and keeping the right talent, to training and reorganizing around a new way to do business, the strategic MO leader spends an inordinate amount of time building a team and gathering the right set of skills. In all my interviews and work with MO leaders, talent is often cited as a top challenge. Why? Because finding technical, analytical, marketing and business skills in one person is difficult.

Team building is expressed in a number of ways, including the actual organizational structure itself. For the MO organization, there is a wide variation in team structure, although the more mature the organization, the more consistent the team composition. More than any other part of marketing, I see constant changes in the MO team structure. We are really still in the Wild West days of MO as a capability. Thus, the MO function is highly defined by the evolving needs of marketing, the needs of the company, and where talent is located. As a result, any MO leader spends a lot of time tweaking the structure.

Looking at a team structure on paper is easy, but building it out is often problematic. The strategic MO leader must determine how to fill in the boxes, which involves making decisions about renting, buying or training talent (or some combination of those). Renting skills short term can help reduce the time to results and provide a training opportunity for less-skilled employees, but there may be problems with bringing in outside talent. Buying talent provides immediate benefit but can be very expensive, and training just takes time. In addition, I have yet to see anyone do training well. (For a deeper dive into talent management, see page 215).

When building talent, "focus on the strength of the team," said Ashleigh Ford, senior marketing manager at Trend Micro, during a recent conversation. "Figure out where their aptitude is, what their passion is, and let them grow. Then encourage them with training and sales. MO professionals are in high demand, and you want to make sure they are happy and that they are growing their career. To do this, you must provide an environment that helps them foster ideas and growth while supporting their passions and strengths."

Another aspect of team building is cross-team integration. I've seen MO leaders build amazing MO teams and then fail because they were not fully integrated with marketing. A particular challenge arises if the MO group reports to IT and not to marketing. At the end of the day, the MO group is a services organization and partners with marketing.

> You need to be the type of leader that can mentor and train and challenge and raise people up in their careers.
>
> —**BRIAN VASS**, vice president of revenue operations at Paycor

One final aspect regarding training and skill building: I often see MO helping the other parts of marketing with data. MO can show these groups how to understand and use data to make more data-driven decisions. I believe this kind of marketing enablement is critical to the success of the entire organization.

FROM SILOED LEADER TO CROSS-FUNCTIONAL FACILITATOR

I've observed an interesting phenomenon in marketing organizations: they have two different organizational charts. One is the traditional chart, which indicates who leads each part of marketing and who reports to whom. The second is not a traditional chart. Instead, it entails mapping a network of collaborative, cross-functional working relationships. In other words, it shows who needs to work with whom to get something done. I call this a collaborative network.

Let's consider an example of that second chart. Say a company has a vice president of marketing operations who is responsible for reengineering the lead management process. Unfortunately, the traditional way marketing approaches lead management is to get into a room and map it out. In this case, no one outside of marketing is involved. In addition, the process is not based on data but rather on gut feelings. When this initiative is led by MO, I see more stakeholders incorporated into the process. MO works with sales leadership, sales, insides sales, customer success and sales operations. Essential parts of marketing beyond MO include demand generation and field marketing. MO orchestrates the development and implementation of lead management by involving all the key stakeholder groups.

Facilitating and involving these cross-functional working relationships can help create smooth processes and avoid obstacles. When I talked to Rohit Prabhakar of Thomson Reuters, he explained that there is a line that blurs between digital ops and sales ops. "It is the line where the martech systems connect with the CRM [customer relationship management] system, and the martech systems connect with ERP [enterprise resource planning] systems," he said. "That's the line where you have to have strong collaboration with your partners on the other side."

As a result of this collaborative process, change affects people both within marketing and outside of marketing. Collaboration often begins in areas of technology, data and process design and continues into the rollout and optimization. People are much more likely to adopt change if they are part of the change process early.

For Dan Brown of Verint, the collaboration role has become so important that he has a dedicated role to fulfill this function called senior analyst, marketing collaboration. Responsibilities include defining the vision, strategies and objectives for marketing collaboration. Other tasks involve analyzing all current means of collaborating both within the marketing function as well as between marketing and other key stakeholder groups. By establishing a collaboration process and technical framework, cross-functional communication is improved. Overall, a sense of teamwork develops.

> I think you need to be the type of leader that can collaborate and partner well with sales and marketing have an understanding and respect for sales and an understanding and respect for marketing.
>
> —**BRIAN VASS**, vice president of revenue operations at Paycor

One final word about collaboration: It must be intentional. In some companies I have worked with, the marketing ops team has a collaboration structure. The setup is similar to an organizational structure but is based on collaboration. The structure delineates all the key relationships, who is responsible, the goals of the relationship, and how to drive the relationship.

A TIME TO LEAD

The time for MO to step forward as a strategic player is now. The changes in marketing, coupled with the evolving roles of MO and its key position to support the CMO's success, create the perfect opportunity for MO to be seen as much more than a button pusher. By putting these behaviors into action, you can be a strategic MO leader within your organization.

In the following pages of this book, you'll learn how to completely fill out that leadership role. The next chapters will take you on a journey to help you understand the challenges CMOs face today and how those obstacles create opportunities for MO to move up. You'll also learn how to build a strategic MO organization and put it into action. I'll introduce an MO maturity model so you can evaluate exactly where you are and what you need to do next. Along the way, I'll point out the skills required for a strategic MO organization and how to develop the right team. Finally, I'll show you what lies ahead and how to put all these lessons into action to succeed.

Let's move on to understand the CMO challenges of today and define the strategic MO.

CHAPTER SUMMARY

A QUICK GLANCE AT WHAT WE LEARNED

- This book is about leadership and will show you how to get marketing a seat at the table.

- MO leadership continues to rapidly evolve and play a key role in company performance.

- The success of the CMO is tied to the leadership in MO.

- The strategic MO leader acts as a business leader, not a button pusher.

- As a business leader, the strategic MO leader acts as a digital visionary, turns data into insights and is a process engineer, change agent, team/skill builder and cross-functional facilitator.

CHAPTER 2

THE CMO CONNECTION

Every executive I know is consumed with how to do business in the digital economy. Their obsession is understandable: technology has forever changed both our personal lives and our professional practices. Advances in technology have been so life altering that what worked in the past no longer is useful, especially in today's engagement economy. Furthermore, those previous uses won't be applicable in the future. Essentially, old ways of addressing competition, working with customers, driving revenue and ensuring profit margins are out the window.

In this uncertain and constantly evolving environment, marketing has more opportunity than ever before. There is a chance to reimagine and reinvent the role and value of marketing to the business—in short, to step up and get that seat at the table.

For marketing to take advantage of this opportunity, two elements need to be in play:

- The right kind of MO leader and MO organization
- The right kind of CMO

In chapter 1, I talked about the right kind of MO leader. In later chapters I go into detail about the MO organization. In this chapter, I'll explore what's going on with the role of the CMO. If you are going to transform into a strategic MO leader and organization, it is imperative you understand CMO pressures and expectations.

I'll start by delving into the three main challenges CMOs face in today's environment. Then I'll explain what CMOs are doing to overcome these obstacles and perform at a high level. To help you understand these strategies, I'll share some key findings from my doctoral studies pertaining to this topic. Along the way, I'll show the connection between the need for a strategic MO leader and MO organization for the CMO to be successful. Let's begin with a look at the CMO's three big initiatives.

THE CMO'S THREE BIG CHALLENGES

The emergence of marketing operations as a strategic marketing capability is partially driven by three game-changing CMO obligations (see Figure 2.1, "Three CMO Challenges"). These main duties are laid out in the following list:

- Drive credible revenue and growth—grow revenue.
- Define and execute the vision for digital transformation—go digital.
- Lead and implement the pivot to customer centricity—engage customers.

THREE CMO CHALLENGES

FIGURE 2.1

Notice that growing revenue is in the center of Figure 2.1, "Three CMO Challenges." Driving revenue and growth ("Grow Revenue") is the result that matters the most for today's CMO. Digital transformation ("Go Digital") is the foundation required to achieve the result and customer centricity ("Engage Customers") is the accelerant to get to the result.

I see validation of the CMO's three challenges in almost all of my interactions with marketing leaders, including the interviewees for this book. All their comments and insights revolve around these three challenges.

Let's look at some quick definitions and the interplay of the three challenges:

- Revenue accountability—"Grow Revenue"—signifies that marketing is an equal partner on the revenue team and has a responsibility to drive pipeline and revenue growth, repeat business and improved margins. The mindset of the marketing organization is that they are revenue marketers responsible for revenue and growth. They run marketing like a business with a P&L approach.

- Digital transformation—"Go Digital"—is the adoption of digital technology to transform services or businesses through replacing nondigital or manual processes with digital processes.

- Customer centricity—"Engage Customers"—is defined as a company-wide competence to sense and respond to customer needs in almost real time. Marketing plays a key role in developing and executing this competency. The mindset is that marketing has ditched the funnel view and instead has adopted a holistic customer journey view to the business of marketing.

As you consider the three challenges, know that they do not stand alone. They are intertwined and have dependencies on how they interact.

Let's now take a closer look at each of the CMO's challenges. I'll start with some more insight into what goes into that main challenge of driving revenue and growth. Then I'll branch into the initiatives I laid out that support this revenue need: digital transformation and customer centricity.

CMO CHALLENGE 1: DRIVE REVENUE AND GROWTH (GROW REVENUE)

The earliest and still most pervasive of the three CMO responsibilities is revenue accountability ("Grow Revenue"). You probably wish it was digital transformation. Trust me, it is driving revenue and growth. Here's why: if marketing can't do this right, they will forever be a second-class citizen. At the end of the day, it doesn't matter how cool of a martech stack you have accumulated. If what you do doesn't help enable and drive credible revenue growth, get ready for a job change—right along with your CMO.

I am unclear on how you can do your job as a CMO if you do not have financial accountability. Thinking more about it, if you do not have financial accountability as a CMO, I do not think that you will be a CMO for a long time in the organization.[3]

The constant and growing pressure for revenue results gives many B2B CMOs sleepless nights and anxiety-filled days. In fact, over 80 percent of CMOs state they feel enormous pressure to show financial results. Only a third, however, report items such as revenue and ROI.[4] Yet marketing is drowning in revenue-enabling technology and data. Both are essential elements to revenue accountability.

The Importance of Having a Number

> **I am unclear on how you can do your job as a CMO if you do not have financial accountability. Thinking more about it, if you do not have financial accountability as a CMO, I do not think that you will be a CMO for a long time in the organization.**

I've talked with many marketing operations leaders about this issue. In our conversations about revenue accountability, I typically hear phrases like "I make it possible" or "We enable the tools and processes so marketing can get to revenue." These responses most commonly occur when the CMO does not have a quota or revenue number and marketing operations is focused on operational metrics.

Now compare those thoughts with a recent situation I came across. I was working with an MO leader and asked him for his current mission statement. He told me it was to "create an environment that allows the global marketing team to operate efficiently and effectively, achieve optimal results and drive revenue."

I learned from him that his mission statement during the previous year had not contained "and drive revenue." I asked him about the impact of adding those three words. He told me marketing operations was now considered an engine for change in implementing company strategies. Moreover, his CMO now had a number to deliver.

> The overall marketing department plan was based on numbers, and so everything in marketing had that number as part of their performance objectives.
>
> **—MITCH DIAMOND,** senior director of marketing operations at SAP Ariba

Note the difference between this MO leader's situation and the previous common conversations I mentioned. *Having* a number rather than *enabling* a number requires marketing operations to act strategically. For example, a strategic MO group tasked with driving revenue might add a revenue analyst to the mix. A revenue analyst is a special data analyst who looks at all the data throughout the entire customer life cycle and identifies areas with the biggest revenue potential and ROI. She helps marketing target those areas. The mindset is very different compared to simply analyzing data.

I'm sure you have frequent conversations with your board and senior executive team on adopting revenue accountability. You might discuss a quota, pipeline contribution or leads sent to sales. In some cases, you may already have a quota (or the marketing team has a quota), and you have revenue accountability. In other instances, you may not have direct accountability, but you know it's coming. In both cases, the pressure is immense. If you believe neither of these scenarios apply to you or your team, pull your head out of the sand.

It's vital for the CMO to adopt financial accountability. Marketing can no longer work on tactics that result in no measurement or "fuzzy math." Companies will not hire CMOs who can't "speak in numbers." If CMOs operate in a traditional sense, they will find themselves extinct.[5]

CMOs Rely on Strategic MO to Drive Revenue

Business-savvy CMOs can envision marketing as the economic and growth engine for the company. They use the strategic MO capability to bring this vision to life. With a strategic marketing operations function in place, the CMO's ability to deliver credible revenue results is enabled, amplified and accelerated. The MO team has a strategic purpose and use, which indicate that technology and data contribute significantly to marketing. In turn, marketing plays a key role in the business.

When I spoke with Dan Brown, vice president of marketing operations at Verint, he discussed this exact relationship. He shared with me a recent conversation he had carried out with his CMO. In it, his CMO expressed, "I cannot imagine doing my job and hitting my numbers without our marketing operations team."

CMO CHALLENGE 2: DIGITAL TRANSFORMATION (GO DIGITAL)

First, let's be clear. Digital transformation is now a strategic imperative, not something that is just "nice to have." While 87 percent of companies view digital transformation as a way to create competitive advantage, 27 percent of senior executives call it "a matter of survival."[6]

Let's also recognize that even with this level of importance to the future of the business, executives estimate they are only 25 percent finished with their switchover.[7] Digital transformation is at the top of every CEO's Christmas list.

For the CMO, the recent pandemic has put this challenge into overdrive. In 2020, 97 percent of business leaders said COVID-19 had sped up their digital transformation efforts (68 percent said by a great deal).[8] The trend brings more budget and more focus on all things digital. In addition, 79 percent of business decision makers said COVID-19 resulted in an increased budget for digital transformation.[9] And marketing is seeing a 10 percent increase in budgets for digital marketing.[10]

Marketing's Opportunity to Be Strategic

There is a bright spot in this accelerated scenario. Think about it: marketing was engaged in digital transformation before it was cool. The rise of marketing automation and other marketing technologies ushered in early use of digital technology to change how marketing addressed the marketing mix. More importantly, the rise of the marketing operations capability in response to the need for marketing to transform digitally can now serve as a wider digital transformation across the company. Keep in mind, however, that this can only take place *if* it is a strategic MO group. The role of a *strategic MO* operation is essentially to use technology and data to create new business models for how marketing responds to a rapidly changing business environment. In many companies, marketing's early use of digital technology is now becoming a proof point for wider digital transformation.

By taking MO's knowledge, experience and skills and including them in the wider digital transformation initiative, an organization can jump-start its digital transformation. A company can reduce the time needed to digitally transform. Moreover, MO can serve as a core part of the digital transformation team. MO can provide invaluable lessons around technology, data and processes. Some of these insights include the following:

- A description of the biggest integration issues
- How to work with data
- How to drive use of technology
- How to measure the impact of the technology
- How to optimize processes
- How to manage the change to digital

CMO'S CHALLENGE 3: CUSTOMER CENTRICITY (ENGAGE CUSTOMERS)

CEOs are waking up to the reality that we live and work in the customer engagement economy. Ultimately, the customer is in control. Companies are pivoting from being product centric to being customer centric. Customer experience is the new competitive battleground. In 2020, customer experience was estimated to overtake price and product as the brand differentiator.

Plus, customer experience pays big. Who wouldn't want to see a 42 percent improvement in customer retention? Or a 33 percent improvement in customer satisfaction? What about a 32 percent improvement in cross-selling and upselling?[11] All of those are possible when a business shifts its focus to the customer.

The pandemic has shed a spotlight on both the need for accelerated digital transformation and the need for accelerated customer focus. New customer behaviors require new business models—now.

Customers are online more than ever. They expect optimal customer experiences, no matter whom they are dealing with. Among marketers, 83.8 percent said in 2020 that their customers were placing more importance on digital interactions.[12] Salespeople have been somewhat disintermediated from customers. Thus, marketing is picking up the slack by creating digital relationships.

As a result, marketers have shifted focus. To shed further light on this, consider the following: in 2020, 60.8 percent of marketers reported shifting resources to build better customer interfaces. Marketers also indicated they are focusing more on customer retention than on net-new customer acquisition. To further support this shift to customer centricity, 95 percent stated they were looking for new ways to engage customers. Moreover, 53 percent of marketers were adding new channels, and 54 percent had increased their omnichannel presences. Finally, spending on customer experience activities rose 10 percent during the course of 2020.[13]

The CMO as Chief Customer Officer

As customer centricity becomes a strategic imperative, there is a need to have a single person or function focused on the customer. More and more, I am seeing the CMO being tapped to assume CCO (chief customer officer) responsibilities. This additional responsibility requires the use of technology and data to understand the customer. Technology and data are also needed to customize corporate responses. These answers

> 💡 We transformed everything we did to really be aligned with the buyer journey.
>
> **—MITCH DIAMOND,** senior director of marketing operations at SAP Ariba

have to be based on where customers are in their journey. They must align with the individuals within the company who are speaking with the customers. Thus, insights need to be gleaned from the customer data. Knowledge can then be shared with marketing and customer-facing groups within the company. Responses and voice must be consistent and in real time. Customer-based, data-driven decision-making becomes the norm. The CMO—who is also now the CCO—can't do this with a regular MO group. A strategic MO group is needed to support the CCO role.

A few years ago, I worked with a marketing operations leader who had been pushing for his company to become customer centric, to no avail. Then in 2019, the CEO finally decided to become a customer-centric organization. The MO team was ready and greatly contributed to the creation of a customer-centric strategy and to the implementation of that strategy. Due to the MO efforts, the company accelerated its pivot to customer centricity.

I work with CMOs and MO leaders every day. I can confirm that the CMO challenges today are greater than ever. At the same time, there has never been a bigger opportunity for the MO team to step up from being button pushers to strategic contributors and enablers. CMOs cannot adopt revenue accountability, succeed in accelerating wider digital transformation and lead customer centricity with a regular MO group focused on operational measures. Today's CMO needs a

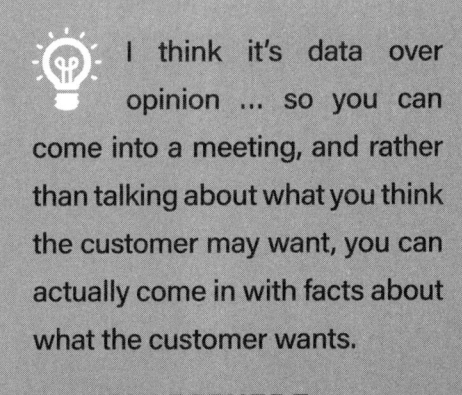

> I think it's data over opinion ... so you can come into a meeting, and rather than talking about what you think the customer may want, you can actually come in with facts about what the customer wants.
>
> —JIM LEFEVERE, international business leader

strategic MO organization that envisions and drives change through the magic formula of people, process, technology and data.

HOW CMOS OVERCOME THESE MAIN CHALLENGES

The CMO's top three challenges represent what today's CMO must deliver. The mantra is: "Revenue and growth powered by digital transformation and accelerated by customer centricity." Moving on, let's pause for a moment and consider: What does today's CMO need to do to address these challenges?

Part of my doctoral research focused on answering that question. Allow me to explain. My dissertation for the doctorate I received in 2018 was called "A Modified Delphi Study: Forward-Looking Strategies for Chief Marketing Officer Accountability in a Digital Environment." For this research, I looked for reasons to explain why CMOs were drowning in technology yet still could not close the revenue accountability gap.

In my research, I identified fourteen strategies that CMOs use to close this gap. Based on my findings, building a technology and data infrastructure serves as a foundation, with thirteen additional strategies completing the puzzle. These findings show that the role of MO reaches past technology. The strategies are what set a strategic MO organization apart from a regular marketing operations group. They help the strategic MO leader know how to best partner with the CMO to drive results.

Let's start with a general look at the fourteen strategies listed in Figure 2.2 ("14 Forward-Looking Strategies for How Future B2B CMOs Might Adopt Financial Accountability"). Two foundational strategies are (1) technology and data as enablers, and (2) the CMO running marketing like a business. From there, two additional strategies support the CMO's new skills: (3) acting like a data-driven company leader, and (4) acting like a digital marketing leader. Strategies 5 and 6 represent the CMO's new scorecard and compensation. Strategy 7 is about working within the current company environment. Finally, strategies 8 through 14 represent the CMO's building blocks for revenue. Let's now look at each strategy in a bit more detail and consider the role of strategic MO in each (of course, this review is only a small part of the research).

14 FORWARD-LOOKING STRATEGIES FOR HOW FUTURE B2B CMOS MIGHT ADOPT FINANCIAL ACCOUNTABILITY

- 1. Technology and Data as Enablers
- 2. Running Marketing Like a Business

New B2B CMO Skills
- 3. Acting Like a Data Driven Company Leader
- 4. Acting Like a Digital Marking Leader

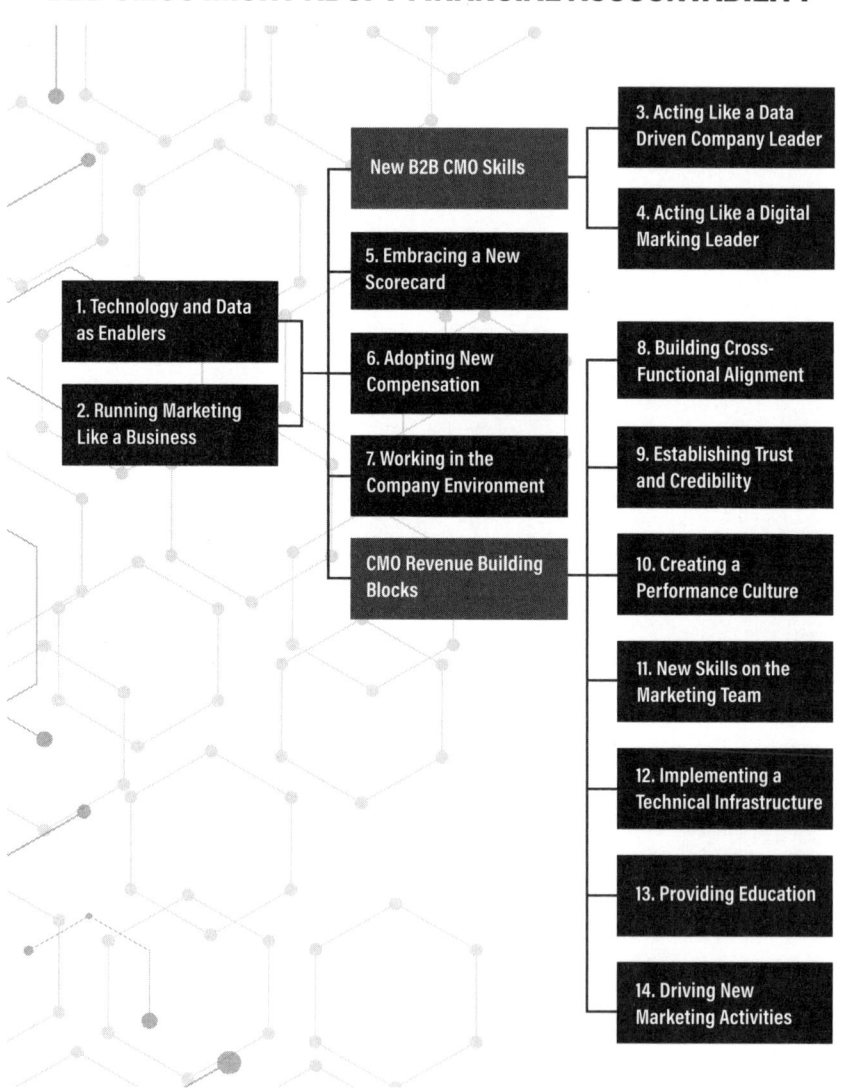

- 5. Embracing a New Scorecard
- 6. Adopting New Compensation
- 7. Working in the Company Environment

CMO Revenue Building Blocks
- 8. Building Cross-Functional Alignment
- 9. Establishing Trust and Credibility
- 10. Creating a Performance Culture
- 11. New Skills on the Marketing Team
- 12. Implementing a Technical Infrastructure
- 13. Providing Education
- 14. Driving New Marketing Activities

FIGURE 2.2

STRATEGY 1: TECHNOLOGY AND DATA AS ENABLERS

For my dissertation research, I asked CMOs to indicate the importance of strategies that lead to financial accountability based on a five-point scale. The five options were (1) not important, (2) slightly important, (3) important, (4) fairly important and (5) very important.

When I analyzed the responses, three key findings emerged. They all underscored the need to use technology and data as enablers. First, over 88 percent of respondents indicated that having the right technology was "fairly important" or "very important." However, I've seen many organizations that don't even know what technology they have.

Second, over 95 percent responded that it was "fairly important" or "very important" to *optimize* the use of technology. Among all the organizations I have worked with, I have found very few that are even close to optimizing their martech stack. From these two data points alone, you can see how critical the MO role is to success. No one can succeed if the foundation is shaky.

CMO financial accountability is directly tied to the rise in digital technologies that help automate and track many of today's marketing functions.[14]

Finally, regarding data as an enabler, the study asked, "How important is it for the CMO to make data-driven decisions?" A full 100 percent of the participants answered "fairly important" to "very important"; of those, 88 percent responded as "very important." Given this incredible focus on data-driven decision-making, the

CMO financial accountability is directly tied to the rise in digital technologies that help automate and track many of today's marketing functions.

role of MO as a teacher and enabler of this new behavior cannot be overstated.

STRATEGY 2: RUNNING MARKETING LIKE A BUSINESS

In chapter 1, I outlined the need for the strategic MO leader to run MO like a business. The approach both supports and enables the CMO to do likewise. A key question in my dissertation research was "How important is it for the CMO to run marketing like a business?" Among the participants, 100 percent answered "fairly important" to "very important"; of those, 88 percent responded as "very important."

My research came across several main elements that allow the CMO to run marketing like a business. These core ingredients are listed below:

- Being data, metrics, and ROI driven
- Aligning to company goals
- Being transparent in reporting numbers
- Proactively managing and adapting the budget
- Applying professional project management practices

Take a moment to consider these CMO requirements. Now consider MO's role as the enabler. Strategic MO is involved in all these essential processes. Furthermore, this list partially defines what it means to be a strategic MO organization.

The budget allocated to the CMO must be invested to maximize shareholder value. Also, the CMO is usually trapping data regarding forward-looking business-growth drivers as well as customer satisfaction metrics. The measurement of marketing's impact on the business must be steeped in the key financial metrics being used to chart the company's trajectory.[15]

STRATEGIES 3 AND 4: ACTING LIKE A DATA-DRIVEN COMPANY LEADER AND DIGITAL MARKETING LEADER

My research revealed two strategies for new skills that CMOs need today. These were to act like a data-driven company leader and to act like a digital marketing leader.

The study found the following elements to be necessary to act like a data-driven leader:

- Being a credible driver of company growth
- Earning a seat and a voice at the table
- Building the right organizational structure
- Acting like a vice president of sales in terms of managing and forecasting a marketing pipeline
- Becoming a credible leader of a revenue center

Show that you're using data to guide your business decisions. Show that you're mapping everything back to impact on revenue.[16]

On this particular topic of leadership, participants were asked, "How important is it for the CMO to be a credible driver of revenue growth?" Among respondents, 100 percent indicated it was "important" to "very important"; of those, over 60 percent said it was "very important." Given the

> Show that you're using data to guide your business decisions. Show that you're mapping everything back to impact on revenue.

CMO's obligation to drive revenue, consider how this focus changes your responsibility as an MO organization.

For the CMO to be a digital marketing leader that contributes to revenue, several elements stood out:

- Hiring new technical talent: 100 percent of CMOs marked this as "fairly important" to "very important" in order to obtain revenue goals.

- Being fluent in technology: 100 percent of CMOs believed it was "fairly important" to "very important" in order to obtain revenue goals.

- Building the right technical structure: 100 percent of CMOs believed it was "important" to "very important" in order to obtain revenue goals.

- Other needed elements included the following:
    - Providing ongoing training to the marketing team
    - Changing the organizational chart by adding new roles
    - Understanding the customer by mining customer data and producing key insights for the organization

The CMO acting like a digital marketing leader was an important finding in my research, as it corroborated what I see in the market. Consider this case in point: I have a longtime friend who had worked at the director and VP level of marketing for many years. A few years ago, we met for lunch to talk about her new and growing marketing operations organization. She began to talk about the technologies she was using, what she was looking at next and how they applied to her business problems. As I listened to her, I was stunned. Here's why: during her entire career, this woman had been more of a traditional marketing leader and certainly not what I would consider "tech savvy." Yet because her knowledge of the technology landscape was critical to her success, she jumped in feetfirst! I also admired her "What technology can help me solve my business problems?" approach.

Not all CMOs may be in this position. I've heard horror stories of MO leaders trying to prep uninformed CMOs for board meetings. In these instances, the CMO ultimately misrepresents the value of marketing. For those CMOs much more uncomfortable with acting as a digital marketing leader, MO plays a critical role. In such circumstances, MO can supply and apply the required knowledge and experience to help drive results.

Digital transformation is driving tremendous change within marketing, and CMOs stand to greatly expand their influence and impact within the C-suite. However, no owner or board of directors is going to empower an individual or department that can't "prove" its value based on financials.[17]

STRATEGIES 5 AND 6: EMBRACING A NEW SCORECARD AND ADOPTING NEW COMPENSATION

Embracing a new scorecard and adopting new compensation are important for one reason: they both are based on driving revenue. You can bet that if a CMO's total earnings are based on these or similar measures, it won't be long before parallel scorecards and compensation plans appear in marketing, and that includes the MO organization. More and more MO organizations now have a specific responsibility for a number. The opportunity for MO is not to build the best martech stack ever conceived. The opportunity for MO is to build a revenue machine, which requires thinking beyond the bits and bytes to connecting the dots to drive growth.

B2B CMOs today are expected to report on results that tie to company revenue and overall performance. Gone are the days of reporting high-level, vanity metrics like website traffic, or reporting solely on things like marketing impact on pipeline.[18]

> **B2B CMOs today are expected to report on results that tie to company revenue and overall performance.**

Nothing drives behavior like compensation. As more CMOs and their teams are given new compensation structures based on revenue results, the role of MO to help engineer the revenue marketing machine becomes more critical. Along with this trend, I am seeing MO organizations add revenue responsibility to their charters. In addition, revenue impact is tied to compensation for all of marketing—even marketing operations.

My study derived four key elements that demonstrate the importance of compensation to drive revenue marketing behavior:

- CMO takes a quota: 88 percent of CMOs believed it was "important" to "very important" in order to obtain revenue goals.

- Marketing team takes a quota: 83 percent of CMOs believed it was "important" to "very important" in order to obtain revenue goals.

- CMO compensation is tied to financial results: 94 percent of CMOs believed it was "fairly important" to "very important" in order to obtain revenue goals.

- Marketing team compensation is tied to financial results: 83 percent of CMOs believed it was "important" to "very important" in order to obtain revenue goals.

There's a momentum to assign direct revenue accountability to all of marketing and to compensate based on revenue performance. Given this, the strategic marketing operations organization is in the hot seat. They must be proactive in what is happening in the funnel. They also need to be forward thinking to show how marketing can improve performance.

STRATEGY 7: WORKING IN THE COMPANY ENVIRONMENT

The study's responses pertaining to working in the company environment revealed the importance of organizational culture, company leadership, innovation and customer strategies. CMOs need to understand the current company environment and culture to be able to implement the adoption of financial accountability. Recognizing the current company environment also enables CMOs to assess just how much change they can affect. The MO leader can then help drive the change.

The remainder of the strategies identified from the study represent basic building blocks required to adopt financial accountability.

STRATEGIES 8 AND 9: BUILDING CROSS-FUNCTIONAL ALIGNMENT AND ESTABLISHING TRUST AND CREDIBILITY

In chapter 1, I explained how building cross-functional alignment is one of the critical behaviors of a strategic MO leader. The CMO has this responsibility, which is based on the needs of the business. The study's respondents rated the stakeholder groups with whom it was critical to build alignments. In order of importance, they were:

- Sales
- Executive team
- Finance
- Board
- Customer support
- IT

I believe alignment between sales and marketing is critical to any firm's future prospects. To achieve that alignment, sales and marketing need to be peers, share common objectives and be compensated on similar measures.[19]

In the study, 100 percent of the CMOs said alignment with sales was far and away the most important relationship to establish. That also included establishing trust and credibility. I see the MO organization doing this better than any other part of marketing. Of course, building alignment, trust, and credibility with the executive team is important, but it was equally important to do so with finance as well.

Always build trust and relationships with finance … never polarize.[20]

> We have a very good relationship and alignment with sales. We really look at planning, decision-making and getting things done together. I think we have built a culture of accountability for both groups.
>
> **—KIRA MONDRUS-MOYAL,** senior vice president of global marketing at Tricentis

STRATEGY 10: CREATING A PERFORMANCE CULTURE

The study asked participants, "How important is it for the CMO to establish a performance culture?" Among respondents, 100 percent said it was "fairly important" to "very important"; of those, 65 percent said it was "very important." As you can tell from the research already shared, a performance culture is about producing results that matter to the business. Marketing can no longer be the pens-and-mugs department. They must evolve into a driver of growth.

Additional ways to create a performance culture, according to the study responses, included the following:

- Focusing on results, not activities: 100 percent indicated this was "fairly important" to "very important"; of those, 77 percent stated it was "very important."

- Establishing financially oriented metrics and KPIs (key performance indicators): 100 percent indicated this was "fairly important" to "very important"; of those, 77 percent indicated it was "very important."

- Supporting an environment of experimentation and continuous improvement: 100 percent indicated this was "important" to "very important"; of those, 64 percent indicated it was "very important."

- Driving process and systems thinking: 100 percent indicated this was "important" to "very important"; of those, 41 percent indicated it was "very important."

- Compensating based on performance, not activities: 100 percent indicated this was "important to very important"; of those, 41 percent indicated it was "very important."

As more and more technologies become tools of the CMO, there is an expectation that is being set that the CMO can and will have more direct influence over a company's performance with the activities of his or her team.[21]

STRATEGY 11: NEW SKILLS ON THE MARKETING TEAM

Talent is so important to the direction of marketing that I have dedicated an entire chapter to the topic (see page 195). I also highlighted the role of the strategic MO leader as a team builder and skill builder in chapter 1. A key question in the study was "How important is it for the CMO to have the right skills on the marketing team—technical and analytical?" One hundred percent of the CMOs replied that it was "fairly important" to "very important"; of those, 65 percent responded that it was "very important."

In addition, another question asked, "How important is it for the CMO to adjust the current marketing organization to include technical/analytical/operational talent?" One hundred percent of the CMOs responded that it was "fairly important" to "very important"; of those, 71 percent responded that it was "very important." As the CMO brings in new skills, many of them will be in the MO group. Some skills will also be in other marketing departments that will have heavy interactions with the MO organization.

The B2B CMO role has changed from a leader in a cost center to a revenue center, and to leading the charge in adapting to the changing buying journey and demand generation model. The skill set has also shifted from the typical liberal arts background to an analytics-driven background.[22]

STRATEGY 12: IMPLEMENTING A TECHNICAL STRUCTURE

For the CMO to be successful, they have to institute the right technical structure. As such, they need a martech stack that is integrated and optimized. The study asked participants, "How important is it for the CMO to build the right technical structure?" One hundred percent of the respondents answered that it was "important" to "very important"; of those, 62 percent responded that it was "very important." One side note: All the CMOs in the study had fairly sophisticated martech stacks. In fact, this was one of the requirements to be able to participate in the study.

> I think that now marketers have to be more technical. They have to be more savvy. They have to be a lot more analytical. Marketers are expected to be able to understand the technical aspect and the tools that are driving all of this.
>
> **—RACHEL CRUZ,** director of marketing automation at Healthgrades

STRATEGY 13: PROVIDING EDUCATION

Throughout this book I talk about the need for ongoing education for all of marketing, not just marketing operations. My research revealed education as a significant theme. Providing education also encompasses continuous training for key stakeholders outside of marketing. When asked about the importance of training the marketing team, 100 percent of CMOs responded that it was "fairly important" to "very important"; of those, 59 percent said it was "very important."

> 💡 What we've done from a training perspective and to foster cross-functional understanding of different things is that we have access to LinkedIn Learning. And within the team specifically developed digital courses. There is a whole series of courses to give people understanding and exposure across a bunch of different topics.
>
> **—JIM LEFEVERE,** international business leader

The study also asked about the importance of ongoing training to key stakeholders. Among participants, 100 percent responded that it was "important" to "very important"; of those, 59 percent said that it was "very important." The MO organization has a key responsibility in training—in MO, across all of marketing, and for key external stakeholders.

STRATEGY 14: NEW MARKETING ACTIVITIES

The final finding from the research relates to marketing adopting new behaviors or a new set of marketing activities. These include activities like working with sales and being revenue focused. They cover everything that is required to transform marketing from being the "make it pretty" department to the driver of growth and revenue. Certainly, MO emerging as a strategic organization represents a set of new marketing activities and behaviors.

Understanding these fourteen strategies helps to decipher the approach that CMOs need to take to overcome today's marketing challenges. In this chapter, I've shown that those challenges tend to center on driving revenue. Both digital transformation and customer centricity are closely tied to the revenue initiative. By reflecting on what strategies the CMO is taking in the current environment, a strategic MO can play the supporting role to ultimately bring success.

> Twice in my career in marketing operations, my CMO said to me, "You're not only running marketing operations; you're my chief of staff." If the CMO is looking for somebody to help run not only the department but also the entire organization, marketing operations becomes a good place to look.
>
> **—REUBEN VARELLA,** vice president of business systems at Veracode

Now that I've outlined what it takes to be a strategic MO leader and shown the connection between strategic marketing operations and the CMO, it's time to get started on building the strategic MO organization. To do so, it's important to understand how marketing operations has evolved and where exactly you fit in. In the next chapter, I'll give you a chance to evaluate your current position. I'll then give you a path to follow to ultimately become a truly strategic MO organization.

CHAPTER SUMMARY
A QUICK GLANCE AT WHAT WE LEARNED

- Technology changes have created big opportunities for marketing operations to step up.

- To get that seat at the table, the right kinds of MO leaders, MO organizations and CMOs are needed.

- CMOs face challenges related to driving revenue, effecting digital transformation, implementing and customer centricity.

- To overcome these challenges, CMOs take on numerous strategies, beginning with using technology and data as enablers.

- Specific activities can help the CMO take on revenue accountability and turn marketing into a growth engine for the company.

- A strategic MO organization supports the CMO's strategies and helps guide and orchestrate revenue accountability.

- There is a strong and direct connection between CMO success and the strategic MO leader.

CHAPTER 3

THE MARKETING OPERATIONS MATURITY MODEL (MOM)

I still remember the day I heard the phrase "marketing operations" for the first time. It occurred in 2009 when I was working with a national sports team. They introduced me to a group of people they referred to as "marketing operations." Back then, the term felt like an oxymoron. However, I was fascinated by what they did and how they used technology to drive actual revenue. At that time, I thought marketing operations was a fit for B2C marketing but would probably never work for B2B marketers. Was I ever wrong.

Fast-forward to today. If you haven't been paying close attention, it may feel like the rise of the MO function as an essential part of every marketing organization occurred almost overnight. One day we woke up to find more than eight thousand marketing technologies (and counting). Suddenly we have a culture in which marketing spends more than the IT department. We now have conferences like MarTech that are dedicated to developing MO as a strategic capability. From a sheer numbers perspective, a quick Google search tells us there are nearly one billion pages that mention "marketing operations." New practices come to market almost weekly. LinkedIn shows more than twenty thousand job openings if you search for "marketing + technology + management" (and that number has doubled since 2018).

Yet however sudden it may seem, we did not get here overnight. The progress has really been an evolution that took place over time. In this chapter, I'll spend a little time peering into the history of marketing operations and going over its progression. Understanding this background helps us see how we arrived at our current environment. You can also use it to build a strategic marketing operations capability today. To do so, it's critical to know exactly where you are in terms of MO maturity—and what to do to reach that goal of being strategic.

The current chapter and the chapters that follow will help you identify where you are. You will then learn, step by step, how to move up. I'll do that by providing a model I developed and have used time and again with marketing operations leaders. I continually get rave reviews about this model, which I call the Marketing Operations Maturity (MOM) model (see Figure 3.2). Users find it clear and easy to follow. They tell me it provides the vision they need to move into that coveted strategic position.

Since this MOM model is so important, I consider it the foundation of this book. Once you've reviewed it and have read the information that corresponds with it, I think you'll agree. Using this model is like having a North Star. The MOM model acts as a guiding light that will direct you on the path to create a strategic marketing operations capability.

EVOLUTION OF MARKETING OPERATIONS

> It was around 2012 when we created what was the first marketing operations team. There were maybe thirty-five of us, not a big team at all. And then similar groups began to pop up across American Express. In 2016, we went through a reengineering initiative and all the CoEs [centers of excellence] were created. Part of that move was to create the global marketing operations team my group got pulled into. I took over this function in 2017, and we continue to evolve.
>
> **—HEATHER COLE,** vice president of enterprise marketing products and solutions at AMEX

As I mentioned, marketing operations has evolved drastically during recent years. Beginning in 2004, I had a front-row seat to this transformation. Since then, I've witnessed the market progress and go through what I call four periods of organizational evolution. These four phases are reactive, proactive/decentralized, proactive/centralized, and strategic.

Based on my observations, I developed the following evolutionary timetable (Figure 3.1: "A Decade of Growth: Timetable Outlining the Evolution of Martech and Marketing Operations").

FROM BACKROOM TO BOARDROOM

A DECADE OF GROWTH:
TIMETABLE OUTLINING THE EVOLUTION OF MARTECH AND MARKETING OPERATIONS

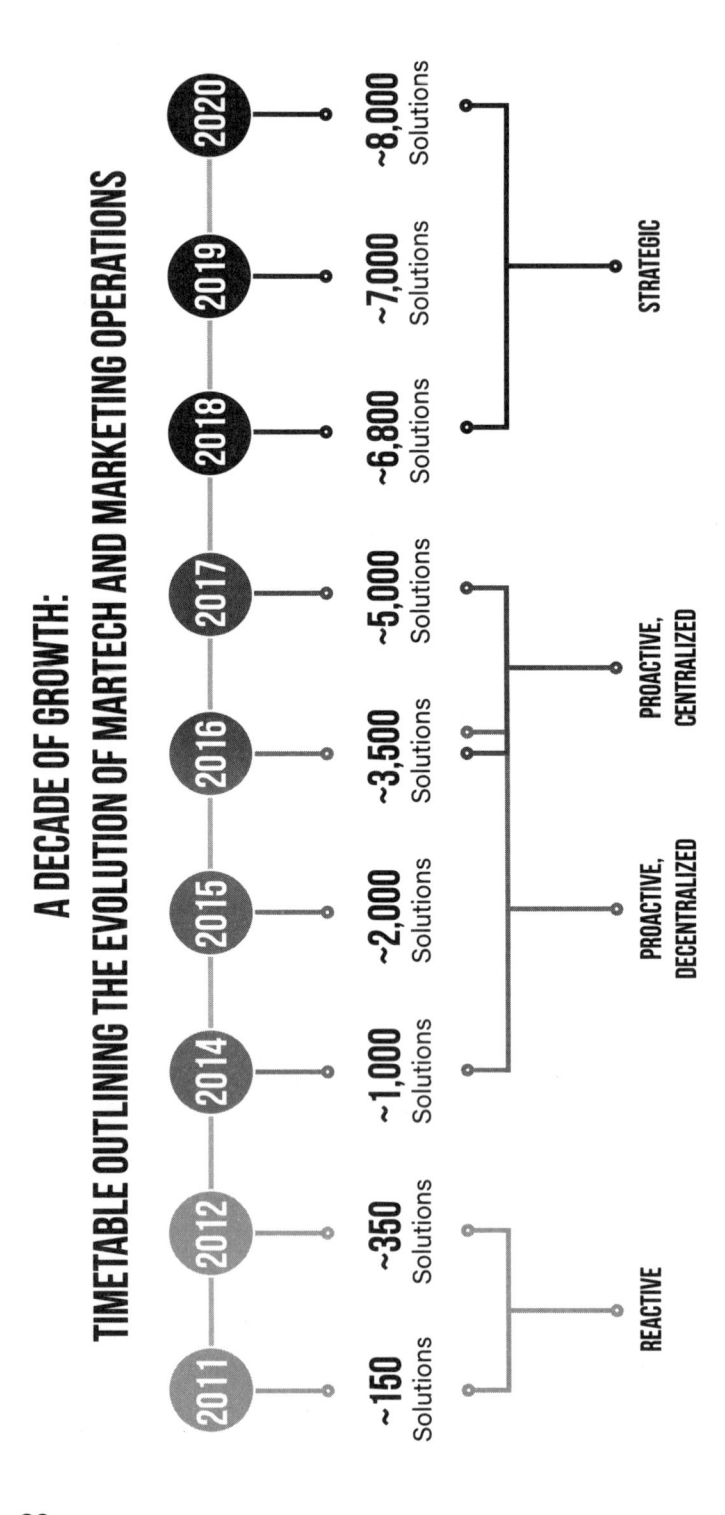

Year	Solutions	Phase
2011	~150 Solutions	REACTIVE
2012	~350 Solutions	REACTIVE
2014	~1,000 Solutions	PROACTIVE, DECENTRALIZED
2015	~2,000 Solutions	PROACTIVE, DECENTRALIZED
2016	~3,500 Solutions	PROACTIVE, CENTRALIZED
2017	~5,000 Solutions	PROACTIVE, CENTRALIZED
2018	~6,800 Solutions	STRATEGIC
2019	~7,000 Solutions	STRATEGIC
2020	~8,000 Solutions	STRATEGIC

FIGURE 3.1

"A Decade of Growth: Timetable Outlining the Evolution of Martech and Marketing Operations," helps you visualize the increasing number of martech solutions available. You can see the corresponding evolution of marketing operations as an organization. Note that as the number of solutions grew, marketing operations moved into more advanced periods of development.

For the purpose of understanding the background of marketing operations, let's spend some time looking at these four periods listed in the timetable. I'll then explain what was going on during each of these stages in the marketing operations world and my personal observations from these periods.

THE REACTIVE PERIOD: 2004–2012

In 2004, I bought my first marketing automation system. In my case, this purchase wasn't something planned. In all honesty, prior to that year, I didn't even know this technology existed. However, I was about to discover the technology and the benefits of having a marketing automation system. I was a CMO at the time and had a very enterprising CEO, who challenged me to help drive revenue for our company. After some research, I found a company called Eloqua. For marketing automation, it was the only game in town in 2004. I bought it, integrated it with Salesforce, and was off to drive revenue. I had previously worked as a vice president of sales, so this option seemed to me like the right way to go. In fact, the first year that we had a marketing automation platform, we closed one of our largest deals in the history of the company.

All this took place at the beginning of the reactive period. For this phase, my story was pretty usual (aside from the revenue part). From 2004 to 2011, the number of marketing technologies grew to about 150. I call this the reactive period because marketing was reacting in an ad hoc manner to these new technologies. In a typical company during this time, the marketing group bought marketing automation. Then they assigned someone on the team who they considered to have a "technical" aptitude to be the power user. The person took on the role of power user in addition to the job they already had. At that time, only about 50 percent of systems were integrated with CRM. What's more, there was no long-term strategy for technology. Both the term "marketing operations" and the concept of this function were scarce.

THE PROACTIVE, DECENTRALIZED PERIOD: 2012-2016

As we entered the proactive, decentralized period, Gartner, a leading research and advisory firm, predicted CMOs would spend more on technology than CIOs by 2017.[23] My mind was blown at this thought. Not everyone, however, believed the prediction. I actually had an argument with my business partner about whether this would indeed occur. I said it would happen, and he believed it wouldn't come true. The prediction held true, and I won the argument. As further proof, the number of technologies for marketers grew from 150 in 2011 to 1,000 in 2014.

I call this the proactive, decentralized period because marketing organizations began to realize they needed a proactive approach to secure, digest and optimize their martech spend and direction. Organizationally, some tasks and roles in this period became more dedicated. For example, I began to see roles fully dedicated to the marketing automation systems. Marketing also began to take ownership of other new technologies like CRM. There might be a manager with a small team, but it was still decentralized. The marketing team "borrowed" capabilities that they needed, such as analytics, reporting, data normalization and technology integrations. Any technology used by marketing lived in the marketing silo (except for integration with CRM).

THE PROACTIVE, CENTRALIZED PERIOD: 2016-2017

During this period, the number of technologies for marketing surged, increasing to five thousand in 2017. I vividly remember attending the MarTech Conference and waiting for Scott Brinker to unveil his chart. Each year, this chart showed the latest number of technologies available for marketing. Just when we thought we reached the limit, more technology appeared on the chart!

Marketing operations as a more defined and dedicated organization began to evolve around this time. There was now a commitment to both a budget and a formal function. In these years, I watched marketing operations teams grow fast: in one case, the team grew from three people to one hundred almost overnight. Leadership requirements—like a dedicated VP position—developed, and cross-functional collaboration began to happen. In addition, the breadth of responsibilities started to reach beyond the marketing tech stack.

During this period, I really began noticing companies call what they were doing "marketing operations." I conducted interviews with ten different leading firms, such as Lenovo, Microsoft, LexisNexis, MediaMath and McKesson. Based on those conversations, I published my first white paper, "The Rise of The Marketing Operations Function." My research showed that marketing operations as an organization and a strategy was now entrenched.

THE STRATEGIC PERIOD: 2018–PRESENT

Today, with over eight thousand pieces of technology, we are in the strategic period. I call it strategic because marketing operations is no longer a nice-to-have. Marketing operations is a must-have for any and all modern marketing organizations. In addition, marketing operations is becoming part of the strategy for marketing, sales and customer success organizations. I now see more dedicated and seasoned teams. There are also structures—both formal and collaborative—that allow for MO success. Marketing operations has a growing number of opportunities to lead in the areas of digital transformation, customer centricity, and revenue accountability.

These four periods in time represent a rather simple look at the evolution of marketing operations as an organization. While it's true that the tsunami of technologies has played a key role in driving the evolution of marketing operations, it is equally as important to note that other external drivers have had an effect as well. In chapters 1 and 2, I outlined many of these nontechnology drivers.

THE MARKETING OPERATIONS MATURITY (MOM) MODEL

After watching this development of marketing operations from 2004 to 2017, by 2018 I knew it was time for a new playbook. I could see that marketing operations had come a long way. More importantly, it was finally in a position where it could credibly contribute and get marketing that seat at the table.

By this point, I had also worked with marketing leaders for years and carried out extensive studies and interviews on marketing's progress. While it was great to understand the evolution of the MO structure, I could see a few lingering questions in the air: "What does MO do, and more importantly, what should they do?" In essence: "What are the capabilities of a strategic MO organization?"

To answer those questions and provide marketing leaders a guide for what's ahead in their world, I developed the Marketing Operations Maturity (MOM) model (see Figure 3.2) in 2018. As I stated previously, this model is really the foundation for the remainder of this book and one you will be referring to frequently. The MOM model provides a picture of the different stages of maturity for marketing operations *capabilities*, not just structure. MO professionals can use it to think about where they are, where they need to go and how they will get there.

THE MARKETING OPERATIONS MATURITY MODEL (MOM)

MARKETING OPERATIONS MATURITY MODEL

NEXT GENERATION

CUSTOMER CENTRIC

GET REVENUE

EFFICIENT/ EFFECTIVE

UNAWARE

STRATEGIC CAPABILITY

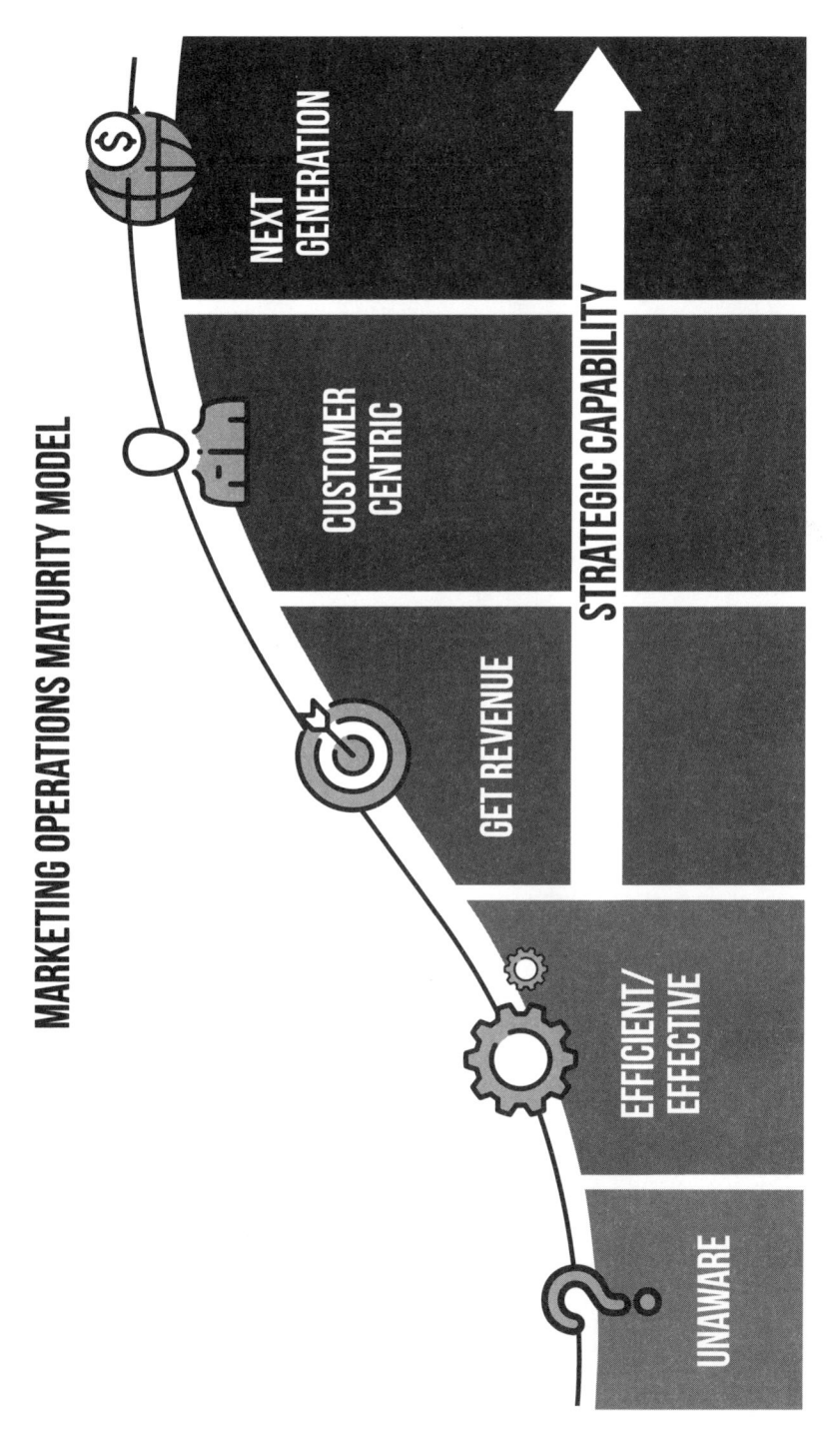

FIGURE 3.2

67

The MOM model helps you understand the complexity of marketing operations capabilities at different stages of maturity. There are five stages: Unaware, Efficient/Effective, Get Revenue, Customer Centric, and Next Generation. I will present the final four stages at an in-depth level in upcoming chapters. You can find a full listing of the characteristics for each stage in Figure 11.5 ("MOM Model Characteristics by Stage") in the appendix. For now, I'll provide a brief description of each stage in the model.

STAGE 1: UNAWARE

In 2019 while visiting Chicago, I had lunch with the CMO of a large global company. A mutual acquaintance set up our meet-and-greet. While we dined, I asked the CMO about her marketing operations team. Imagine my surprise when she gave me a puzzled look. Finally, she replied, "We don't have one." I was stunned. I was also brought back to the reality that the modern marketing organization and the marketing operations role are still in their infancy.

Stage 1 is the first step in the strategic marketing operations journey. I call it the "bless your heart" stage. ("Bless your heart" is a deeply southern saying that is a precursor to soften an insult.) At this point of maturity, marketing ops is an ad hoc response to the tsunami of technology and change. Disparate groups perform uncoordinated MO tasks with no central vision or leadership. The Unaware stage typically begins with the use of a marketing automation platform that is used as a glorified email system. A team member is selected and dedicates a few hours a week to be the technology specialist. No plan exists for the martech stack and data. There is an overwhelming lack of awareness that MO can and should be a dedicated capability and no thought to it being a strategic capability.

In parallel, at this stage of maturity, the company go-to-market strategy is typically product focused rather than customer focused. Tasks are performed in silos (think marketing versus sales versus IT) with big walls in between. The most basic martech stack is in place. While marketing is now gathering data about prospect and customer behavior, no one takes the time or initiative to use this valuable data. It sits in the data graveyard.

Finally, key MO metrics in this stage are nonexistent. Marketing is low on the totem pole within the company. All marketing activity represents a cost to the business. I actually considered removing this stage from the MOM model. Some marketing organizations, however, are in this stage, so I left it in the model. To marketing organizations that are still in the Unaware stage, all I can say is, "Bless their heart!"

STAGE 2: EFFICIENT/EFFECTIVE

> 💡 Our immediate charter is to improve the efficiency and effectiveness of marketing by establishing a sound operational foundation through technology, data, templates, best practices and a new structure. With this foundation, we'll be able to successfully move into the next stages of our journey. This is key because we do have a revenue number, and we must lead in understanding our customers.
>
> —**MEAGHAN AMATO,** director of marketing operations at TraceLink

Enter Stage 2, which is the Efficient/Effective stage. At this point, everyone is focused on building the operational foundation, driving operational excellence, and learning and preparing for the next stage. They eagerly establish a sound technology and data foundation. In addition to doing things well (i.e., efficiently), marketing operations begins to question if they are doing the right things (i.e., effectively). At this point, reengineering core processes and enabling them with technology take center stage.

In the efficiency part of this stage, there is acknowledgment of the need to develop an MO function, along with an organizational commitment and budget. Here is a typical marketing operations charter for this stage: "The charter of the efficient MO is to select, implement, integrate, and optimize various marketing technologies while also introducing an analytics and data capability into the marketing organization."

The second part of this stage consists of being effective, or doing the right things. The charter for an effective MO is typically as follows: "The charter of the effective MO is to improve the efficiency and effectiveness of marketing operations, including reengineering core marketing and sales processes that enable marketing and the company to obtain stated goals."

> **The charter of the efficient MO is to select, implement, integrate, and optimize various marketing technologies while also introducing an analytics and data capability into the marketing organization.**

> **The charter of the effective MO is to improve the efficiency and effectiveness of marketing operations, including reengineering core marketing and sales processes that enable marketing and the company to obtain stated goals.**

Acknowledgment of the need for an MO capability has now morphed into an operational imperative and includes reengineering core processes such as demand generation and use of multichannel marketing. There is a larger commitment to a budget and a formal, dedicated function. There is a robust martech architecture in place. The MO group leader is more strategic. Performance is tied to establishing new processes and continual improvement of operational metrics. Broader responsibilities include campaign optimization, data analysis and insights, mostly for marketing. Efficiency and effectiveness in driving marketing goals is the mantra.

STAGE 3: GET REVENUE

In the get-revenue stage, the training wheels come off. Leveraging the foundation established in the Efficient/Effective stage, this stage is all about applying people, process, technology, and data to drive a business result: revenue. Beki Scarbrough, vice president of demand strategy and operations at SecureAuth Corporation, describes the charter for this stage as follows: "Our charter is to enable the rest of the organization to hit the number through process, technology and analytics."

Reengineering core revenue processes for marketing and sales processes are critical. Analytics are much more sophisticated, and data-driven decisions are rampant. The get-revenue stage is also about a new mindset that questions what is best for the business, not just what marketing has to get done today. Marketing operations becomes *proactive* in driving business results instead of *reactive* to the needs of marketing.

> **Our charter is to enable the rest of the organization to hit the number through process, technology and analytics.**

During this stage, marketing operations begins to use data to proactively provide guidance and insights. These are used to improve marketing and sales performance as they relate to revenue. This stage is an early precursor to a revenue operations organization (see more on revenue operations on page 188). By using data-driven decision-making and insights, the marketing operations team significantly improves the relationship between sales and marketing.

One key process that highlights this stage of maturity and contributes to the rejuvenation of the sales and marketing relationship is the lead management process. You'll hear this from me many times in this book: nailing the lead management process, along with the subsequent enabling technology and data, is critical to the value of marketing operations.

> Our charter is to enable the marketing team to achieve our overall goals. And our goals are—all around—creating pipeline and delivering on our revenue contribution. So it's making sure that we can get that done.
>
> **—KIRA MONDRUS-MOYAL,** senior vice president of global marketing at Tricentis

In the get-revenue stage, the martech stack is architected to be a repeatable, predictable and scalable (RPS) revenue engine for marketing. The stack is optimally integrated with CRM and other internal systems to help drive credible revenue performance. A vision and a plan for future martech that is cross-functional in nature is in place. Marketing operations is a dedicated and critical function in marketing and has a significant budget and team. Additionally, the MO team typically has some direct accountability to drive revenue, not just set up the infrastructure for a revenue machine. Finally, the get-revenue stage is an important precursor to the customer-centric stage.

STAGE 4: CUSTOMER CENTRIC

In this stage, the MO function/capability becomes an unexpected and valuable source of customer data and insights for business decisions to all customer-facing parts of the organization and for executives. In our current customer-centric world, this represents a significant opportunity for marketing operations. Essentially, MO can drive extraordinary value by harnessing prospect and customer data they already have. They can also bring in data lying around in other areas of the business. Setting up digital conversations through multiple channels, tracking and gathering customer/prospect behavior and creating actionable insights are invaluable for a customer-focused company. Customer data and insights allow for better and quicker decisions to be made in response to market and customer changes. Strategic marketing operations makes all this possible.

> It's critical that my team really know the customer. We need to take time to understand them at an individual level and to understand their behaviors. With this knowledge, we can plan to meet them where they are.
>
> **—JIM LEFEVERE**, international business leader

At this stage, the customer focus becomes the lens through which the martech stack, data and strategy must be viewed. Since the customer journey touches all customer-facing parts of the company, a broader view must take place. As a result, marketing technology is more deeply integrated into all systems that touch the customer. Likewise, data integration is critical, as is a broader collaboration of functions.

To see a great example of how marketing operations has responded to the shift to customer centricity, look at the Stackies, a contest run by ChiefMarTec.com. They take submissions that are graphical representations of an organization's tech stack. A few years ago, they began to see these representations based on the customer journey. In 2017, Allocadia presented a great example of a martech stack fueled and informed by their customer's journey. A picture paints a thousand words, so check out the Stackies for updated examples.

Meaghan Amato, director of marketing operations at TraceLink Marketing, shared the following charter for this stage: "We harness priceless intelligence that predicts customer behavior; fuels exceptional, end-to-end customer experiences and shapes our understanding of key personas and customer journeys. Our data-driven approach and customer insights accelerate pipeline creation and revenue delivery in a new value-based world."

STAGE 5: NEXT GENERATION

While the customer-centric stage is about up-leveling the sophistication of marketing operations and realigning a larger, cross-functional team around a customer focus, the next-generation stage is about breaking down silos to drive an even better result. The hallmark of this stage is a radical structural reorganization. In it, some combination of customer-facing ops teams (marketing, sales, and customer success) are brought together. Marketing operations is part of an organization that is a strategic enabler.

> The typical combined operations organization is centralized and reports up through the COO [chief operating officer] line. This gives any combined ops team the ability to be very objective about what needs to be done in terms of what is best for the business and what is best for customers.
>
> **—ALEX SIMOES,** RevOps pioneer

I began to hear about these kinds of reorganizations in early 2017. In March of that year, I interviewed Brian Vass, the vice president of revenue operations at Paycor, on my radio show. When Brian explained what he and Paycor had done with the marketing operations organization, I was fascinated. To achieve true line of sight to the customer, they combined sales ops and marketing ops. The combined ops team helped marketing contribute 45 percent of the total bookings and helped drive double-digit growth at Paycor. The company's success, along with the success I have seen in other combined ops organizations, is why this is the stage to watch in the future.

Whatever stage you are in, the degree of integration you believe you have established in a siloed operations environment only gets better when the silos come down. Once they are removed, the lens through which the martech stack and data is reviewed and optimized changes significantly. The impact on the business improves as well.

In this chapter, I've reflected on how marketing operations has evolved and where it is at today. More exciting, however, are the possibilities of what's ahead. To help you face the future, I created the MOM model, which lays out the steps to build your own strategic MO capability. While I touched on all five stages here, I want to point out that in the next chapters, I will give you a closer look at the final four: Efficient/Effective, Get Revenue, Customer Centric, and Next Generation. The last three are strategic capabilities. I want to give you action steps for each one that will help you progress in your journey to becoming a strategic MO leader.

CHAPTER SUMMARY
A QUICK GLANCE AT WHAT WE LEARNED

- I first heard the term "marketing operations" in 2009.

- Today, there are more than eight thousand marketing technologies, and that number is growing.

- The evolution of marketing operations consists of four phases: reactive, proactive/decentralized, proactive/centralized, and strategic.

- The Marketing Operations Maturity (MOM) model allows you to easily see where you are and where you need to go to build a strategic marketing operations capability.

- The five stages of the MOM model are: Unaware, Efficient/Effective, Get Revenue, Customer Centric, and Next Generation.

- The MOM model is a key tool for this book and will help you shift marketing from the backroom to the boardroom.

CHAPTER 4

THE EFFICIENT/EFFECTIVE STAGE

To build a strategic marketing operations function, you need a solid foundation. That's what the Efficient/Effective stage is all about. During this stage, you lay a framework that can support the next stages.

When you're in the Efficient/Effective stage, you'll notice there tends to be a buzz of excitement in the air. There's potential and opportunity seemingly everywhere. Careers take flight. Everything's new, and the energy is palpable.

I love the Efficient and Effective stage of the Marketing Operations Maturity (MOM) model (see Figure 3.2). Look at its placement in the model. You'll see that it comes after the Unaware stage and before the three strategic stages.

MARKETING OPERATIONS MATURITY MODEL

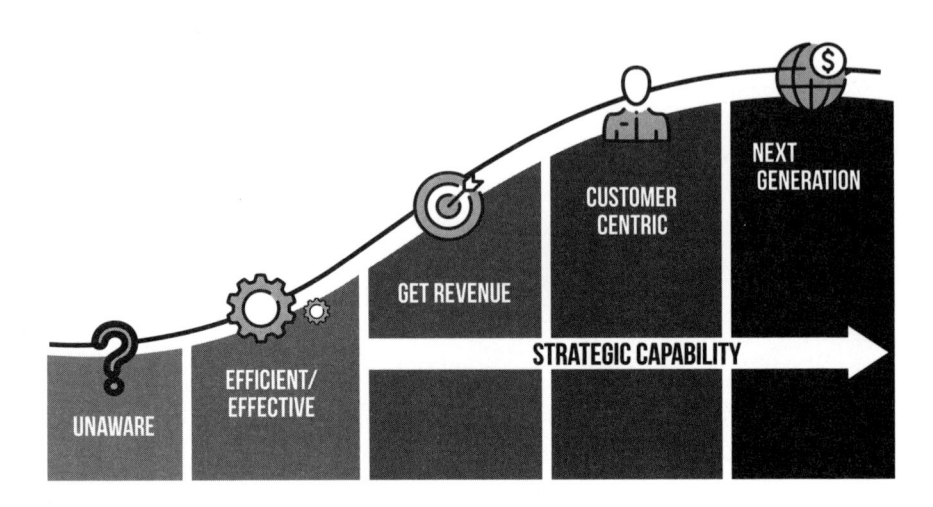

FIGURE 3.2

A lot happens in the Efficient/Effective stage. Put together, these actions prepare marketing to address the CMO's main challenges (see more about the CMO's challenges on page 31). These main challenges tend to be effecting digital transformation, driving revenue and being customer centric. The Efficient/Effective stage is especially helpful in digital transformation efforts. This is because the stage is all about building the critical digital base that enables driving innovative business results in the later MOM model stages. Resolving this challenge can then help the CMO face the other two objectives of driving revenue and being customer centric.

To fully explain what goes on in this stage of the MOM model, I'll share an overview of this stage. I'll provide charters associated with being Efficient/Effective and give an example of a company in action. I'll point out competencies that begin in the Efficient/Effective stage and go over how to build and manage the martech stack—the right way. I'll close with some MO team structure and roles that develop during this stage.

OVERVIEW OF EFFICIENT/EFFECTIVE

During the Efficient/Effective stage of the MOM model, marketing operations is still a cost center that serves the needs of marketing. The focus centers on operational metrics. At this point, a dedicated MO structure and team is in place. The CMO is typically operational in nature.

As the MO team matures, they bring in new talent for technical, analytical and process orientation roles. The MO team can then create a data-driven approach for decision-making. The MO group also begins to infuse this data focus for decision-making across the marketing organization. Once this takes place, marketing starts using data to improve core marketing processes such as campaign performance.

The key metrics at the Efficient/Effective stage are operational in nature. They include items such as the following:

- Percent of systems that are fully integrated
- Percentage use of functions in applications
- Percent of the database that is usable
- Speed to getting a campaign developed
- Basic campaign tracking through dashboards
- Certification in a marketing operations platform

At the beginning of this stage, the perceived value of the MO person or group is to help with automation. They are sought after to automate previously manual processes with technology. They are also expected to provide clean data and some rudimentary marketing metrics.

I have found there are two charters associated with the Efficient/Effective stage. I separate them into a charter for being efficient and a charter for being effective. I do this because I have observed that many MO organizations will work at the efficient level for a time before moving into the effective level.

Charter for Efficient: To begin digitally transforming marketing by selecting, implementing, integrating and optimizing various marketing technologies. An analytics and data competency is introduced into the marketing organization.

Charter for Effective: To digitally transform marketing by marrying process and technology to improve the efficiency and effectiveness of marketing operations. Reengineering core marketing processes that enable marketing to obtain stated goals is essential to this part of digital transformation.

EFFICIENT/EFFECTIVE IN ACTION

Early in 2020, I worked with TraceLink, a company that was creating their first dedicated marketing operations capability. Their goal was to have an Efficient/Effective marketing operations organization. Getting to this level would serve as a precursor to the more strategic stages of the MOM model.

Prior to 2020, TraceLink had invested in a very good martech stack. The limited MO capability was distributed globally across end users of the marketing automation platform and a very small team at corporate. The organization worked well for the original business model of the company. However, the company began a significant transformation that required an equal transformation in MO to support new goals and objectives.

The new business model involved selling new solutions to new buyers in a rapidly evolving market. Given this shift, TraceLink required a different marketing ops capability. Thus, marketing had to develop a dedicated, world-class marketing operations organization.

The founding program had a lot of moving parts and required many operational actions. Therefore, our plan for successfully creating an Efficient/Effective MO function involved numerous steps. These included the following:

- *Assess and remediate the MO team structure, roles and responsibilities and how they work with others.* This action had three primary considerations. First, the dedicated MO team was in India, with MO leadership in the United States. As such, a global execution model needed to be developed. Second, as MO became a consolidated capability, new responsibilities and workflows had to be defined. Third, a ticketing system needed to be developed and instituted to handle the new processes. A new RACI chart (responsibility assignment matrix) was developed and institutionalized.

- *Assess and remediate the current martech stack.* TraceLink had a very good foundational martech stack. Like many companies at this stage that do not have a dedicated MO function, the optimization in terms of integrations and use was not as good as it could have been. With a dedicated MO function, optimal and integrated use of systems to drive results became a reality.

- *Define data governance and health plan.* Customer data now moved to the top of the list. TraceLink needed a way to better understand new personas and new digital behaviors. With the analytical competency of MO, TraceLink Marketing would be able to provide insights into the company's changing business model.

- *Institute templates, processes and best practices.* While templates, processes and best practices were in place, they represented the old business model. New templates, processes and best practices were required to support and drive the dedicated MO function. The dedicated MO function could continue to evolve these items.

- *Create training.* The MO team needed training for new templates, processes, and best practices. Training was also created for key stakeholders participating in the new processes.

- *Define operational metrics.* A list of operational metrics was developed and instituted in dashboards.

- *Create reporting and dashboards.* Reporting and dashboards for operational metrics and value were made. Weekly marketing meetings could then start with a review of the dashboards.

- *Create a culture of metrics.* The move to a dedicated MO function helped the marketing team embrace a culture of metrics. These metrics focused on operations, the customer and revenue.

- *Lay the foundation for marketing to drive revenue.* TraceLink's end goal for marketing was to be able to drive credible revenue and growth in new markets with new solutions. Building an Efficient/Effective MO function served as the baseline for TraceLink's next marketing evolution.

MO COMPETENCIES IN THE EFFICIENT/ EFFECTIVE STAGE

As I mentioned earlier, a lot happens in the Efficient/Effective stage. One of these changes consists of starting to build the core competencies required of a strategic MO organization. A competency is defined as having the skills, knowledge and capacity to perform. To understand how this works, look at the MO Skills Chart (Figure 4.1). It represents all the core competencies required of a strategic MO organization.

FROM BACKROOM TO BOARDROOM

MARKETING OPERATIONS SKILLS CHART

INTERPRET AND DRIVE BUSINESS GOALS

TECHNOLOGY, DATA & ANALYTICS

MarTech Stack
- Cross-Functional Strategy
- Cross-Functional Road map
- Vision
- Interpreter
- Selection
- Integration
- Optimization
- Manage Infrastructure
- Admin
- Vendor Management
- Scanning

Data
- Cross-Functional Strategy
- Cross-Functional Road map
- Strategy
- Governance
- Insights
- Quality
- Cleanliness
- Optimization
- DB Management
- Data Management
- Predictive
- Warehouse
- BI

Performance Management
- Reporting
- Analytics
- Insights
- Metrics & KPIs
- Dashboards
- Funnel Management
- Operational Insights
- Customer Intelligence

PROCESS ENGINEERING

Across Functions
- Funnel Management
- Lead Management
- Lead Life Cycle
- Lead Conversion
- Customer Buyer Journey
- Personas
- Campaign Operations
- Segmentation
- Content Operations
- Shared Services Ops
- Ticketing System
- Insights
- Optimization
- Consulting
- Best Practices
- Performance Management

PROJECT MANAGEMENT & TRAINING

Project Management & Budget
- Professional Project Management
- Budget & Budget Tracking
- Financial Compliance

Training and Education
- Training on New Systems
- Training on New Processes
- Training on Marketing Operations Skills
- Marketing Enablement in Tech and Data

CHANGE MANAGEMENT & CUSTOMER INSIGHTS

Across Functions
- Change Agent
- Visionary
- Strategy to Action
- Collaboration, Communication & Influence with Key Stakeholders
- Empower Accountability
- Dive innovation
- Create Actionable Customer Insights for All Key Stakeholders

FIGURE 4.1

86

In the Efficient/Effective stage, digital transformation begins by building the baseline through technology, data and analytics. In the following sections, I'll give a detailed look at the competencies required to build and manage a martech stack. I'll also point out the competencies needed for data and performance management. As you read through explanations of these competencies in the next sections, keep in mind they will evolve as MO matures.

MARTECH STACK COMPETENCIES

As I mentioned earlier in the book, there are over eight thousand pieces of technology in the martech world. The martech stack is the set of integrated technologies that provides the foundation for marketing success. The stack may include technologies owned by marketing, as well as tech that marketing doesn't own.

Regardless of who owns the technology, the martech stack competency begins with a cross-functional strategy and road map. The MO team spends a lot of time on these two elements.

As MO matures, the need for both a martech strategy and a road map is essential. These must be tangible, well thought out, documented, socialized, actionable and updatable. The strategy and road map documents signal that MO is growing up and becoming part of the fabric of the larger organization. They also set up MO to fully participate in strategic conversations. With them, MO can be more than just the downstream recipients of actions required. For this reason, I'll give you a closer look at both in the next sections.

Martech Strategy

In the Efficient/Effective stage, the martech strategy supports the charter of operational excellence. As MO evolves, the martech strategy does too. In the get-revenue stage, for instance, the martech strategy is based on what it takes to drive revenue. In the customer-centric stage, the martech strategy is based on what is needed to pivot to customer centricity.

You cannot and should not have a martech strategy that is not informed by the business. You also should not have one that was built in marketing isolation. Everything marketing does is in service to drive company goals. Once the company strategies are understood, marketing's overall strategy and goals can be defined. The step happens in close collaboration with marketing leadership, sales leadership, services, and the customer success team. The key input finalizes the martech strategy. At this point, cross-functional collaboration on how everyone's technology will be optimally integrated to serve company goals is critical. Keep in mind that while this happens a little at this stage, it occurs a lot in later stages.

Martech Road Map

Once the martech strategy is in place, the martech road map is created. In this sense, a road map is the action plan. It refers to what is going to happen and when it is going to happen. In my experience, this typically begins with a martech catalog and assessment.

Regarding a martech catalog, I always tell my clients that you can't measure what you can't see. Yet it is common for us to work with MO groups that do not have either a catalog of systems or a sense of the wellness of their ecosystems. Here is a quick challenge: Can you pull up, on one page, a document that represents the total picture of your martech systems? If you have a list of technologies or—even better—a graphic of all the systems you have and how they work together, bravo! You are way ahead of many organizations. If not, your job starts with creating a martech catalog.

A martech catalog is similar to a martech inventory, but it has more information than just a list of systems. Include in your catalog a reference to who uses the system and why. Consider how optimized the use of that system is and whether there is another system that might be used to accomplish the same thing. Is it the best system to accomplish the goal or task? Who else needs to accomplish a similar task? What are the costs? And don't forget to ask: Where are the gaps—what technologies do you not have that you need?

Once you have the catalog developed, look for ways to save money by consolidating or getting rid of systems. Check for opportunities to gain more productivity by sharing and optimizing systems. Make sure you have the right technologies that will support achieving the goals set out by marketing and the company.

After creating the martech catalog, the next step is to assess the overall wellness or optimization of your martech ecosystem. Look at integrations, examine all relevant technology functions, find the gaps and prioritize the next steps to take. One tip: I always like to create the road map by quarters. Doing it in less than a three-month timeframe is just too difficult.

There are many, many ways to represent a martech road map.

The following example, Sample Martech Road Map (Figure 4.2), includes more than the martech stack. The sample also shows the complementary actions of marketing and MO. Having these makes it highly effective for evaluating the overall effectiveness and input of the team as a whole.

As you get started, consider the Functional Martech Stack (Figure 4.3) to see what a martech ecosystem looks like. The example represents both marketing and sales. Of course, it varies widely by company. Getting a similar graph of your own ecosystem is fundamental to understanding the potential for your own company.

FROM BACKROOM TO BOARDROOM

SAMPLE MARTECH ROAD MAP

PHASE 1
MONTHS 1-3

PHASE 1
UP-LEVEL INFRASTRUCTURE AND MARKETING OPERATIONS CAPABILITIES

Marketing Operations - Tech
- Across functions, consolidate overlapping functionality in data analytics and management.
- Audit and remediate Marketo Engage/SFDC integration deficiencies to amplify lead management.
- Implement Jira for ticketing system.

Marketing Operations - Process
- Up-Level the Marketing Operations function that meets current needs.
- Design processes for development of content and campaign execution including all relevant engagement channels.
- Create intake process for shared services for campaign building and execution.
- Collaborate and build Personas and Customer Journeys for new market.

PHASE 2
MONTHS 4-6

PHASE 2
SCALE CONTENT AND CAMPAIGNS TO OPTIMIZE NEW CUSTOMER INTERACTIONS

Marketing Operations - Tech
- Implement web personalization in CMS.
- Expand email personalization in MAP.
- Consistent utilization of A/B testing in MAP to optimize email engagement.
- Evaluate additional platforms for web personalization, video engagement and chat capabilities.

Marketing Operations - Data and Analytics
- Enable a centralized customer data repository.
- Identify and adopt a middleware for data integrations in support of segmentation, personalization and data analytics.
- Ongoing maintenance of data architecture and data quality.
- Development of standard dashboards for Operational, Management and Executive reporting.
- Consider implementing Data Science capabilities.

PHASE 3
MONTHS 7-9

PHASE 3
GET REVENUE

Marketing Operations - Technology
- Identify and evaluate additional platforms or services to meet evolving business demands.
- Optimize what you have.

Marketing Operations - Process
- Optimize lead scoring.
- Optimize lead management.
- Empower ownership of platforms and responsibility for documentation and enhancements to continue to meet changing demands of the business.
- Develop internal processes using resourcing platform to better predict realistic project timelines and resource allocation and increase campaign creation velocity.

Marketing Operations - Data and Analytics
- Improve adoption of Domo or select and implement an alternative platform for data visualization and self-serve data analytics.
- Continue improving integrations to enable a better 360-degree view of customers and prospects.

FIGURE 4.2

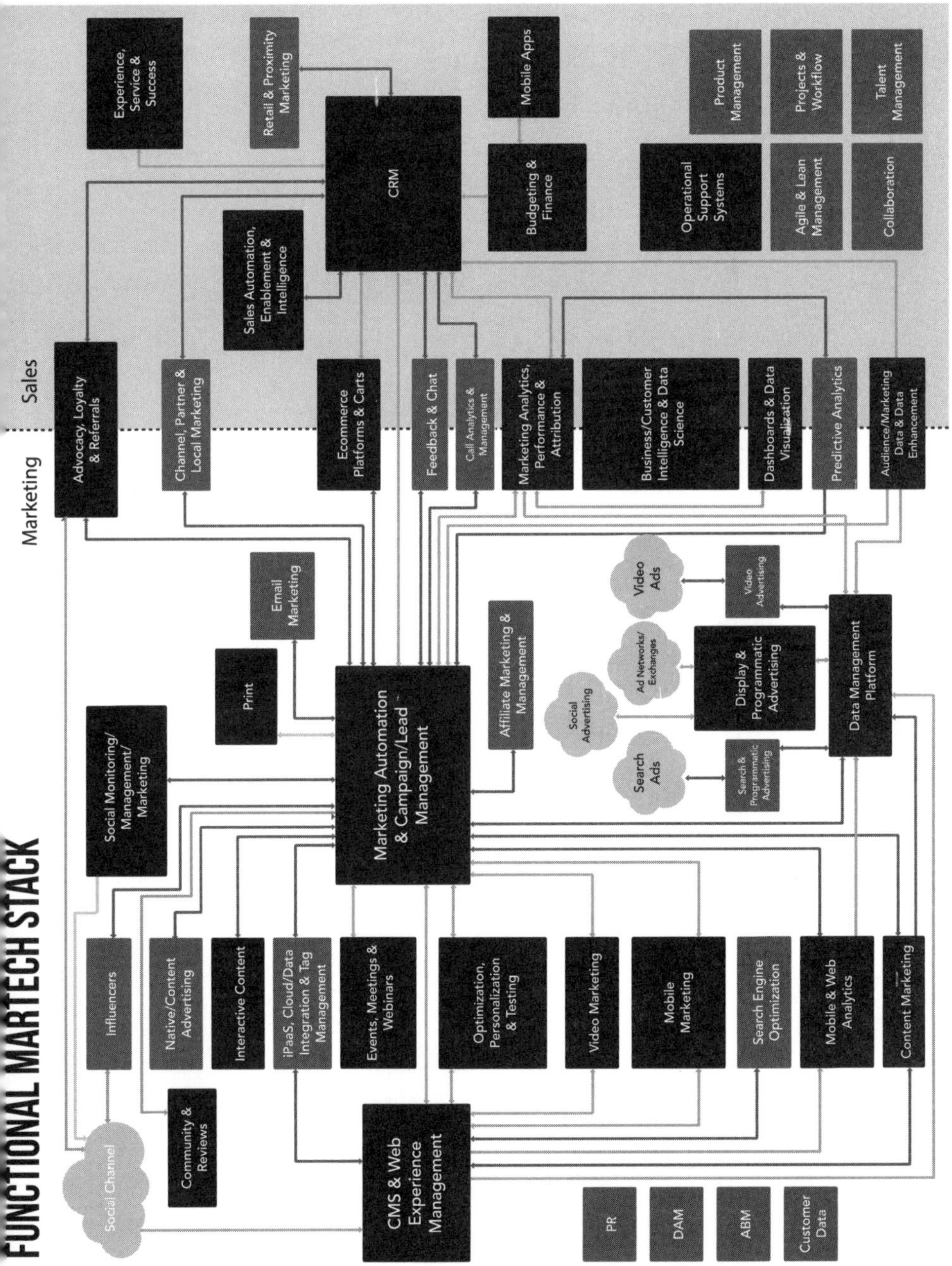

THE EFFICIENT/EFFECTIVE STAGE

FIGURE 4.3

Visionary and Interpreter

While you might think that the role of visionary and business interpreter falls solely on MO leadership, that would not be true. The entire MO team needs to be proactive in helping to shape and reiterate the vision of what martech can enable. Doing this makes the vision practical and usable for marketing. In this role, MO becomes an educator and a consultant.

A simple example of this in the Efficient/Effective stage can be seen in campaigns. If whoever is designing the campaign does not understand the full range of competency in the marketing automation system, they will not get the best campaign results. The MO team has knowledge about both the technology and marketing. Given this, the MO group can work with a campaign manager to improve campaign design based on what the marketing automation system can do. Helping everyone see the vision for what can be and helping to interpret how to drive business results with martech is extremely important. In fact, it is so important that it should be a management business objective (MBO) for the entire MO team.

> We have to continue to ground ourselves in: What is our company's business challenge? What is our purpose for existing? And how does my slice of the pie of the company within marketing and/or MO continue to drive that?
>
> —TOM DELMONTE, head of North America marketing operations at SAP

Selection, Integration and Optimization

These three little words mean so much to the MO function! If you have developed a martech strategy and road map collaboratively with key stakeholders, then selecting, integrating and optimizing becomes much easier. I've seen technology ecosystems that were a nightmare of legacy and ownership. When different parts of marketing buy disparate pieces of technology with no cohesive strategy, it results in a "Frankenstack" of technology. The end results are waste, inefficiencies, and additional costs.

Beyond the martech strategy and the road map, you may be selecting new technology as a corporate collective—not just for marketing. If there is a need in the company that one piece of technology can fulfill, it might become shared. The MO team might find that selecting new systems by working with a cross-functional team is very different. Yet it is a good thing. Integration and optimization will be much smoother in the end.

The Wrong Way to Buy Martech

In the Efficient/Effective stage of the MOM model, it is critical to develop good habits that will then carry over into the more strategic stages. One habit to develop early is how to buy martech. As I reflect on why marketers buy technology, I see two types of marketers with the wrong reasons for buying technology. The first is "I have to have the bright and shiny toy." It is very important to keep up with technological changes. But buying technology because it's the "latest thing" creates a cluttered, underutilized environment. Another kind of marketer is the technology hoarder. They will pick up any piece of software, bring it home, and never want to let it go, even though it serves no purpose except for taking up space. Clearly, these marketers represent the wrong way to buy technology.

The right reasons to buy martech always support the business strategy. CMOs must ask, "How does this technology enable my organization to change, improve or do something new?" The need to change something might be the ability for marketing to be accountable for revenue. The reason to improve something could be to produce higher quality MQLs (marketing-qualified leads) that convert to opportunities at a higher rate. The purpose of doing something new might be adding inbound and social as part of your omnichannel program. In every case, the reason to buy a new piece of technology fits into the business strategy.

How to Implement Martech

Given a clear business reason to buy a new piece of marketing technology, let's now look at the elements of "how." This includes problem definition and participation. The purpose of the technology solution is to solve a business problem that you have. By clearly defining the problem, you can develop a use case for what the technology needs to accomplish.

I built my first set of technology use cases in 2004 when I bought my first CRM. I have used this technique for every software purchase I have ever made. Why? Because I need to see how a piece of technology will solve my business problem. An out-of-the-box demo is not going to impress me. I've seen marketers use a similar process with great results. They take the time to understand what the technology does and specifically how it will help them do something new or better or change something. They then stand a better chance of buying a solution they will actually use and from which their department will benefit.

From my observations, there are—on average—more than thirty martech tools in a marketing group. I've seen research that indicates the average number of martech tools is close to ninety. If you do the calculation on the time and effort required to build a use case for every piece of technology, you might throw up your hands and exclaim, "I don't have the time!" But you do have the time. You must make the time now, or you will need to make the time later. Figuring out how a piece of technology will improve an element of your business is a sunk cost. Doing it early ensures you buy the right technology the first time.

Participation is also a frequently overlooked element in buying martech. If you are not involving all the key stakeholders in the buying process, you are doing it wrong. I cannot state this strongly enough. Too many times I arrive at a client site, and in discussions with the marketing team, I hear that they have technology they are resistant to using. They typically were not involved in the buying decision. In some cases, this included the people who were supposed to be using the technology on a daily basis.

Participation in the buying process ensures improvement in two areas. First, participation gets everyone on the same page and gains commitment to the technology. As a result, your team will work for a flawless implementation. They will also work to optimize the use of the technology. Second, participation will secure a higher probability that you are buying the right technology. Other stakeholders add valuable insights to how the technology may be used. You can then make the best decision for the entire organization.

Who Buys It?

I have referenced working with key stakeholders during the buying process. The other "who" refers to the people engaging in the unfettered buying of marketing technology across the organization. I often help clients define, map and build a martech architecture. I always have them begin with a hunt to discover the various technologies used throughout the marketing organization. They must also understand who uses the technologies and for what purpose. Doing this audit takes time and effort, but it is critical.

The accidental marketing technology landscape in a company is often a legacy hangover. It can be resolved with a documented martech map. Having a documented current and future architecture corrals and defines the "who" of the buying process. The buying of all marketing technologies now becomes a centralized effort. The purchase doesn't just occur randomly. Defining a buying process and a team to lead the process ensures buying the right technology at the right time to solve the right business problems.

In the history of digital technology, volumes on the right way and the wrong way to buy technology have been written. Around 99 percent of that material has been written for the IT department. However, marketing is now a major buyer of technology. In some companies, the CMO has a larger technology spend than IT. Given this, it is time for marketing to develop a comprehensive and agile process for buying marketing technology. We are in a fast growth market. Being able to responsibly source marketing technology is a key skill for MO, both today and for the foreseeable future.

Martech Fatigue Syndrome (MTFS)

I can't leave this section without talking about martech fatigue. While I can't take credit for the phrase, I think it's time to look at what is happening to the collision between marketing, technology and the marketer. As we consider the eight-thousand-plus distinct pieces of technology available to marketing, we must also recognize the impact of all that technology on the marketer.

Some marketers are still very excited about all the possibilities from this intricate martech landscape. In contrast, others are beginning to feel fatigued by it all. Symptoms of martech fatigue syndrome (MTFS) are beginning to appear. I began to see marketers with this syndrome as early as 2017, but it now seems to be going viral. I'm seeing symptoms such as the MO team with glazed and hopeless looks in their eyes. They are skittish around martech vendors. They hide when they see their CMO coming down the hall because they think she might have an idea about a new piece of technology. They begin hallucinating anytime they see the MarTech Lumascape. They count martech vendors to go to sleep at night.

For the victims of MTFS, just trying to survive the tsunami of technology and expectations is grueling. The good news is that there is a cure. Here are three ways to overcome this syndrome:

- Put your head down, and optimize what you have.
- Develop a martech scanning competency.
- Develop a martech vendor management program.

If you suffer from MTFS, try one (or more) of these cures. I explain them in detail below.

PUT YOUR HEAD DOWN, AND OPTIMIZE WHAT YOU HAVE

The first way you can cure MTFS is to realize that your world will not end if you don't immediately buy the latest technology. The martech landscape is like the weather: if you wait a bit, it will change. A recent statistic states only 58 percent of marketers report that they are optimizing their martech stack.[24] There is room for improvement! Taking the time to analyze your current state and then optimize it is essential. The productivity gains from this single action can be substantial.

A simple example that can increase efficiency and effectiveness lies in the use of all the features and functions in various applications. Too often I see marketers with powerful systems using them almost as doorstops. Another way to optimize what you have is to ensure that your marketers are fully trained in the use of core systems. Investing in training is a sure way to optimize your investments in systems and to improve performance.

DEVELOP A MARTECH SCANNING COMPETENCY

Marketing leaders need to develop an always-on martech scanning competency. They must have some level of fluency in the technology. For the MO team, they must be extremely fluent and knowledgeable in the different martech options. The martech scanning competency must be at a category and detailed level.

One way to resolve MTFS is to develop a similar competency. If you don't have a natural curiosity and desire to learn about various technologies, give this assignment to someone else on the team. There is so much published about martech today that anyone with a healthy curiosity can keep up at a scanning level. Finally, this scanning competency needs to be tied to the goals of marketing, which are tied to company goals. Otherwise, you can spend *all* your time just looking at options in the market.

DEVELOP A MARTECH VENDOR MANAGEMENT PROGRAM

One area of a marketer's everyday life that is adding to MTFS symptoms is managing the sheer number of martech vendors. Five years ago, most marketers were perhaps using four or five systems. Now, the average number is above twenty and climbing. Furthermore, that number represents a major portion of the budget. Added to this volume is the importance to achieving new marketing goals and how technology helps. Some technologies are mission critical. Either way, this is a lot to manage.

IT views vendor management as a core discipline, which includes knowing how to negotiate, how to renegotiate, how to bring on board, how to monitor performance, how to handle technology issues, support and so on. In large marketing ops teams, there is one person almost fully dedicated to this discipline. To help alleviate MTFS, take an intentional approach to developing and running a vendor management program.

Start with managing infrastructure and administration. For the MO function, managing the infrastructure and serving as the administrator of systems comprise the most basic set of skills. Doing this well ensures the good health, continuity and use of systems for their intended purposes.

Today, marketing organizations are managing twenty to fifty different vendors. Taking the time to be intentional to create a vendor management program often results in huge savings. From contract negotiations for better pricing and terms to keeping up to date on new features and functions, this can be an almost full-time job.

We see this come into play in just about every company we work with. One of the things we do when we catalog the different martech systems is to review contract terms. Carrying out this task leads to significant savings.

DATA COMPETENCIES

Data is the lifeblood of every organization, even more so in our digital and connected world. Historically, understanding data, using data and having good data have not been strengths of the marketing department. As such, the rise of the MO function has been as much about data as it has been about systems. Today's marketing organization simply cannot be successful without data. MO brings this important competency to marketing.

When I sat down to talk with Kira Mondrus-Moyal, senior vice president of global marketing at Tricentis, she talked about what MO brings to the table in terms of data. "MO helps marketing be data driven and use data for all of our important decisions," she said. "Where the organization matures and becomes more advanced is through really understanding the data and using it to drive future decisions, future investments, future direction and so forth."

During the decision-making process, MO groups present data in a nonbiased way. Kira mentioned to me that the honesty of data could often be valuable to a company. "Sometimes, the numbers really aren't positive, and that's OK," she explained. "That means it just needs time to pivot."

Data Strategy, Road Map and Governance

Like the martech stack, the MO team needs its own data strategy and a road map. There is also one additional data element to address, and that is data governance. Let's look at all three.

The data strategy paints a very clear picture of the perfect state of data and lists why the data is valuable to marketing. More importantly, it should include the decisions and actions the data set will enable.

The data road map represents all the actions required to achieve the desired data set, the priority and the timing. One thing to note: Work on data is *never* done. While your road map may be finite, the actual task at hand is ever growing and changing.

Together, the data strategy and data road map are a cross-functional collaborative effort. Everyone in the company has data, although in different formats and for different reasons. The third element—a strong data governance group—can be highly beneficial here. The more marketing activities cross and affect other functions, the more a cohesive data strategy and road map need to be in place. In the past, marketing has had a difficult time contributing to the conversation around data. With a strategic MO organization, marketing now has a seat and a voice at the table.

Quality, Cleanliness and Optimization

The lament of every marketer I know is, "Our database is horrible." They have records that are wrong or incomplete. They have duplicate records and ones that are out of date. They have many data types and very little consistency. Marketing cannot be successful in this scenario.

The time and effort that MO spends in correcting this long list of wrongs—while tedious—is time well spent. Giving marketing an optimized database is the best gift ever. They will forever love you for it.

To make this happen, you may need to onboard more talent. "Three years ago, I hired a full-time data analyst to do nothing but make sure that we have good, clean data in our database," Brian Vass, vice president of revenue operations at Paycor, shared with me during a conversation about data. "He's the expert on bringing data in from our third-party vendors, keeping it clean, deduplicating it, segmenting it from an industry standpoint, sourcing data for our sales and marketing campaigns, all those kinds of things."

Brian went on to explain that his organization had recently hired a second data person. "There's such demand across the business for having good quality data," he said. "So that's really important. Without good quality data, nothing else matters."

Data Management and Database Management

Data management involves understanding marketing goals and ensuring the use of data is optimized to drive results. In contrast, database management is about the nuts and bolts of the software or platform. A strategic MO organization has both and has at least two people (but ideally a team) dedicated to this effort.

Advanced

The strategic MO team definitely has advanced competencies with data. They work with tools and processes for predictive actions. They understand how to store and access data, as well as work with BI tools. With all these in their tool belt, the strategic MO organization is a powerhouse of data competencies and resources.

PERFORMANCE MANAGEMENT COMPETENCIES

Performance management is a game changer for MO. If I called this "reporting and analytics," it would not really represent this category or show the value that MO brings to marketing. Once MO gets out of the mindset of "I have to create reports and dashboards" and moves to "I have to improve marketing performance in terms of business value," more sophisticated skills are required. The perfect combination of technology expertise, analytical skills, marketing know-how and business acumen are needed.

In many ways, the MO team is the enabler of performance and this step begins in the Efficient/Effective stage. Building a performance-based versus activity-based culture should be high on the CMO's to-do list. In a CMO study, 95 percent of CMOs believed it was "very important" to "critically important" to build a performance culture.[25] Without the support and guidance from a strategic MO organization, however, this shift is almost impossible.

During the Efficient/Effective stage, MO can begin to help marketing on their digital transformation journey. When I spoke with Tom DelMonte, head of North American operations at SAP, he shared how MO was a key partner in digital transformation. "We're very KPI focused and numbers driven, so performance management is very key," he said. "How many leads? How much value and volume did we get from leads that are opportunities? What's the conversion rate?" Having an MO group that can produce solid KPIs enables marketing to up its performance.

Reporting, Analytics, KPIs and Dashboards

MO people are much more analytical, data driven and tech driven than traditional marketers. These skills are needed to put the metrics and KPIs in place for the marketing organization. Once these are established, the MO team can move to creating reports and dashboards that help marketing consistently stay on task. The MO team can develop operational as well as revenue-oriented dashboards.

Taking this one step further, MO can provide the most value by taking the data, analyzing it, and providing actionable insights to marketing and sales. Instead of executing a reactive set of activities to see what happened in the past, insights are provided to help predict the future. Data and analytics regarding customer behavior across all channels must be pulled together to deliver these future-oriented insights. The MO function provides a type and level of customer intelligence that only marketing can provide.

Putting this into motion enables marketing to take on more of a leadership role. When I spoke with Brian Vass of Paycor, he told me how his team had grown to be a leader. "My team builds out all the reports and dashboards in Salesforce and Marketo Engage that are consumed by the marketing organization every single day," he explained. "We have an analyst who can take that data and do things with it in Excel and help identify trends and conversion rates that you can't do so easily in CRM."

Funnel Management

Funnel management is a marketing view for how the customer takes their buyer journey. The role of marketing is to influence the prospect/customer at each stage of the funnel to move them through to become a lead for sales. The MO team is responsible for ensuring it works as it should. From a process perspective, how it is engineered and supported by data and technology ensures marketing meets their goals. The MO team engineers this process to make it repeatable, predictable and scalable (RPS).

> Our MO is all about managing the technology. We really depend on technology to be better marketers. They manage the sort of flow of the funnel for making sure that leads are flowing through the different stages.
>
> **—DANNY ESSNER,** vice president of revenue marketing at Sisense, Inc.

MO ROLES IN EFFICIENCY/EFFECTIVENESS

In the Efficient/Effective stage of the Marketing Operations Maturity (MOM) model, structure and roles tend to be basic and operational in nature. The MO team focuses on the pieces of the puzzle versus solving the entire puzzle. Team structure and roles might include some of the following:

- Director
    - Reports to the CMO (marketing leader) or to the demand generation leader
    - Focused on team building, practice building and execution
- Marketing technology admin
    - Reports to the director
    - Focused on marketing automation and integration with CRM campaign manager
    - Might report to demand generation group or to marketing operation
    - Responsible for creating, building and executing campaigns in marketing automation system, or
    - Responsible for creating a campaign and then handing off for build and execution to another group
- Campaign builder
    - Might report to demand generation group or to marketing operations
    - Focused on building and executing campaigns
    - Expert in marketing automation
    - Reports to director or to the demand generation team
- Data analyst
    - Reports to the director
    - Focused on data quality and segmentation for campaigns
    - May work with other parts of the company on data issues

THE EXPANDED ORGANIZATIONAL AND COLLABORATIVE STRUCTURE

In the Efficient/Effective stage, along with the other more advanced stages, a bit of tug-of-war goes on in terms of where the MO function should sit in large organizations. On one side is corporate marketing, who believes all MO functions are best kept as a centralized and shared services type of function. On the other side, field marketing believes they should own their own destiny and the technology to go with it.

Who is right? There are pros and cons to each structure. In the next sections, I'll outline some of the main advantages and disadvantages to be aware of.

Pros of a Centralized Structure

Clearly, the number one benefit of a centralized structure in a large organization lies in the economies of scale. The benefits include centralized vendor management, system administration and integration, data and skills. Remember, the average marketing department uses north of thirty different pieces of technology—although this number is much larger in big companies.

Given the escalation in the number of disparate systems that need to be managed, a centralized vendor management program is common. Larger companies may find it very cost effective. In addition, system administration and integration can be greatly "simplified" in a centralized model.

Centralized systems can also greatly help in centralizing data. As large companies move to a customer-centric strategy, gaining that *one* view of the customer journey—no matter where they interact with the company—becomes a strategic imperative. Having a centralized architecture helps accomplish this extraordinarily difficult task.

Finally, centralizing the skills required to manage and use all these systems can be a huge benefit to a company. Finding and growing marketing technologist talent is one of the biggest challenges that marketers face today. Creating a centralized and deep talent pool has real advantages for a large company.

Cons of a Centralized Structure

The major con of a centralized MO structure is a lack of local specificity and alignment in terms of market conditions, goals, and agility. No personalization can be a death knell to any marketing campaign: it fails to speak directly to the prospective buyer about specific challenges that need to be solved. Using this generic approach often leads the prospect to respond with an immediate "delete."

Pros of a Decentralized Structure

While there are economies of scale in a centralized structure, there are also unique benefits to a decentralized structure. These include knowledge of and responsiveness to local markets.

One of the most important roles of the field marketing team is their working knowledge of sales, local market conditions, and local customer idiosyncrasies. In contrast, corporate marketers are so often removed from the local reality, especially from customers, that they make decisions in a vacuum. These determinations do not always represent the best interests of local marketers. A decentralized MO structure helps minimize the knowledge and results orientation gap.

Cons of a Decentralized Structure

Of course, all the pros for the centralized structure are actually the cons for the decentralized structure. Besides the economies of scale, the biggest drawback is the lower skill level typically seen at a local level. The lower skill level suboptimizes the possibilities of leveraging technology and best practices to solve the prospective buyer's problem.

A Tale of Two Global Companies and Their Marketing Operations Approach

I've watched companies take various approaches when organizing the structure of MO. For the sake of comparison, I'll point out two global companies I worked with that were both embracing revenue marketing. During their transitions, they made very different MO decisions. These decisions were based on their company environment and business conditions.

In one company, they decided to centralize all systems and demand-generation services. Their centralized MO team grew to about seventy-five people in six months. During this process, the field marketing organization was not happy. They believed they needed to own their "MO" organization and structure to best support field initiatives and goals.

The number one reason this company adopted a centralized MO had to do with the goal of getting all customer data centralized to create one view of the customer. With this overarching, company-wide strategy, centralizing the MO organization made sense. The move allowed them to act as one company, rather than a set of loose associations.

The other global organization took the opposite route. In this company, marketing automation and the relating MO structure were pushed down to a field level. Each major field office had their own instances of marketing technologies they managed, integrated and used, with an overarching strategy based on speed. In this company, enabling the field organization with their own mini MO organizations allowed for speed and agility. Both were required in their marketing environment.

In the second company, one reason for decentralizing MO had to do with how the company functioned. There were very different business units that acted like sole companies. In this case, decentralizing MO made sense.

The Distributed Marketing Operations Structure: A Shared Services Capability

In addition to the two examples I just described, there is a third example that sets up the best of both worlds. Called the distributed MO capability, it begins with corporate centralizing MO functions such as vendor management, system administration and integration, data and skills. Yet it does this in a shared services model. Corporate then sets up best practices and governances that can be accessed by field marketing. At the same time, field marketing has their own mini MO organization that allows them to optimize local results.

There are many different organizational structures in MO as a shared services capability. You don't necessarily have to find the one right or wrong answer. The key is to allow for local independence while establishing easy access to a very high level of expertise in people, data and systems.

FOLLOW THE BOUNCING ORG CHART

As B2B marketing accepts new responsibilities in terms of digital transformation, customer centricity and revenue generation, the B2B marketing org chart will continue to evolve. We've seen the fast growth of the MO organization as a logical response to marketing's need to use technology to drive change and business impact. Where the MO capability lives is a critical component of marketing success.

I've seen all kind of models work, so it's not the model itself that helps predict accomplishment. Rather, success is predicted based on how the MO organizational model serves the need of marketing and of the company. The question is "Where does MO live in your company, and is it in the right place?"

The Efficient/Effective stage can be pictured as a bit of a frenzy to get all the gears in place. And while there are many benefits that come during this stage, the best part may lie in what's ahead because once these gears are in place, they can start turning, and the strategic motions can begin. I'll cover these next steps in the following chapter, where I'll discuss Get Revenue, the next stage in the MOM model.

CHAPTER SUMMARY
A QUICK GLANCE AT WHAT WE LEARNED

- The Efficient/Effective stage comes after the Unaware stage of the Marketing Operations Maturity (MOM) model and before Get Revenue, Customer Centric, and Next Generation stages.

- MO teams in the Efficient/Effective stage can help CMOs address the main challenges of driving revenue and being customer centric by building the digital foundation.

- In this stage, marketing operations focuses on operational metrics.

- The competencies for managing a martech stack, along with data and performance management, begin in this stage.

- In an Efficient/Effective MO function, structure and roles tend to be basic and operational in nature.

- In large companies, there is frequently a bit of a battle when deciding where the MO function should sit.

- There are pros and cons to both centralized and decentralized structure; determining the right place within your own organization will depend on the company's specific situation.

CHAPTER 5

THE GET REVENUE STAGE

If you know nothing about me, know this: I began as a revenue marketer in 2004 and have not stopped since. A revenue marketer is a marketer or a marketing organization that is proactively responsible for driving revenue by building a digital foundation and accelerating customer centricity. A majority of my work, my business and my academic research revolves around revenue marketing. For more on revenue marketing basics, see the Revenue Marketing Journey (Figure 11.6) in the appendix.

Here's why I'm sharing this with you: it's my belief that you must understand and focus on what it takes to help marketing drive revenue and growth. Creating a repeatable, predictable and scalable (RPS) revenue machine—being revenue marketers—is the only result that ensures marketing a voice and a seat at the table. Yet nothing continues to plague today's CMO as much as achieving credible revenue results. Make no mistake: as a *strategic* MO organization, this is your North

Star, your guiding light, your daily mantra, and your top goal. Generating revenue is your reason to come to work every day.

In the Marketing Operations Maturity (MOM) model I first introduced in chapter 3 (listed again below in Figure 3.2), this stage is called the Get Revenue stage. This stage comes after the Efficient/Effective stage and is the first *strategic* stage on the model. *Strategic* in this context means driving business results versus operational results.

MARKETING OPERATIONS MATURITY MODEL

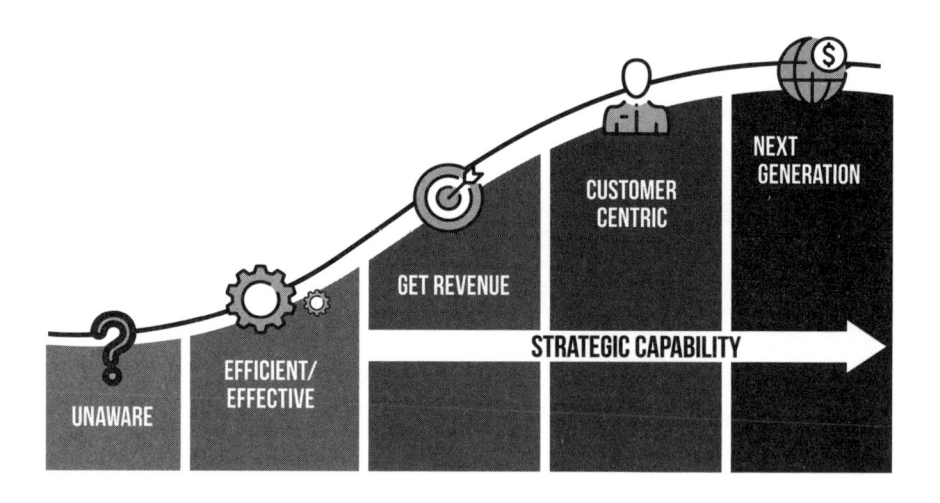

FIGURE 3.2

Getting revenue does not happen by snapping your fingers; on the contrary, it is an intricate journey. Done well, however, it produces amazing—even magical—results. To fully lay out what's needed to start that ascent to the boardroom, I'll go over a detailed description of the Get Revenue stage. Next, I'll show how *strategic* MO is the arbitrator of the relationship between sales and marketing and why this is a game-changing dynamic. I'll explain my take on revenue management and the role strategic MO plays in moving the focus from leads to revenue. Finally, I'll show you the action steps strategic MO can pursue to fully embrace this stage and move forward as a leader.

> I am really excited about the future of marketing operations because it will be a key function for organizations as they shift to become revenue marketers. As a revenue marketer, it is imperative to develop defined processes and to measure and analyze results. Marketing is shifting; there is now a critical role for quantitative analytics and process management in order to compete and succeed. This is the role that marketing operations contributes.
>
> —MITCH DIAMOND, senior director of marketing operations at SAP Ariba

AN OVERVIEW OF THE GET REVENUE STAGE

When I think about revenue marketing pioneers, one name that always comes to mind is Danny Essner, vice president of revenue marketing for Sisense. I recently sat down with Danny to talk and asked him to describe how he views marketing operations today. I love his answer. He said, "The way I define marketing operations is probably narrower than others. I see it as managing the systems, data and possibilities to make a scalable revenue machine as efficient as possible."

Danny and the entire team at Sisense—up and down the chain—understand the need to get revenue. What's more, they are using revenue marketing methods to optimize and scale their revenue engine.

In the Get Revenue stage, the CMO is responsible for revenue and growth. Accountability cascades down into every part of the marketing organization. The newly formed partnership of marketing, MO, and sales creates a new and exciting way to drive revenue in a digital world (also called digital revenue). The Get Revenue stage is the first stage of the MOM model in which the MO focus extends beyond marketing to embrace sales and tie more directly to company goals. Strategic MO has a dedicated and substantial structure, which includes a collaborative, cross-functional method of working. After all, revenue is a team sport.

Here's a typical charter for the Get Revenue stage of the MOM model: "With digital transformation as the baseline, marketing becomes part of the revenue team and applies martech technology, process and analytics to drive repeatable, predictable and scalable (RPS) revenue results." You can see the other characteristics of the Get Revenue stage in the MOM Model Characteristics by Stage (Figure 11.5) in the appendix.

> **With digital transformation as the baseline, marketing becomes part of the revenue team and applies martech technology, process and analytics to drive repeatable, predictable and scalable (RPS) revenue results.**

During this stage of the MOM model, the marriage of technology and revenue-specific processes such as revenue management take center stage for the strategic MO organization. Marketing might focus on net-new client acquisition, customer retention or both. In the prior stage of Efficient/Effective, data was used to improve marketing performance around operational metrics. At this stage, data is used to inform decisions and performance for both marketing and sales in terms of driving revenue and growth.

A better understanding of the customer also develops during this stage. Marketing is able to effectively use technology, data and analytics to understand digital body language. Marketing can then use these insights to inform sales and marketing pursuit decisions—both personal and automated.

Metrics at the Get Revenue stage indicate that marketing is now running like a business. Two radical changes in metrics include tracking sales efficiencies and marketing revenue numbers. For sales, the strategic MO organization can help impact operational metrics such as time to close, average deal size, and percentage of salespeople meeting quota. At the same time, marketing adopts revenue metrics such as marketing contribution to pipeline, revenue, and growth. Everyone in the marketing organization has some portion of their compensation tied to marketing's revenue performance—including MO.

STRATEGIC MO AS THE ARBITRATOR OF THE SALES AND MARKETING REVENUE RELATIONSHIP

One of the most thrilling roles MO plays during the Get Revenue stage is to mediate and forever change the sales and marketing revenue relationship. Note that in the previous sentence, I stated "revenue relationship" and not "good working relationship." I share this distinction based on experience. In my early days of consulting with marketing organizations, I typically asked marketing if they had a good working relationship with sales. When I closely examined the situation, I discovered a very different picture. I found they might be cordial, but the relationship was not one based on revenue. Marketing was simply the "yes" organization to anything sales required. As marketing pushed to create a revenue relationship with sales, they were often not viewed as an equitable or serious partner in revenue.

Now let's turn to see what happens when *strategic* MO enters the picture.

First, in the Get Revenue stage, strategic MO brings immediate credibility into any conversation with sales. Using data rather than gut intuition, they can make a case for change and demonstrate the benefit to sales. Moreover, strategic MO can make the required changes in the technology to drive new behaviors from both sales and marketing. Second, strategic marketing operations takes a project management approach to working with sales, which is transparent and commonly understood. As such, strategic MO mitigates the drama and emotion. Instead of having heated arguments, everyone can focus on figuring out what is wrong and how to fix it. The revenue management process—a core element to the revenue engine—becomes scalable and predictable in terms of revenue results. Marketing can move past being a lead factory and turn into an essential part of the revenue process. I consider this one of the *strategic* MO leader's most critical successes.

CHANGING THE LEAD DYNAMIC

Another revenue marketing pioneer I greatly admire is Brian Vass, vice president of sales operations at Paycor. In a recent conversation I had with Brian, he succinctly laid out the familiar sales and marketing dilemma the firm faced in the past. "Marketing throws leads over the wall to sales, and then marketing complains that the salespeople don't follow up with the leads," he said. (We've all heard this tale.) "And salespeople say, 'Marketing doesn't understand what we need—these leads are worthless.' And marketing responds, 'Why aren't you following up with my amazing, quality leads?'"

While this is typical in many companies, Brian said at Paycor they worked to eradicate this dynamic. "We wanted to have a really strong alignment between sales and marketing," he explained. To make that a reality, Brian and his team created one go-to-market strategy.

"It's a combined sales and marketing strategy," Brian noted. "Our chief revenue officer has responsibility for sales and marketing. And our revenue operations team (a combination of marketing ops and sales ops) is responsible for supporting both sales and marketing."

The new approach and organizational structure helped establish a solid alignment with tangible results. "When you look at our strategic initiatives and pillars for the fiscal year, sales and marketing are combined, and when we present to the board, it's a sales and marketing update," Brian said.

Brian's story exemplifies the role that strategic MO can play to help marketing become a team player in the Get Revenue stage. The action steps he and his company took enabled marketing to get that seat at the table.

DIGITAL REVENUE MANAGEMENT

Brian's description of the typical "throw leads over the wall" is exactly what I've seen in many companies. Marketing diligently works to produce sales-ready leads. In doing so, they spend large amounts of time, money and resources. Yet over 50 percent of leads given to sales receive no follow-up.[26] Or sales says, "We have it—we know all of our customers!" Both cases represent unnecessary costs to the company and lost opportunities for revenue and growth. They also ensure marketing loses business credibility and is still seen as a cost center.

From a marketing operations perspective, this common scenario represents a massive failure. Today's strategic MO organization is about more than implementing and optimizing the right technology and ensuring data quality. Their charter is to enable marketing achievement of revenue goals. Strategic MO must embrace, drive, and optimize an end-to-end revenue management process.

To build this essential process, marketing operations must reimagine the term "lead management process" and give it an updated name, one that represents revenue as a team sport and one in which marketing plays a critical role.

LEAD MANAGEMENT IS DEAD

For many years we have called the lead management process, well, the lead management process. Marketing solely worked to pop out as many MQLs as possible. Today, more needs to be done. As marketing moves to embrace revenue marketing and MO moves into the Get Revenue stage, we need something beyond a lead process. We need a digital revenue process.

To further support my argument, let's look at the difference between lead management and revenue management. Lead management is the coordination of people, process, and technology in marketing that allows marketing to generate MQLs for sales. Once that handoff is completed, marketing's role is done. Most often this approach sets up the "us-versus-them" dynamic.

A revenue management process comprises a larger cross-functional team dedicated to driving systematic revenue and growth. In this dynamic, marketing is measured on the team result of revenue across the entire customer life cycle. By changing the word "lead" to "revenue," you can more easily recalibrate the role of marketing in revenue. For this reason, I believe the name should be changed from lead management to revenue management.

Revenue management is both a methodology and a capability. By naming it a methodology, I mean it is a cross-functional process of finding, sharing, and processing qualified leads that result in predictable revenue results. Both net-new acquisition and growing exiting accounts are included. In other words, it encompasses any point in the customer life cycle. Getting this process right and working to continuously optimize it are critical for marketing to achieve revenue goals.

While lead management is a basic capability, revenue management is a *strategic* capability. Consider an MO team that develops a repeatable, predictable and scalable (RPS) way to create leads, MQLs and opportunities that convert at a predictable rate. Those results are a tremendous gift to the business and a game changer for marketing.

Revenue management is also a shared capability between marketing ops, marketing, sales ops, and sales. Since it is such an important cross-functional process, ongoing change management efforts should be utilized. Done well, revenue management often represents big changes in marketing and sales.

> MQLs are a driver for us. We also measure how many of those are converted. We don't have a qualification team, so MQLs go directly to sales, and they do the qualification. One of their required steps is to mark the MQLs as qualified or unqualified. Within that step, we have reason codes for why something might be unqualified. For example, in one market where we are doing the high-demand creation across a very large market, we use an ideal client profile to help us determine if they are qualified or unqualified. Using the ideal profile narrows down our market to about 10 percent; as a result, we are much more efficient.
>
> —RANDY TAYLOR, director of marketing operations at Aderant

THE ROLE OF STRATEGIC MARKETING OPERATIONS IN THE REVENUE MANAGEMENT FRAMEWORK™

Now that I've reviewed the basics of revenue management, I'll show you how strategic MO fully fits into the scene. To do so, I'll use the Revenue Management Framework, listed below in Figure 5.1. The framework details six key areas: establishing metrics; defining a sales-ready lead;

creating a common funnel with stages and statuses; architecting lead processing and routing; developing lead scoring and implementing service level agreements (SLAs). Together these six elements create a holistic and interrelated framework that forms the foundation for an effective revenue management practice. I'll give a brief description of each of these areas so you can see how they play out and interact with each other.

THE REVENUE MANAGEMENT FRAMEWORK

SALES & MARKETING ALIGNMENT

1. ESTABLISHING METRICS
2. DEFINING A SALES READY LEAD
3. CREATING A COMMON FUNNEL WITH STAGES & STATUSES
4. ARCHITECTING LEAD PROCESSING & ROUTING
5. DEVELOPING LEAD SCORING
6. IMPLEMENTING SLAS

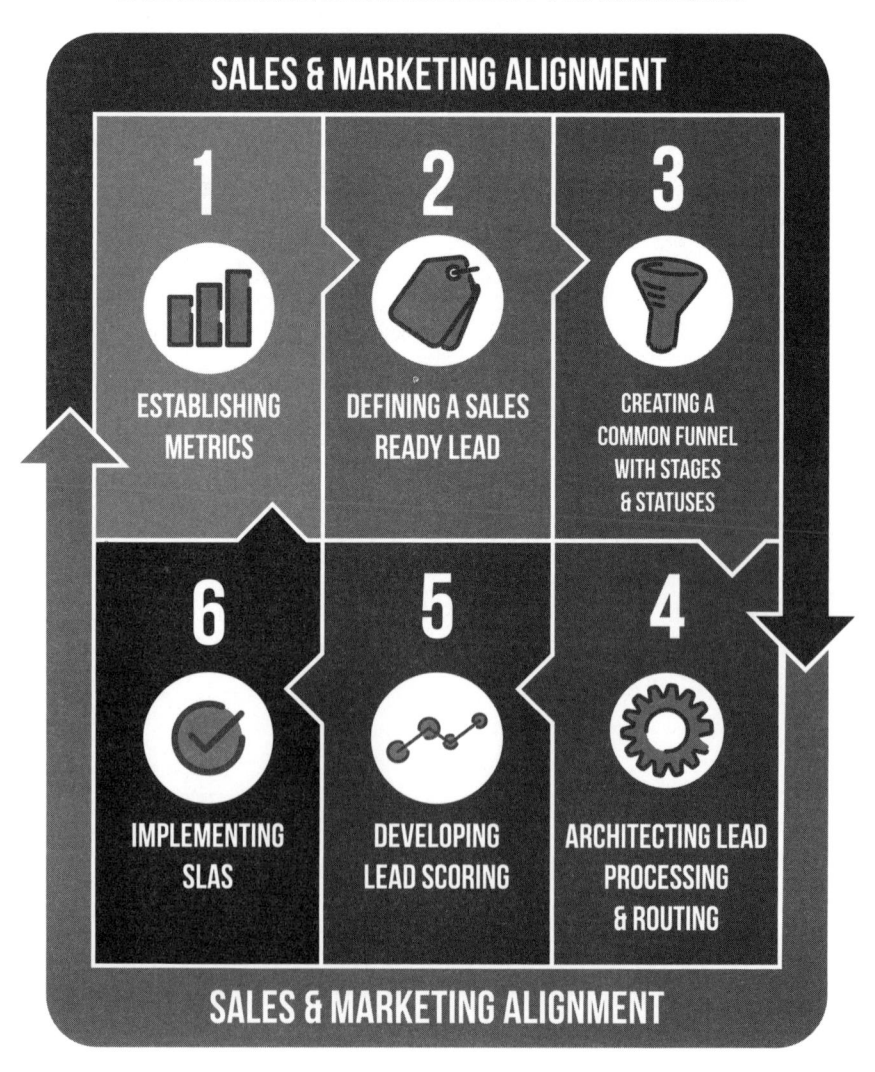

SALES & MARKETING ALIGNMENT

FIGURE 5.1

1. ESTABLISHING METRICS

The first step is to set up a system that can be tracked and reported on. As Peter Drucker said, "If you can't measure it, you can't manage it." For this reason, it's essential to take the time to develop a set of key performance indicators (KPIs).

A KPI is a value you choose to measure. The KPI might be tactical and measure the effectiveness of your marketing activities. For example, you can track the number of newly engaged leads that are added to the database or the volume of marketing sourced in a set period. A KPI can also be operational and measure efficiencies in your processes. For instance, you can establish a KPI for funnel performance or funnel velocity. Finally, a KPI can be revenue related and measure attribution, pipeline and revenue. The KPI can include the percentage of contribution to sales' pipeline and revenue. Tie a bow around these by adding dashboards for your selected KPIs.

> The first step was to develop an executive dashboard. Once we had that, it provided a visible set of KPIs with targets. The second step was to create a continuous improvement process where we reviewed the results of all our programs, campaigns, and key strategic initiatives each quarter. We analyzed our results and measured them against the KPIs on our dashboard. Everything we analyzed was aligned with that dashboard: Did it source revenue? Did it influence revenue? Did it source pipeline? Did it influence pipeline?
>
> **—MITCH DIAMOND,** director of sales and marketing operations at McKesson Business Services

Strategic MO is absolutely vital to establish, track, and report metrics to ensure success in the Get Revenue stage. I've seen the simplest dashboards contribute to big changes in behavior as marketing transforms into a team player in revenue management. In companies without a dedicated strategic MO organization, metrics are often challenging. Sadly, without this capability marketing can never prove their impact on revenue and growth.

2. DEFINING A SALES-READY LEAD

Step 2 is to carefully define a sales-ready lead with the revenue team. Don't get hung up on the word "lead." In this case, "lead" is a placeholder for an action any member of the expanded revenue team can take. Defining a sales-ready lead—something sales or another customer-facing part of the company needs to take action on—creates a common language. The step also presents the ideal opportunity to initiate a business collaboration with sales and other revenue-responsible parts of the organization. A sales-ready lead might be a net-new prospect or additional business with an existing customer.

A sales-ready lead is determined by using demographic data (i.e., size of company or title), digital body language (i.e., online behavior) and other kinds of intent data. The value of digital body language is continuous: it helps score a lead and provides insights for better informing revenue decisions. The definition of a sales-ready lead should be updated at least twice a year.

The role of strategic MO is to work with the other operations teams to ensure that the right systems and data are available to define a sales-ready lead, to instigate the right set of actions, and to track and measure those actions. Strategic MO (with their cross-functional team) will also need to constantly analyze results based on established data parameters. They will update the revenue team as changes happen.

3. CREATING A COMMON REVENUE FUNNEL WITH STAGES AND STATUSES

Step 3 uses the common language established in step 2, along with common marketing and sales goals to create one common revenue funnel that spans the entire customer life cycle. In this common funnel, both marketing and sales have unique and cross-coordinating responsibilities. Multiple technologies enable managing one funnel. For example, the marketing automation system provides lead stages, and the CRM provides lead statuses. The most important factor here is to have *one* funnel with assigned responsibilities and outcomes enabled by various technologies from across multiple customer-facing functions.

Step 3 is clearly a strategic MO responsibility. When marketing does not have a strategic MO group, getting the required changes in CRM (and any system outside of marketing) is often a monumental challenge. Without those changes, marketing has no view into the entire revenue process and their role in it. Furthermore, without aligning customer-facing technologies across the entire customer life cycle, the revenue team cannot do their job.

4. ARCHITECTING LEAD PROCESSING AND ROUTING

Step 4 depicts the detailed flow of how a lead is processed (through people, process and technology) and routed for action from any point of the customer life cycle. The development of the flow should include input from sales and be optimized through technology. When an organization uses any kind of telesales or telequalification team—whether sourced internally or externally—this is an especially important step. I see many leads lost when this team is added, when what I should see is a set of greatly improved results.

In step 4, strategic MO defines and operationalizes key lead processing and routing flows. Tracking and reporting on the processing and flows are also critical. The processing and routing may also include other customer-facing functions in the company. Ultimately, step 4 represents the key role in architecting process that today's strategic MO function must embrace.

5. DEVELOPING LEAD SCORING

Step 5 is to develop the lead score for a sales-ready lead with the involvement of the revenue group. After all, they are marketing's partner in the revenue management process. If they do not perceive value in the lead, they will not take the prescribed action. The lead score for a sales-ready lead is determined by using demographic data (size of company or title), digital body language (online actions) and intent data. However, the lead score is not a "set it and forget it"; it needs continuous review and optimization.

Step 5 requires the unique data knowledge of the strategic MO team. Too often, sales and marketing guess on the lead-scoring parameters rather than using data to build the initial lead-scoring program. In addition, sales and marketing are not prepared to review lead-scoring performance and adjust based on data. The strategic MO carries out this role.

6. IMPLEMENTING SLAS

The final step in the Revenue Management Framework is to develop service-level agreements (SLAs). The document describes the roles, responsibilities and KPIs for marketing, telesales and sales (really, the entire revenue team). An SLA is jointly developed with the revenue team. Marketing often faces challenges with getting buy-in and behavior change around this document.

The role of strategic MO in step 5 is to ensure the revenue management program is based on data and can deliver the stated KPIs. With this assurance and oversight, there is a higher probability that all parties will adhere to the SLAs.

REAL WAYS STRATEGIC MO HELPS MARKETING BECOME REVENUE MARKETERS

While earlier in the chapter, I pointed out the typical sad case of marketing woefully shoring up leads that sales appears to toss aside, I want to emphasize here that it doesn't have to be that way. In fact, I've watched standout companies find creative, collaborative solutions to use marketing as a key part in the revenue machine. Guess where the foundation of this change lies? In strategic MO, of course. Consider the following three companies in action to see how strategic MO is stepping up within companies today and enabling marketing to truly act as revenue marketers in the Get Revenue stage.

COMPANY IN ACTION 1: FULL ALIGNMENT TO SET TARGETS

"Lead to cash." That's the name of the model that Dan Brown, vice president of marketing operations at Verint Systems, told me his company uses to drive revenue through marketing. He went on to explain, "In our Americas region, my team worked with the Americas marketing function and defined a model that we call Lead to Cash. The model allows us to sit down with sales and business development, who do a lot of the lead qualification, and start with a revenue goal."

After establishing the goal, they back up and consider questions. For example, according to Dan, they ask, "How many leads are the sales team responsible for, through their own prospecting? And how many leads need to come from campaigns? How many do we need to qualify? How many opportunities do we need to create?"

By backing up all the way to the beginning, everyone is able to think through the process and establish real numbers. "It's an interesting way for us to get everybody aligned around our goals and for everybody to understand—up front—what the targets are," Dan told me.

COMPANY IN ACTION 2: LOOKING BEYOND MQL METRICS

"Measuring key metrics is extremely important," Brian Vass of Paycor told me when we discussed revenue marketing. He went on to map out the shift in measurements over the past years. "There was a time where we spent a lot of time looking at campaign responses and MQLs," he said. "While those are still important in certain scenarios, the MQL has become a vanity metric as it relates to conversations with senior executives and stakeholders. Really, it's all about pipeline, bookings, conversion rates from stage to stage, and ROI."

Wow, I thought, he really understands what it takes to get revenue. "We've matured over time with the metrics that we care most about," Brian said. "Revenue contribution and campaign ROI are presented at the executive or board level, and the 'vanity metrics' stay within the tactical marketing team meetings."

COMPANY IN ACTION 3: NO DATA, NO DECISION

Latane Conant, CMO of 6Sense, described herself to me as an "accidental CMO." Here's why: she came into marketing from sales. As such, she runs marketing like a sales organization.

"I have this saying: no data, no decision," she shared with me during a recent conversation. "The week of a salesperson is pretty standard. They might complain about entering CRM data, but they use it every single day and live and die by the forecast. We have decent data after an opportunity opens. In marketing, we have what I call 'the Dark Funnel™,' and by that, I mean all the activity that's happening anonymously as prospects do their research. For most, this data isn't in any system."

Given this, Latane said it was of utmost importance to fully comprehend what's going on in that Dark Funnel.™ "The majority of the sales cycle occurs in the Dark Funnel™," she said. "Without a marketing or sales ops role, the right technology to dissect and understand the patterns in your Dark Funnel™, and reporting to bring insights from it forward, it's like we're still just using a Ouija board."

Once Latane and her team established a system to truly understand the data in the Dark Funnel™, a significant shift occurred. They can now predict who's in-market for their solution and in what timeframe they will most likely buy. "This takes me from a Dark Funnel™ to a known and predictable funnel," she explained to me. "I see ideal-fit accounts mapped to buying stages. This takes me from waiting for inbounds and passing questionable leads to sales to partnering with sales on how we prioritize and actively influence accounts in-market for what we do."

MO ROLES IN GET REVENUE

In October 2016, I published an article in *B2B Marketing* magazine called "The B2B CMO's Second Chance: The Dawn of MarTech." The article highlighted that CMOs have been applying a right-brained approach to get a left-brained result. In their defense, these were often the only skills they had on the team, but that is totally different today. With the meteoric rise of marketing operations, the CMO has a second chance to get it right. Every CMO needs to invest in a strategic MO organization that will ensure success the second time around.

The role of *strategic* MO in the Get Revenue world is not to be caught up in bright and shiny toys or to be so far down in the weeds they can't see the big picture. Their role is to work in a highly collaborative manner to operationalize the revenue marketing approach. To do so, they need a strategic role that encompasses four main areas: process engineer across functions, lead life cycle management, revenue analyst and training and education. I'll explain what it means to be *strategic* in this Get Revenue stage and then map out the four key roles.

STRATEGIC MO ROLES IN GET REVENUE

An important change happens in the MO team as they move to the Get Revenue stage. There is a significant shift from being technology focused to now being process-, business- and revenue focused. The team becomes responsible for enabling marketing ROI and contributing to revenue, margins, customer acquisition, customer retention and ultimately, shareholder value. The leap is often challenging for the MO team and can be supported with a new organizational chart, a collaborative working structure, and the addition of new roles on the team.

By the time the MO organization has arrived at the Get Revenue stage, there is typically a vice president of marketing operations reporting to the CMO. After all, accepting revenue accountability is a massive change and requires specialized leadership. As a result, the VP of strategic MO now has a team with more depth and breadth in all MO areas. Additional roles can be added in digital transformation, process, revenue management, training, vendor management, project management and budgeting. For more information, see the MOM Model Characteristics by Stage (Figure 11.5) in the appendix.

Process Engineer Roles across Functions

Many of the marketing leaders I speak with and know personally are passionate about the role of MO in process engineering. Process engineers address two key areas. First, they reengineer core cross-functional business processes such as revenue management. For any strategic MO leader, getting revenue management up and running is critical to driving revenue, yet getting sales and marketing on the same page takes a lot of work. I've seen everything from passive-aggressive behavior to lots of yelling when sales and marketing get together to address this topic. Once I even had to eject a person from the discussion.

Second, process engineers help develop a new, collaborative work structure that cuts across functions. For example, the role of field marketing versus corporate marketing often changes as the MO function matures. For organizations with global and field marketing operations, defining who owns what MO skills and responsibilities and how things will be executed is a key business process. These relationships—both formal

> Going through, function by function, and asking, "What are you trying to do?" and "How do you know if those things are getting done?" I think marketing ops can help organize all of that—that process, that planning and then the data capture on the back end, to try to get to that place.
>
> **—BRANDON JENSEN,** director of marketing operations at Plex Systems

and informal—need to be adjusted continuously.

Adding processes to the mix for the strategic MO group is best organizationally represented by a dedicated process role (think lean manufacturing). Because so many processes in marketing and between sales and marketing are broken and suboptimized, this role makes sense. In addition, calling out the importance of process reengineering through a dedicated role demonstrates the importance of process optimization.

Keep in mind that the role of the process engineer is flexible. The role might be at a director level and report directly to the VP of marketing operations. The position could also be at a manager level and report to a director level. You will rarely see it as a full-time position. Maybe it should be.

FUNNEL MANAGEMENT

Funnel Management is a marketing view for how the customer takes their buyer journey, both as a net-new customer and a repeat buyer. The role of marketing is to influence the prospect/customer at each stage of the funnel to move them through to become a lead for sales. Since it is a necessary aspect of marketing performance, it is the responsibility of the strategic MO team to ensure it works as it should. From a process perspective, how it is engineered and supported by data and technology ensures marketing meets their goals. The strategic MO team's job is to engineer this process and make it repeatable, predictable and scalable (RPS).

> Our MO is all about managing the technology because we are really dependent on technology to be better marketers. They manage the flow of the funnel to make sure leads are flowing through the different stages. They check that things are not getting stuck or lost.
>
> **—DANNY ESSNER**, vice president of revenue marketing at Sisense, Inc.

Lead Life Cycle Management

The lead life cycle represents the set of actions that marketing and sales take to interact with a prospect or current customer. The lead life cycle involves not only getting a new customer but also the keeping and growing of an existing customer. Many marketing organizations seem to either focus on getting new business or selling new solutions to existing customers, but both strategies need to be supported by strategic MO.

What I am beginning to see—especially in more customer-centric organizations—is a desire to have a holistic and shared view over all parts of the buyer journey. In this scenario, collaboration across systems and data becomes the main goal for the strategic MO team. Dan Brown from Verint gave me a great description of the role of MO in the lead life cycle. He shared, "From the very beginning, we've had to consider if people know how to use Eloqua to properly set up campaigns."

Dan discussed how his team needs to know that they're setting up the campaigns properly, that they're pulling the right segments from the database and that they have defined all the elements that need to happen in the campaign. "My team is also responsible for creating the integration algorithm that exists between Eloqua and Salesforce," he explained. "My team also has to worry about, 'Do leads flow correctly from Eloqua into Salesforce? Are they assigned correctly?' Once we send leads over to Salesforce, we have lead stages that are set up, where they work through qualification, get to marketing-qualified leads, and get assigned over to sales." After this they become a sales-accepted lead and ultimately get converted into contacts or opportunities.

> I think this is what a lot of marketers make mistakes with—they see great numbers for their own set of KPIs, but they aren't relating those KPIs to the business. Marketing operations can step in here and say, "That's great. Let's pat ourselves on the back for a great campaign. We got a lot of interest in this campaign, but we didn't convert anything. So why didn't we convert anything?" It's about taking those analytics and refining them so that it's not so much a volume game as it is about a value and revenue game.
>
> —CLAUDINE BIANCHI, chief marketing officer at LeanIX

Revenue Analyst

In the Get Revenue stage, the focus should be on just that—getting revenue. However, some MO groups struggle to get out of the solo technology mindset and into a results-oriented frame of mind. One addition at this stage helps everyone on the MO team adapt to the change. Enter the revenue analyst.

The focus of the revenue analyst is to optimize not just general marketing performance, but also a specific revenue number. The number might be contribution to pipeline or closed business in terms of percentage or dollars. Either way, the revenue number becomes their focus. Thus, the person in this role should have a sales background and intimately know how a sales funnel works. They will spend time collaborating with sales to ensure adherence to SLAs, just as they will spend time with marketing to ensure they provide quality and on-target leads to sales. They will track activity through the revenue management process to ensure systems and processes are optimized, and they will walk and talk like a VP of sales who always knows exactly where the revenue team is on achieving quota and achieving revenue goals.

In addition, the revenue analyst must be an opportunity spotter. Translation: They use data to continuously examine the entire customer life cycle from acquisition to expansion to advocacy. Based on this, they determine the best opportunities where marketing can invest and get the greatest return. With a deep analytical acumen that is passionately applied to spot the best ROI opportunities, the revenue analyst is poised to help optimize martech for its ultimate purpose: making marketing accountable for revenue.

Because the role is so critical, the revenue analyst most typically reports to the VP of marketing operations.

Training and Education Roles

Often the strategic MO function has a dedicated head count for training and education. Strategic MO might oversee training on the systems (from novice to advanced), the new processes and basic marketing skills. One key aspect of strategic MO assuming an educational role is teaching marketing how to use data to make data-driven decisions. I love seeing this position on the org chart because it tells me the group is on a mission for growth (for a full look at this, see page 195).

> Training is a requirement. Today, employees expect us to invest in them. I think it goes with how they want different assignments, they want variety ... they want to be challenged, and that's all part of managing the workforce.
>
> **—JIM LEFEVERE**, international business leader

As I've pointed out, the Get Revenue stage of the MOM model is really where the *strategy* begins. Moreover, it's a bit of a magical step. Participating in generating revenue in a real way is what starts to raise the platform for MO and marketing. Suddenly they are a bigger player and act as a collaborative leader that has meaningful targets and results to share. When asked to prepare a presentation for the boardroom, they'll be ready.

If this excites you, it should. Getting revenue is a big, game-changing step in the MOM model. Mastering this stage helps drive momentum to push into the last two stages of the model. I'll cover the first of these next two stages, Customer Centric, in the next chapter.

CHAPTER SUMMARY
A QUICK GLANCE AT WHAT WE LEARNED

- Driving revenue is the single most important factor to getting that seat at the table.

- Get Revenue is the first stage that is *strategic*, and this is where revenue marketers get created.

- In this stage, strategic MO mediates the relationship between sales and marketing, which is a must-have step to create a revenue machine.

- Revenue management is replacing lead management and is both a methodology and a capability.

- The Revenue Management Framework details six key areas: establishing metrics; defining a sales-ready lead; creating a common funnel with stages and statuses; architecting lead processing and routing; developing lead scoring and implementing SLAs.

- The strategic roles MO plays in the Get Revenue stage include being a process engineer, managing the lead life cycle, providing a revenue analyst and participating in training and education.

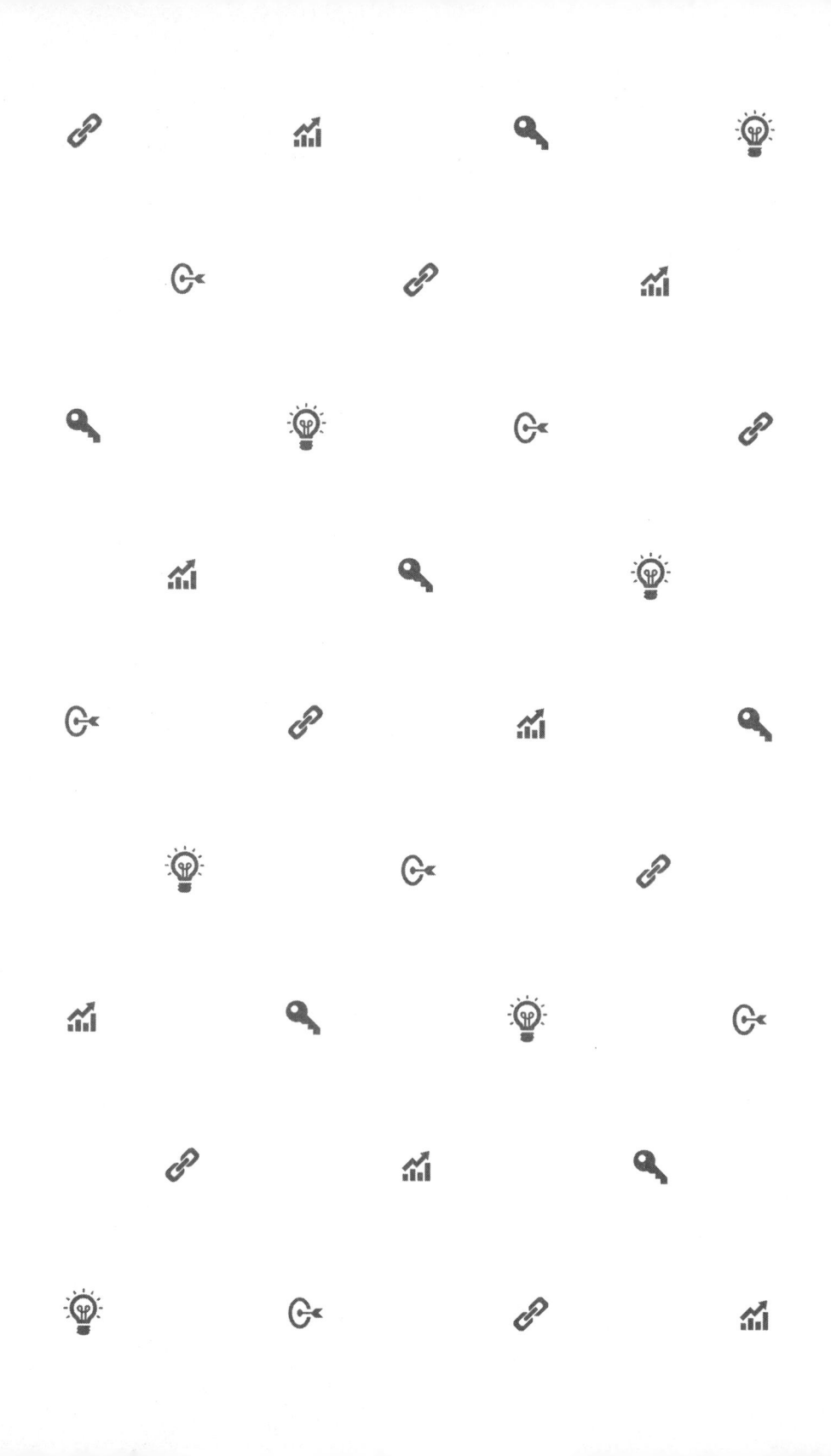

CHAPTER 6

THE CUSTOMER CENTRIC STAGE

For decades, companies took a product-centric focus. Marketing flooded prospects with product slicks, product messaging and product conversations. Today, companies are fleeing from this approach. Instead, they're shifting to a business model that centers on the customer. Rather than talking about product features, the conversation is about customer problems and how a particular product can directly address workplace issues. I've seen this transformation take place in all types of organizations, most significantly in the tech, financial services, insurance and health industries. Organizations typically make it one of the highest-priority initiatives.

For strategic MO, this is good news. Here's why: once you've mastered being efficient and effective and lain the groundwork for becoming a revenue-generating machine, the next step is to focus on the customer. The Customer Centric stage is listed in the Marketing

Operations Maturity (MOM) model (pictured below in Figure 3.2). Being customer centric is the second stage in the strategic part of the model, and success in this stage accelerates revenue growth.

MARKETING OPERATIONS MATURITY MODEL

Stages along the strategic capability curve: UNAWARE → EFFICIENT/EFFECTIVE → GET REVENUE → CUSTOMER CENTRIC → NEXT GENERATION

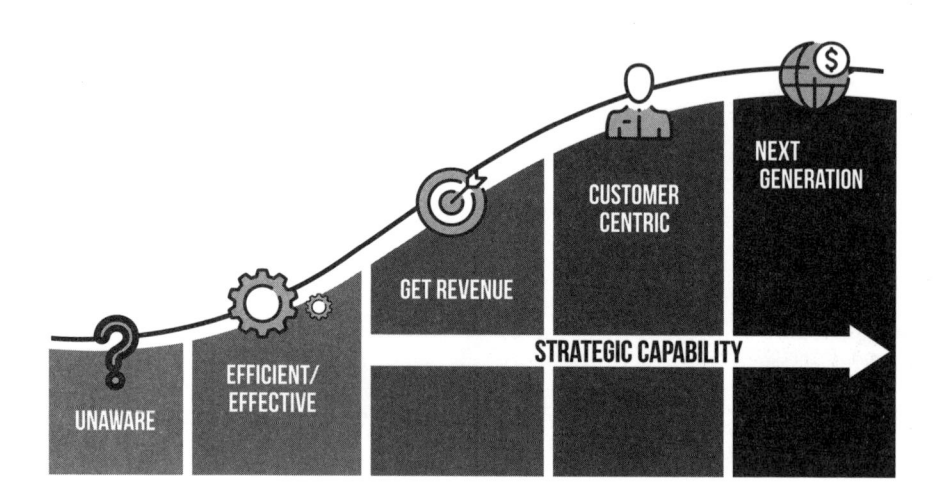

FIGURE 3.2

Companies place a high value on becoming customer centric for two reasons. First, CEOs are realizing that in our digital world, the customer is in control. Companies can no longer win on product strategy alone.

Second, CEOs know that customer centricity pays. Reports, surveys, analysts and case studies provide an abundance of evidence to support this. Overall, customer-centric companies enjoy higher margins, higher client satisfaction scores, reductions in cost to serve, improved revenue growth, and an increase in employee satisfaction. Check Google for these statistics.

Still, CEOs and executive teams must figure out how to transform from being product centric to being customer centric in a digital world.

They need to create a corporate capability that allows the company to sense and respond to customer changes in real time. They must have actionable customer data. They also require customer-based processes that are coordinated across their company. Furthermore, they need systems that allow, track, and report on smart engagement with the customer. Given this, I firmly believe the strategic MO organization has a unique opportunity to step up and play a critical role in this significant business transformation.

> Business growth is a good outcome of improved customer experience.
>
> **—ROHIT PRABHAKAR,** vice president of digital marketing at Thomson Reuters

Of course, stepping up may be easier said than done. To become customer centric, strategic MO must change their current mindset, broaden their skill set and sharpen their tool set. I use the Customer Pyramid model (see below in Figure 6.1) to help show the interconnectivity of these moves.

THE CUSTOMER PYRAMID MODEL

CHANGE YOUR MINDSET

STEPPING UP: LEADING CUSTOMER CENTRICITY

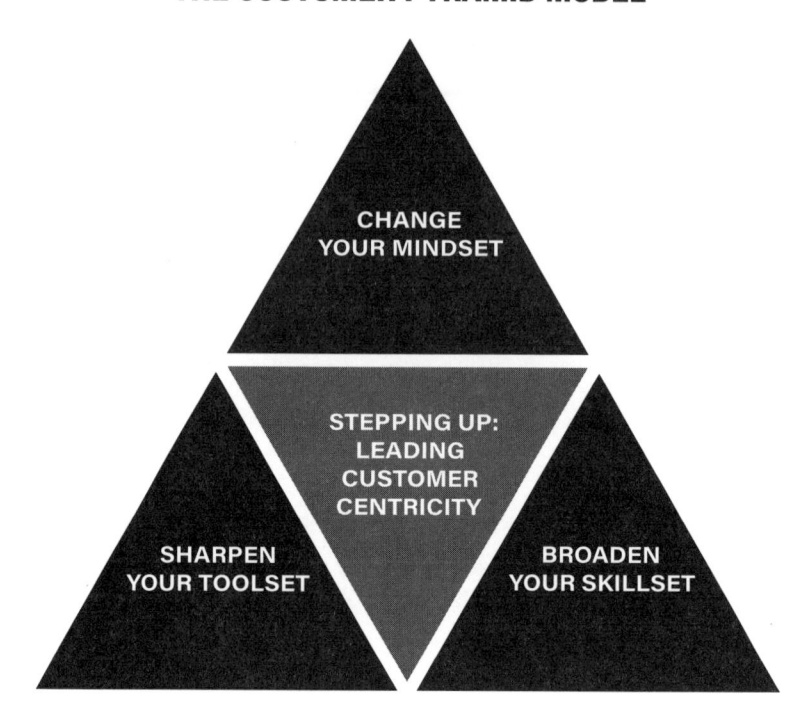

SHARPEN YOUR TOOLSET

BROADEN YOUR SKILLSET

FIGURE 6.1

Mastering each element of the Customer Pyramid model enables MO to embrace the customer-centric movement and help the company transform. The components of the Customer Pyramid model are so significant that it's worth spending some time on each of them. In the following sections, I'll explain what it means to change the mindset. Then I'll lay out the logistics of broadening the skill set. Finally, I'll provide guidelines on how to sharpen the tool set in this Customer Centric stage.

CHANGE THE MINDSET

Before delving into the ins and outs of shifting a mindset, it's important to understand what the term "mindset" means. Mindset involves how you see and think about the world. Consider the parable of the three blind men and the elephant. In the parable, each of the three blind men touches part of an elephant. One feels the trunk. Another one grabs the ear. The third man handles a leg. Based on their individual experiences, they develop how they view and think about the animal. The first blind man states the elephant is like a snake. The second believes it is similar to a leaf. The last one suggests it is a strong column of wood. They each hold firmly to their viewpoint and go on to argue about who is right.

Like the men in this parable, we are all ruled by our experiences. Thus, changing a mindset that we have developed over time can be quite challenging. Many change efforts fail for this reason. Believe me, your company pivoting from a product focus to a customer focus represents a huge change effort.

Before you attempt the shift to becoming customer centric, make sure your company is doing more than just talking about this critical pivot. Check that they are willing to change their mindset. To take on a customer-focused viewpoint, it's essential to want to understand the customer.

I spoke with Rohit Prabhakar, vice president of digital marketing at Thomson Reuters, about this need. He shared that he had developed an approach to really

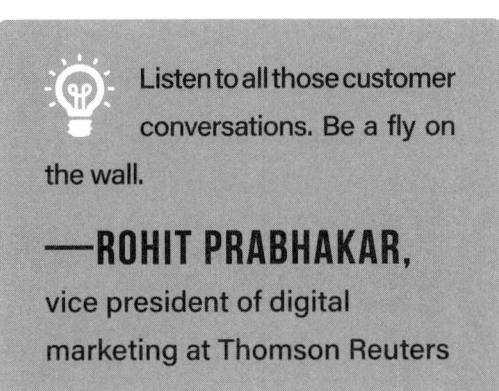

> Listen to all those customer conversations. Be a fly on the wall.
>
> **—ROHIT PRABHAKAR,** vice president of digital marketing at Thomson Reuters

learn about a customer in a holistic way. "In my previous company," he said, "my team had to go and sit on customer service calls. They had to go and spend time on the road with sales reps." By listening to conversations with customers, he and his team were able to develop a true picture of the personas they were targeting.

THE COMPANY MINDSET

Strategic MO cannot lead the pivot to customer centricity if the entire organization is not on board and engaged. Once they are engaged, they will be ready for tangible action and adoption—not just talk. I recently spoke with Claudine Bianchi of LeanIX in a podcast that covered this topic.

During the episode, Claudine shared how her company adopted a customer focus that stretched from the CEO down to every person in the organization. Claudine gathered evidence to show this operationalized customer strategy.

The evidence included the following:

- A set of corporate-wide KPIs based on customer names baked into the management by objectives (MBOs) for every person in the organization

- Senior management sharing the effectiveness of a customer-centric approach for every person in the company

- Employees across the company empowered with decision-making responsibilities in terms of delighting customers

- Peer-to-peer recognition and rewards for individuals who delight the customer

- Obsession around customer net promoters scores and customer satisfaction (CSAT) scores

Ensuring that the corporate mindset and resulting actions are real is the first step for the strategic MO team to take. Once they have verified this is a real transformation, the MO team is ready for the next step. To do so, they must consider their own mindset.

THE STRATEGIC MARKETING OPERATIONS MINDSET

I worked with a large tech company on their martech stack in 2011. MO was years away from being cool at that time. The terms *martech* and *stack* weren't even in play.

During our meeting, my contact handed me a single sheet of paper. The page listed twenty different logos. Each of the logos represented a technology they used to support marketing. Then she asked me, "What should we keep, and what should we get rid of?" She added, "Keep in mind that this will be a battle to get alignment on any changes."

I picked up the sheet of paper and looked at the logos. Then I looked back at her. "I have no idea," I said.

She was a bit taken aback; after all, it was part of my job to be guiding her on martech management. However, like many tech stacks, this one was put together over time. The stack had many different owners and was based on different goals. Without a unifying mindset, they didn't have a basis to use for making decisions on what would stay and what would go. They also didn't have a single approach to evaluate how things were used and how they were integrated. The tech stack was merely a set of disparate, costly, and ineffective systems representing different fiefdoms.

Fast-forward to today. We know that MO as a capability has quickly matured. Even so, MO groups are still all over the board in creating "unifying mindsets" to envision and optimize their stack. I now see three primary unifying mindsets in action. I'm listing them below and will go on to give details for each:

1. Technology mindset
2. Funnel mindset
3. Customer-first mindset

Mindset 1: The Technology Mindset

If the MO team uses "technology" as their unifying mindset, they act more like a traditional IT group. You might see characteristics like chasing the next bright and shiny toy, poor communication protocols, and a fiefdom mentality. You'll often see an "I know best" set of behaviors.

I recently witnessed a clash between a tech-centric MO group and a marketing group at a company. One issue that exacerbated the disagreement was that the MO group was actually part of the company's IT organization. Legacy IT function thinking bled into the MO function, and they were entirely too tech centric. They did not understand marketing. They didn't grasp how and why various marketing technologies could help marketing attain their new and bodacious revenue goals.

The MO group's perspective fueled their priorities, urgencies, and actions. They were not in sync with what marketing needed to accomplish. The MO team didn't understand how technology drives the larger business goals and initiatives and how technology enables marketing to meet those goals.

Many MO groups may consider this scenario to be far away. Keep in mind, however, that marketing technology is rapidly becoming more sophisticated and powerful. Given this, there is a real danger for the MO function to become too tech centric.

Mindset 2: The Funnel Mindset

As both marketing and the MO group mature, there is a shift to what I call the funnel mindset. B2B marketers now use this mantra. In many ways, the marketing funnel is the center of the B2B marketing universe—just look at the metrics that are tracked and reported. Typically, those metrics will answer some mix of the following questions:

- How many people are in each funnel stage?
- What is the rate of conversion from one funnel stage to another?
- How do we create content by funnel stage?
- How many MQLs were sent to sales?
- What is the conversion rate of those MQLs to closed/won business?

Make no mistake: when the idea of a funnel managed by marketing first came out, it was revolutionary in the B2B world. The funnel became a key driver of marketing accountability in revenue. With the rise of the MO function, the marketing funnel was finally able to be fully operationalized and optimized.

As MO acts as a service function that enables marketing goal attainment, let's look at how a funnel-centric view affects the MO group's responsibilities. First, in most cases, the funnel-centric view focuses on only part of the customer journey. The funnel either looks at the first part or the net-new acquisition. From a systems and data perspective, this has a huge impact on what and how MO buys, implements, integrates with and manages. Tech fiefdoms are created through this myopic approach. As a result, marketing may be at odds with sales, with customer service, and with IT. Data, of course, is a big issue across these fiefdoms.

MO certainly needs to be supporting marketing's funnel-centric approach. Still, more needs to be done in the customer digital economy where the battleground is customer engagement. Marketing must understand that with the tools they have, they can affect every part of the customer journey. They can also have a bigger revenue effect. Once marketing comprehends this, the MO responsibilities expand.

Mindset 3: The Customer-First Mindset

Let's go back to the story of the tech company that asked for my input on their tech stack. You'll recall I told my contact that I could not advise them on what was written on the paper listing twenty different logos. The conversation didn't end there.

I went on to reimagine what was on that slip of paper. I took out my pen and drew a person's head in the center of the paper. I wrote "customer" under the head. Then I turned the paper so my client could see the image.

I advised her that the only way to unify and make sense of all their technologies was to take an external—not an internal—perspective. She needed to look at the customer and think about how they take their journey. She could then develop a unifying mindset for the martech stack to stop turf wars. Following this path was the only way to optimize the tech stack to drive actual marketing results.

Having a customer-centric mindset affects a multitude of MO decisions. Here are three quick examples of how this plays out:

- Buying technology: Rather than assessing a piece of technology for what it can do just for marketing, strategic MO has to assess technology for marketing and other groups. Was the sales team looking at something similar? Were there needs in customer success that might be incorporated into the tech review? Does another group have something they might use in marketing?

- Implementing and integrating technology: Rather than implementing and integrating to meet marketing needs, a bigger picture must be evaluated. Who needs to be involved in implementation if multiple uses across groups were established? What needs to be integrated into what, and how will that work?

- Optimizing technology: From a customer-centric viewpoint, optimizing a tech stack that holistically maps the customer life cycle involves collecting data from sources throughout the life cycle. Optimization also consists of analyzing that data and working with stakeholders. The process and practice are very different when spread across functions versus just within the marketing silo.

In the last sections, I've discussed three main mindsets I've seen in MO teams. Take a moment to ask yourself about your own MO team mindset. Are you tech centric, funnel centric or customer centric? As you read the rest of this chapter, consider where you are as well as where you need to be and how to get there.

BROADEN THE SKILL SET

In addition to changing the mindset, the skill set must be expanded when taking on a customer-centric approach. Essentially, your skill set consists of the capabilities you have developed, based on knowledge and experience. By placing the customer at the center of the MO universe, you naturally broaden your skill set.

In the Customer Centric stage, the strategic MO has four distinct capabilities. They are as follows:

1. Tech/data/analytics DNA
2. Marketing experience
3. Business acumen
4. Customer knowledge and insights

The best way to describe a truly customer-centric capability is when there is a company-wide capability to sense and respond to customer changes in real time. The most mature and successful MO organizations use that fourth characteristic: customer knowledge and insights. With it, they begin establishing a customer-centric mentality, a set of processes and supporting structures for the organization. Think of Amazon.

Having the skills to envision and operationalize the customer-centric strategy is key. Moreover, owning the skills to produce and share customer insights for better decision-making across the company represents a powerful step. Being able to do this will help you reshape the value of MO to your organization.

CUSTOMER CENTRICITY IS A CAPABILITY

When I describe MO skills for a customer-centric organization, the place I start might surprise you. I begin with process—in particular, the process called the customer journey. Why? Because this is the single most important element in understanding customers. Yet marketing does a remarkably bad job in this area. In contrast, the strategic MO organization is armed with all the skills, knowledge, data and technology to help build and manage the customer-centric capability.

For every organization moving to a customer focus, the shift is beyond simply gaining a set of new activities. The change is about building a strategic capability. A strategic capability is a set of capacities, resources and skills that creates a long-term competitive advantage for an organization. These capabilities are created as a response to new strategic directions and/or big changes in the market.

One such market-breaking change and new strategic direction is today's digital customer. I'm not referring to a single customer who buys online. I'm discussing the broader sense of how customers behave in a digital and mobile world. With a few clicks or swipes, the digital customer is in firm control of their own journey with your company.

As a response to this new market dynamic, the B2B CMO needs to develop and own a different strategic capability. The capability must include mapping, auditing, and optimizing the customer journey. Still, it is the role of the strategic MO organization to actually make it happen.

> I was a marketing major for a while. One thing they don't really teach you is what's actually of value from the customer's perspective. And I don't mean to say that as a blanket statement about every marketer. But the way the goal has been taught is, "See, Debbie, you need to get the content out there, and it needs to be perfect." Not, "See, Debbie, you need to understand who Abby is so that you can hand-deliver that content and it makes the most sense to her."
>
> —**ABBY RYAN,** global director of marketing operations at SAP Concur

FUNNEL SKILLS VERSUS CUSTOMER JOURNEY SKILLS

If you thought your job was hard before, getting marketing (and other groups) to move away from their siloed customer view and adopt a holistic customer view is an almost Herculean task. Yet the company cannot pivot to customer centricity without this change. To make it a bit easier, let's consider the long-held, sacred view of marketing: the funnel.

The marketing funnel has become the standard of measurement, performance, and contribution from marketers. Whether you depict a vertical or horizontal funnel, the marketing funnel has become the mantra of marketers today. I will say it was good for its time. Once marketers embraced the funnel approach, they became more accountable for affecting revenue growth.

However, as companies pivot away from product-centric strategies to embrace customer-focused strategies, I think it's time for us to *reimagine* the funnel. Rather than a funnel that ends with delivering an MQL to sales, the customer engagement economy now requires a holistic view of the customer journey. Instead of having marketing and the rest of the company work in silos across the customer's journey, there needs to be a highly coordinated effort to get to one view of the customer.

To clarify this, I like to use two pictures. In Figure 6.2, you'll see the classic marketing funnel. You'll also view the holistic picture of the customer journey.

THE CUSTOMER CENTRIC STAGE

FUNNEL-CENTRIC VS. CUSTOMER-CENTRIC

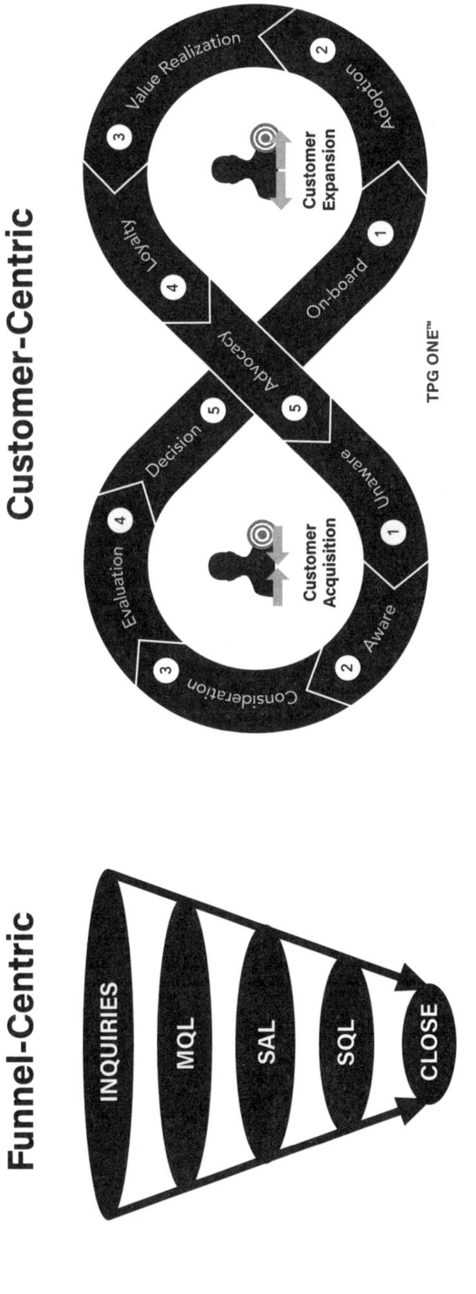

Funnel-Centric

Customer-Centric

FIGURE 6.2

Let's say that you are a funnel-centric marketing organization, as represented by the picture on the left. Your approach is to segment your activities based on the top, middle and lower sections of the funnel. Generating new business is your world. Although you've done a lot of work to identify your customer in this way, your responsibilities and your view of the customer journey are limited.

However, if you are a customer-centric marketing organization, as represented by the picture on the right, your roles and responsibilities are very different. They are much more expansive. Now you have a holistic view of the customer journey, and you have responsibilities in net-new acquisition, account expansion, retention and renewals.

I'm personally very familiar with this approach. Several years ago, The Pedowitz Group began talking to customers about this holistic customer journey view. Consequently, we developed an infinity loop. We call it "the Loop," and it presents a complete picture of the customer journey with a company. More importantly, it visually sets up the set of coordinated responsibilities for marketing, sales, service and other customer-facing elements of a company. The Loop represents a new mindset for marketing and the role of marketing in building customer relationships. Most folks we talk to quickly onboard with a broader approach and then look to their MO team to help them get it done.

As a strategic MO organization shifts to the customer-centric funnel, the changes are monumental. Working with marketing on the classic funnel is in many ways a siloed effort with limited possibilities. The data and systems the MO organization is responsible for are fairly restricted to marketing and are only a section of the customer journey.

In comparison, if the MO organization is supporting a company-wide customer approach, different data and tech needs are mandatory. Data now must be centralized, shared and used. Every customer-facing function in the company needs to work with coordinated processes and views of the customer journey. In this scenario, the MO organization is not operating in a marketing silo. Instead, they are working in collaboration with all customer-facing parts of the company.

CUSTOMER JOURNEY MAPPING AND MANAGEMENT ARE A SKILL SET

With a customer-centric mindset, a key skillset of the strategic MO organization is the mapping and management of the customer journey—holistically. In this case, the working definition for the customer journey becomes much more detailed.

Think of it this way, a customer journey includes all the touch points a customer makes with your company throughout the full customer life cycle. The journey includes becoming a client for the first time, as well as continuing to do business with a company. Each connection a customer makes with anyone, in any function, both within your company and externally, presents an opportunity to create an optimal customer experience leading to a customer for life.

The typical customer-mapping process is based on gut feel and singular experiences; it is not data driven, nor is it customer focused. Few customers are asked how they actually *do* take their journey. However, the strategic MO team can change this dynamic by taking a data-based and analytical approach that is continuous.

> The customer journey is typically looked at as a marketing-oriented initiative. I think marketing will have to pull that journey together. And that's one of the early values they can deliver—showing all of the different disparate data sources and how they connect in that full customer journey.
>
> **—TOM DELMONTE,** head of North America marketing operations at SAP

A key component of the customer journey map is the persona. Who is the customer? What do they want? Why? Where do they go to find out? Whom else do they work with?

Marketing has a mountain of behavioral data to use when developing personas and customer journeys. However, the data is often overlooked. With some mining, it can provide powerful insights.

Making this shift requires a good sense of what sales really needs and how marketing-controlled data can help meet those needs. A few years ago, I worked with a technology company in which sales "owned" the customer. A new MO leader with a highly quantitative and analytical background was hired. Her first focus consisted of helping to improve MQL conversion. She began by looking at how lead scoring was done in the marketing automation system.

She found a "tribal information" approach to create the lead-scoring algorithm. Using data already at hand and some quick analysis, she rescored leads to MQLs based on behaviors. She showed the sales team that things they thought were predictive of a lead becoming a quality MQL were just not so. At first, the sales team was doubtful. However, after a short pilot demonstrating that leads scored with the new data-based algorithm converted at a 19 percent higher rate, the sales team got on board. From that point on, shared customer ownership became the norm.

These touch points are core to the map. Additional elements on the map include roles and responsibilities for each function at each touch point. Others involve the technology used, the data collected and the messaging used.

I experienced a similar situation in 2004 when I bought a marketing automation system and integrated it with our CRM. The sales team told me one of the best leads I could uncover was the head of training, a role that was identified as a key on-ramp to an active sales cycle. I began to build up demand-generations efforts. I also did quite a bit of analysis with CRM and sales data to figure out the customer journey and the personas involved. Imagine my surprise when the data revealed that interactions with the head of training as the way into the rest of the organization never paid off. Not even once. As a result, we removed this persona from our buyer journeys.

One of the greatest skills of the strategic MO team is to ask questions. Constantly challenge the status quo. For developing personas and their customer journeys, questions will need to be asked, and sacred cows will need to be examined. In this type of change scenario, it is all about data and analytics to educate and inform.

CUSTOMER INSIGHT SKILLS

I have a background in sales: I've been a salesperson, a sales manager, and a VP of sales. In each of these roles, I strongly believed that sales held the keys to understanding the customer. No one in the company, I thought, knew the customer like my team or I did.

Then, in 2004, I saw a demo of a marketing automation system. As I watched it, I suddenly understood the power of digital body language. My belief that sales held the customer in the palm of their hand was shattered.

In its place, I developed a new set of beliefs. I now see that marketing owns the power of customer knowledge like no other single part of the organization. Too often, however, marketing hasn't had the skills or the technology to mine and use that data for actionable customer insights.

If you want to deliver value to executives, bring them actionable customer insights. Every executive I know who is leading the transformation to customer centricity is trying to understand what customer data they have, where it is, how it can be harnessed and what is still missing. Too often, they only consider the demographic data types. They ignore (or are unaware of) the horde of behavioral data in marketing. Strategic MO has a great opportunity here to bring immense value to the company.

> In a prior company, we were attacking the same customer with different groups and different offerings. All uncoordinated efforts. What if, instead of organizing by our own internal products or our own internal sales process, we organized by groups of like-minded customers? So customers with the same problems. And then we sold them things that made sense to them.
>
> **—BEKI SCARBROUGH,** vice president of demand strategy and operations at SecureAuth Corporation

SHARPEN THE TOOL SET

With a new mindset and an understanding of some of the new core skills required to help a strategic MO lead the pivot to customer centricity, it's time to look at the tool set. I define the tool set simply as the methods and tools you use to get things done. Keep in mind that change is inevitable. As you place the customer at the center of the martech universe, and as the customer changes and technology evolves, you will need to sharpen and/or replace some of your tools.

I've seen MO organizations move to a customer-focused approach. When they do, they significantly change how they buy, integrate, manage and administer their martech stack. Huge switches aren't necessarily made in the actual technologies used (although this can vary). The biggest changes in the tool set involve how technology is purchased, managed, integrated and administered. Essentially, you aren't necessarily switching the tools you are using. You tend to be sharpening the ones you have based on a customer-centric view.

THE MARTECH TEST

The way your martech stack is configured is a highly visible indicator of your company's true intentions to being customer centric. I suggest a simple test to see if your martech stack is aligned to support and enhance the customer journey. (The exercise is also a great tool to use in an executive meeting to help nontechnical executives understand the consequences of a legacy martech configuration. You can also use it in a business case for investments required to bring your martech stack up to speed.)

To start, take a blank sheet of paper (you can also whiteboard this activity in a meeting). In the middle of the sheet, draw a picture of your customer's journey from being a prospect to a repeat buyer.

Around this customer journey, list your various technologies. Explain how they support, connect to, and enhance the stages of the customer journey.

List the stages of your customer journey. Note all your technologies around the customer journey. Tell the story of how your martech stack supports and enhances your customer's journey on a single sheet of paper. If you cannot do this, you are not prepared.

At its simplest level, the Customer-Centric MarTech Stack might look like this generic graphic created by our team at The Pedowitz Group (Figure 7.3). The stack takes the entire customer journey and places it in the center. Generic placeholders are used for different kinds of technologies needed by marketing at each stage.

THE CUSTOMER CENTRIC STAGE

CUSTOMER-CENTRIC MARTECH STACK

FIGURE 6.3

There are some great examples of what a martech stack looks like when it is centered around the customer. To see some models, check out the Stackies at ChiefMarTec.com.

One of the roles I see in the strategic MO function in this stage is the strategic martech leader. The role might report to the head of digital transformation. Or it may report to the head of global MO.

CUSTOMER DATA

A similar exercise can be conducted with data. Take a sheet of paper, and draw a customer journey from prospect to repeat buyer. Around this customer journey, list the customer data sources and the type of data generated. For example, while in the prospect phase, a customer data source might be your website or your marketing automation system. The type of data generated might be digital body language data. Next, list how each data source and data type is used to enhance the customer journey. Include where and how data sources connect. Also note who uses the data and how they use the data.

You should be able to paint the picture of the customer's journey through the dataflow. If you cannot, it may be a sign that your organization is not yet customer centric. The concept of a customer focus may be only talk—and no action.

KEY ROLES FOR THE CUSTOMER-CENTRIC STAGE

For the strategic MO organization leading the pivot to customer centricity, there are several key roles. These cover the customer journey mapping and management, persona creation and management, and creating customer data insights. There may or may not be a specific role associated with each of these areas. I would argue for there to be roles dedicated. In the following sections, I'll point out two that are especially valuable: the customer intelligence role and the consulting role.

CUSTOMER INTELLIGENCE ROLE

Even if the CMO is not the chief customer officer (CCO), when a company pivots away from a product orientation to a customer orientation, MO plays a key role. Adding a customer intelligence leader is a very smart move. Yet I rarely see this as a dedicated role. In my opinion, if no one person has the accountability for customer intelligence, no accountability actually happens.

In companies where I see a customer intelligence leader, there are usually responsibilities that exist with the role. Some of these include the following:

- Developing all personas and customer journeys, based on data
- Developing a customer knowledge management practice that includes the following:
    - Collaboration with key stakeholders to identify specific customer data, intelligence and insights that need to be monitored, collected and shared
    - Collaboration with key stakeholders to determine how, when and with whom customer data, intelligence and insights are shared throughout the organization
    - Collaboration with key stakeholders to define how customer data, intelligence and insights will be utilized in different parts of the organization
    - Collaboration with key stakeholders to describe the process for updated and optimizing customer knowledge, intelligence and insights throughout the company

The customer intelligence role might take on additional importance if the CMO is also the CCO. I am seeing this trend more and more. A large West Coast technology company we work with recently made their CMO also be the CCO. As a result, the MO organization took on a larger responsibility to know the customer from every angle. The responsibility included knowing the customer from every perspective and across all channels and customer journeys. Practically, the customer intelligence role might report to the CMO, to the CMO/CCO, or to the head of MO.

THE CONSULTING ROLE

Inherent in the definition of a strategic MO group is a new skill critical to creating cross-functional value: consulting. At first, you might think this is an odd skill to add to the ever-growing list of MO skills. However, as you consider the ever-expanding responsibilities of the strategic MO team, you see they are becoming a shared services function in more than technology.

Beginning in the Get Revenue stage, and especially in the Customer Centric stage, MO becomes a valued internal consultant to different parts of the company. MO might consult on something as simple as campaign best practices that drive business results. Or they might offer insight on something as complex as revenue management.

Let's look at the core definition of consulting and see how it applies to the MO team. I consider this an especially important section, as consulting is foundational to strategic MO.

Consulting 101

The hallmark of a consultant is the ability to provide specialist expertise with an objective perspective to help a business improve. According to the Institute of Consulting, the definition of consulting is:

> *The provision to businesses of objective advice and assistance relating to the strategy, structure, management and operations of an organization in pursuit of its long-term purposes and objectives. Such assistance may include the identification of options with recommendations; the provision of additional resources and/or the implementation of solutions. In a nutshell, a consultant provides external advice for organizations that require specialist expertise or an objective outside perspective on their business.*

For the strategic MO that also acts as a shared services function, knowing how to act like a consultant creates great value. Interestingly, when I spoke with the contributors for this book, the topic of consulting often arose. Slightly more than 50 percent of the leaders interviewed had consulting as part of their work experience.

Now, let's break down the definition of consulting a bit further and see how it applies to the strategic MO team.

Specialist Expertise

Consultants are experts in specific areas. Within marketing, the MO group has a unique skill set. Their skills include technology mastery, data analytics, process improvement, problem-solving and overall operational efficiency and effectiveness.

In many organizations, the MO group is a centralized function and is separate from the demand-generation team. As marketing embraces new technologies, one part of marketing may be the users of the technology. The MO group is concerned with the implementation, integration and optimization of systems. For example, I've worked with many companies where the MO group acts as a campaign optimization consultant to the demand-generation team. The MO group knows the systems. They can analyze the data. By using their problem-solving and process improvement skills, they can help the demand-generation team optimize campaign performance and revenue.

Another example of the MO group acting as an internal consultant involves customer data. Marketing creates and gathers an enormous amount of data about prospects and customers. Yet as we've seen, most marketing groups do little with this data. The MO team, being the data scientists that they are, know how to collect and analyze data to produce stakeholder-specific customer insights. I've seen the MO group work with the demand-generation team in defining personas. I've watched them work with the product marketing team to understand customer response to product launches. They've also helped the sales team establish data-based sales approaches.

Objective Advice

As the strategic MO organization matures into this internal consulting role, their objectivity in terms of approaching a problem without bias is highly valued. Whenever I talk with these internal MO consultants, they sound just like external consultants. I can tell they are bringing an objective lens to each project. The organization values objective advice given to other parts of marketing, to sales or to other leaders of the business.

A great example I recently observed centered on the implementation of a lead management program for an organization. For any lead management program to be successful, it requires full participation from both sales and marketing. In this particular case, the marketing department had been historically viewed as not being helpful to sales. During the process, the MO organization acted as an objective consultant to both the demand-generation team and to sales. The strategic MO team provided key data to better align their conversations and to reach a mutually agreed-upon lead management process. MO's objective advice based on data prohibited the "he said, she said" arguments that so often arise between sales and marketing.

Proactive Problem Identification

The best consultants bring to light problems the client may not have yet recognized. Internal MO consultants do this as well. In companies where there is a well-oiled working relationship between the strategic MO team and the demand-generation team, the strategic MO team proactively looks for problems that prohibit optimal goal attainment.

In one large company I worked with, this was an extremely useful role played by strategic MO. While the company was ramping up their demand-generation / revenue marketing capability on a global basis, the centralized MO team constantly reviewed best practices. The strategic MO team also looked at the performance of the various demand-generation teams. With this central view, they were able to proactively identify ways to improve performance. They carried this out through systems optimization, systems integrations, process improvements and the application of best practices. The often overworked regional teams welcomed their input.

Problem Resolution

Of course, like any really great consultants, strategic MO consultants don't just identify problems and provide advice on what to do. They also work to resolve the problem. Key stakeholders associated with the problem are involved with this step.

A great example I recently saw in action involved lead scoring at a company. Both the demand-generation team and the strategic MO team recognized that lead quality needed improvement. The original lead-scoring program had been in place for two years and was implemented before the MO team was established. The program had developed as part of a one-day workshop involving sales and marketing and lots of "best guesses" on prospect and customer digital behavior.

The strategic MO team analyzed the lead-scoring program. Then, based on detailed data analysis, they made recommendations for improvements. Once the recommendations were accepted, the MO team set up a pilot series to further add to the data set. After that pilot was complete, the strategic MO team implemented the new, data-based lead management program. As a result, the demand-generation team improved MQL conversion by 11 percent.

Growing the Internal Marketing Operations Consultant

While it's true that the strategic MO team has a unique skill set, recognizing the cross-functional nature of the MO role is the first step to growing this skill set. Communication skills—including active listening as your partners turn to you for advice—are fundamental. A strategic MO group may find this challenging because they always want to jump in to fix a problem. Taking the time to listen can be tough. As more of your team members act in this consulting capacity, send them to a good communications class. They'll be able to learn how to listen and effectively communicate.

The cross-functional nature of the strategic MO group will continue to expand. As such, understanding how to act like a consultant to other parts of your company is extremely important. Being able to carry out this skill will help both your company and your career.

The Customer Centric stage is really one that allows strategic MO to act as a guide. Companies will continue to shift to a customer-focused approach to be able to operate in today's digital world. During and after this transition, the data, tools, and capabilities strategic MO possesses become critical. Putting them to use within marketing and for other parts of the organization can help strategic MO take on higher levels of leadership.

I've mapped out the beginning stages of the MOM model. I've laid out the details for the Efficient/Effective stage, the Get Revenue stage, and the Customer Centric stage. One stage remains: the Next Generation stage. In it, there is a true sense of excitement and opportunity for growth. I'll outline how this all happens in the next chapter.

CHAPTER SUMMARY
A QUICK GLANCE AT WHAT WE LEARNED

- More companies are shifting from a product-focus strategy to a customer-focus strategy.

- To become customer centric, strategic MO must change their current mindset, broaden their skill set and sharpen their tool set.

- Mindset is defined by how you see and think about the world. Strategic MO is tasked with helping shape the company mindset and their own mindset. Strategic MO teams typically have one of three mindsets: technology mindset, funnel mindset and customer-first mindset.

- In the Customer Centric stage, strategic MO broadens their skill set. Strategic MO has four distinct capabilities in this stage: the tech/data/analytics DNA; marketing experience; business acumen and customer knowledge and insights.

- As strategic MO becomes more customer centric, there is a need to sharpen and/or replace some of your tools. Two ways this can be done are through a martech test and by mapping the customer's journey through the dataflow.

- Strategic MO tends to take on new roles during the Customer Centric stage. Two that are especially valuable are the customer intelligence role and the consulting role.

CHAPTER 7

THE NEXT GENERATION STAGE

"Structure follows strategy." Historian and author Alfred Chandler coined the maxim back in the 1970s. His book *The Visible Hand: The Managerial Revolution in American Business* came out in 1977, decades before the current technology revolution. His concepts touting the need to restructure as key strategies shift hold true today.

In fact, this maxim of "structure follows strategy" is exactly what takes place in the Next Generation stage. (Going forward, I'll refer to it as NextGen.) NextGen is the final stage of the Marketing Operation Maturity (MOM) model (see below in Figure 3.2). Once you've lain the groundwork to be efficient and effective, built up a revenue machine and moved into a customer-focused mindset, your organization is ready to fully embrace a new strategy. You can take into account all of the previous building blocks on the model. In fact, the desire to be even more revenue and customer focused is what drives the NextGen stage.

MARKETING OPERATIONS MATURITY MODEL

Stages along the strategic capability curve: UNAWARE → EFFICIENT/EFFECTIVE → GET REVENUE → CUSTOMER CENTRIC → NEXT GENERATION

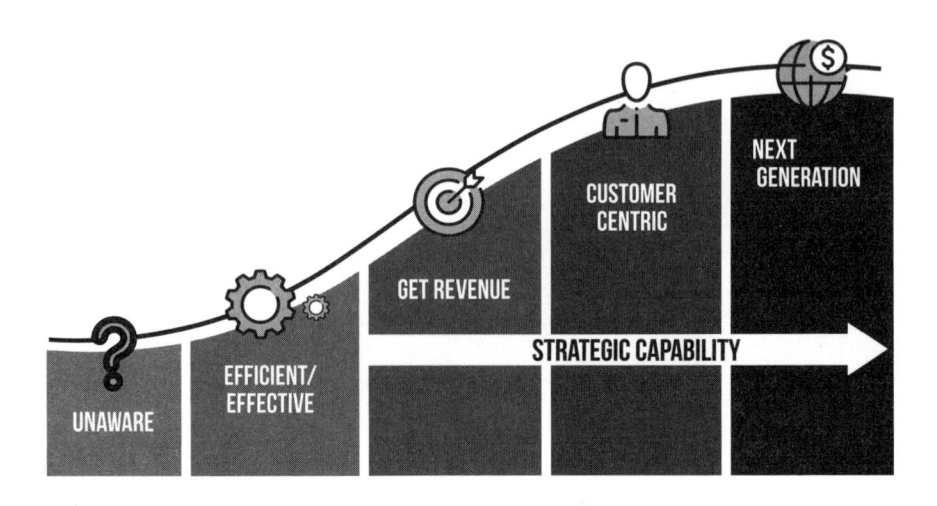

FIGURE 3.2

When an organization embraces a different strategy, the decision typically calls for a reorganization. A change in strategy will not automatically bring any results if no other adjustments are made to the structure of the organization. Legacy structures developed to support prior strategies will only hamper new strategies. In our current digital world, this is especially true.

The NextGen stage offers the opportunity to reimagine the current structures within an organization. Generally, companies in the NextGen stage make a shift to create a combined function of marketing operations and sales operations designed to support forward-thinking strategies. The new function includes MO and others. Implementing this combination in an effective way allows you to operationalize a strategy focused on revenue and the customer.

To fully appreciate what's involved in the NextGen stage, it's worth going over some background on this concept of combining functions. I'll walk you through the main characteristics, benefits and responsibilities that come with this stage. I'll close by spending a little time explaining how this combined function evolves into a revenue operation and the steps to take to get started.

EARLY COMBINATIONS

In 2015, the combination of sales and marketing operations first appeared on my radar. As I investigated this new group further, I found two places that seemed to be light-years ahead of the rest.

One of these occurred at McKesson, and I learned of it through an interview with Mitch Diamond. His title was a dead giveaway: he was the director of sales and marketing operations. As Mitch described his role in this combined operations organization, the evolution of it and the benefits, it just made sense.

I was fascinated with his story. While it was clearly unique to his situation, I had the feeling we would see more of this type of combination. How could we not, when it seemed so logical for business?

One year later, in 2016, I spotted a trend of other firms following suit. In particular, I witnessed a number of smaller companies combine sales and MO. For many of these organizations, it was their initial approach to forming MO. As you can see, some organizations don't go through each stage of the MOM model in sequential order.

In early 2017, I came upon the second place that was really paving a path in this emerging field of combining operations organizations. During that time period, I had the pleasure of meeting Brian Vass, who was then vice president of sales and marketing technology at Paycor. I interviewed Brian on my radio show for a segment I titled, "Paycor: Achieving Line of Sight by Combining Sales and Marketing Operations."

The introduction for that episode reads as follows:

"Here we are in 2017, and marketers are still struggling with driving the expected revenue results and improving alignment with sales to achieve revenue goals. What is still missing from this equation is a clear line of sight to both functions and the customer. Clear line of sight is defined as a 'straight line along which an observer has unobstructed vision.' Join us as we interview Brian Vass, VP of sales and marketing at Paycor, and find out how a strategy of combining the marketing and sales operations has helped gain this view and contributed to double-digit bookings and company growth." (You can listen to the interview at www.pedowitzgroup.com/resources/revenue-marketing-radio.)

Brian shared with me that having one combined team be responsible for strategy, technology, reporting measurement and analytics was a very practical approach. "You get less politics and less of a me-versus-you or us-versus-them attitude," he said. Another perk lay in reducing the duplication of effort, as there weren't two different teams trying to solve the same problem in different ways.

Brian also touted the advantages of having higher levels of collaboration, communication and teamwork. "At the end of the day, because one combined team is aligned with those strategies, you're much more effective, and you're able to scale," he said.

NEXTGEN IN ACTION

Brian had experienced the classical revenue marketing journey. When Paycor, an already successful organization, decided to aggressively pursue double-digit growth, they knew they needed a different approach to drive revenue. At this point, they began their journey, and Brian assumed the role of VP of revenue marketing (later to become the VP of sales operations).

To start with, he built a center of excellence based on a white paper authored by myself and Kevin Joyce. Brian focused on forming the demand gen team, the sales development rep team and a combined sales ops and marketing ops team. Brian himself assumed responsibility for creating the sales ops and MO team. "It really started as a combined sales ops and marketing ops team because in many ways, we were starting from scratch," he explained.

As the owner of both sales ops and marketing ops, Brian had what he called "line of sight," which I referenced in my radio interview with him. Through this line of sight, he could see and affect the performance of the top, middle and later stages of the classic marketing funnel and the entire customer life cycle. He helped both the marketing and sales teams become more effective and efficient through the use of technology and data.

For Paycor's marketing team, this created strong alignment of the customer-facing functions of the organization. Suddenly they were able to track everything through the funnel and credit attribution. The arrangement also improved productivity for sales. For any CMO, this type of alignment creates strong growth and accountability for the marketing function in the organization.

At Paycor, having one person (or one team) with line of sight to the complete customer life cycle, whose focus was to improve efficiency and effectiveness, resulted in double-digit growth to sales productivity. To achieve it, there was a strong level of teamwork between operations and the VP of revenue marketing across both the sales and marketing teams.

After meeting Brian and hearing his story, I was hooked. While Mitch got me interested in the topic, Brian helped me see a significant future for combining the operations functions in companies. Given their long history in combined operations organizations and accomplishments, I consider Mitch and Brian to be front-runners in the field of combined sales ops and marketing ops.

DEFINING THE NEXTGEN STAGE

The move to the NextGen stage on the Marketing Operations Maturity (MOM) model is characterized by a radical rethinking. At this stage, a reimagining of business models to drive revenue and growth takes place. The shift leads to a major reorganization of functions.

The main distinction between these new business models and the previous ones used in MO can be seen in what I call the "outside-in" factor. In an outside-in model, the company listens and responds to what is happening outside their company. The setup affects every part of the business from strategy to technology to organization. The focus of the outside-in business model is the response to customers; thus, it requires digital transformation, pivoting from product to customer focus and finding new ways to drive revenue. Contrast this to "inside-out" business models, which tend to be the previously used models. In an inside-out model, the company is limited in their perspective and understanding of market dynamics.

With an outside-in approach, companies must consider radical reorganizations to properly respond to the customer. The reorganization may include some combining of MO, sales operations, customer success operations, customer support operations and possibly others.

Over the years, I've seen all types of combinations. In the following three lists, I'll point out some of the different names, definitions and reporting structures I've heard for this radical reorganization.

NAMES FOR THE COMBINED FUNCTION

- Sales and marketing operations
  - SMO
  - Smarketing
  - SMOPs
- Business enablement
- Business operations
- Customer operations
- Digital operations
- Revenue operations
  - RevOps

DEFINITIONS FOR THE COMBINED FUNCTION

- SMO, smarketing and SMOPs: The function combines sales ops and marketing ops. As such, it creates a true line of sight to the entire customer journey. Real-time response and shared insights are possible. The function also drives improved revenue and growth.

- Customer ops: The function is an expanded view of the more traditional customer operations job that provides a holistic and connected view of the entire customer life cycle. Customer ops typically include all customer-facing functions in an organization.

- Digital operations: Another way to view key operational roles is through a digital lens. I first heard the term "digital operations" in a conversation with Rohit Prabhakar, vice president of digital marketing and e-commerce at Thomson Reuters. I believe we'll be seeing this term used more in the future.

- Revenue operations or RevOps: Another transformational role, this function looks at all revenue points. RevOps sets up the operations to support the revenue attainment across the entire customer life cycle. RevOps tends to include every part of the company that touches the customer, from customer service to sales to marketing—any touch point that can help create revenue.

REPORTING STRUCTURES FOR THE COMBINED FUNCTION

- Report to head of marketing
- Report to head of sales
- Report to COO

I find the reporting structure component particularly interesting. Across the maturity cycle of MO, the common strategies for who does what and who owns what have typically been based on skills and power. As skills, power and needs change, we will continue to see different evolutions of this structure.

> I think the RevOps organization should be owned by operations. This allows the RevOps team to be truly independent and take the best actions for the business. Another choice might be the CFO (chief financial officer). If you don't have a third-party choice to report to, it tends to be a big argument between sales and marketing.
>
> —REUBEN VARELLA, vice president of business systems at Veracode

For example, I've seen the MO team own the marketing automation system and also do all the building and execution of campaigns. I typically come across this when the marketing team is missing some skills. Data analytics is another example: in the early days of marketing ops maturity, this may be a borrowed capability.

From a reporting structure, it is about the power and the emphasis for operations. When revenue is a top priority and the head of sales knows how to use marketing as part of her revenue engine, I've seen the MO function report into the sales structure. Many combined ops teams, however, prefer reporting into the COO function. By doing so, they can provide a broader view into what's going on in the company and more power at the table. I rarely see a combined ops team report to marketing. If it does, it is typically because of a big lack of skill in sales ops.

NEXTGEN VISION, DRIVERS AND CHARTER

In the NextGen stage, you'll find a particular vision and set of drivers. There is also a typical charter to keep in mind when you reach this point of the MOM model. In the following sections, I'll flesh these out a bit more.

NEXTGEN VISION

A consistent thread across all strategic MO organizations and across any NextGen MO organization is that somewhere in the company, there is a visionary. The person either has a unique background in combining operations or has experienced all the headaches of siloed organizations and knows there has to be a better way. Here are some examples of who the visionary might be:

- A VP of sales or VP of marketing who has previously worked in a combined function in a company and grasps the power of a combined operations function
- A VP of marketing who understands the power of optimizing CRM and marketing automation platform (MAP)
- A VP of sales with a marketing background and knowledge of the possibilities
- A VP of marketing who has a grander, more holistic vision for growth

NEXTGEN DRIVERS

From my experience, the drivers for the creation of a combined operations group tend to be consistent. Across all the possible permeations of names, definitions and reporting structures, the drivers for all these organizations were twofold. The first driver is the customer and stems from the need to gain one line of sight to the customer that is shared and optimized across all parts of the company.

> When speaking about a NextGen organization, it really is about being able to create a consistent customer experience across all the customer-facing parts of a company.
>
> —ALEX SIMOES, RevOps pioneer

The second driver is revenue and growth. I never, ever see this combination as a money-saving or efficiency initiative all by itself. Focusing on the customer is the way to accelerate the path to revenue.

NEXTGEN CHARTER

The typical charter for a combined operations team is also consistent and takes into account the two key drivers. Following are a few examples of SMOPs charters that I have seen—notice that most align with the two drivers I mentioned:

- To take a holistic and single-threaded approach to optimize technology, process and data across the entire customer life cycle to drive revenue and growth

- To visualize the customer life cycle through systems and data, thereby ensuring every department can respond appropriately to optimize the customer experience

- To attract more new customers and retain the ones we have by making sure we have the tools, optimized processes and data

- With digital transformation as the foundation, to build a unified operational capability that improves revenue performance through one line of sight to the customer

The biggest difference between an MO charter and a SMOPs charter is the breadth of impact. Marketing ops is largely concerned with marketing, while a SMOPs involves sales, marketing, sales development reps, a customer success team, product development and any part of the organization needing customer data to make decisions. The SMOPs team is much more involved with providing data and insights about every aspect of the customer journey to a wider audience. Also, a SMOPs organization does everything through the lens of sales, so creating a framework that enables sales and overall revenue production is paramount.

NEXTGEN BENEFITS

The chief benefits of SMOPs are the line of sight to the end-to-end customer journey and the nimble changes that can be made based on this line of sight. Imagine sensing and responding to changes in the customer in almost real time, across every part of the organization. Think about your customer having a consistent and thoughtful experience with your company, regardless of where they are on their journey. The ability of a SMOPs team to provide actionable customer insights is a key to creating competitive advantage in our digital world.

The next most important benefit of SMOPs is the resulting alignment and synergy created across sales and marketing. Words like "team," "together," and "unified" all roll off the tongues of SMOPs leaders. What is difficult (or nearly impossible) for many companies is taken for granted and a common occurrence in organizations with a SMOPs practice. The level of communication and trust across teams grows exponentially with a SMOPs practice.

The third benefit of SMOPs is a collective set of credible KPIs. Most organizations experience overlapping and conflicting KPIs, as the goals of each department can be wildly different. However, with a SMOPs practice, one set of KPIs is developed based on the customer life cycle. In addition, data about the customer journey is supplied from SMOPs to every part of the organization. There is a holistic consideration of KPIs to the benefit of the entire company.

Ultimately, a SMOPs organization becomes a revenue and growth engine. I should point out that this becomes a focus and reason for being at the Get Revenue stage. However, it is through the combining of functions with one leader that revenue and growth is now optimized.

THE CHANCE TO MOVE AWAY FROM SILOED ORGANIZATIONS

In many ways, companies today have digital strategies based on revenue and customer engagement. Still, they haven't yet fully operationalized these strategies with the right structure. Current siloed structures represent legacy thinking that will not work in our "always-on" world. As long as these organizational silos continue to exist, teams will struggle with responsiveness, change, data, insights, politics and power—all at the expense of the customer and gaining competitive advantage for the company.

But for those teams who can do it, combining key operational elements of sales and marketing to create one complete line of sight to the customer is a game changer. Furthermore, the breadth and depth of analysis and response in an almost real-time context differentiates the SMOPs team from siloed organizations. These customer life cycle operations groups might be extended to customer support or engineering. As far as revenue achievement, SMOPs leaders are all about the number and see their organization as the best way to make it happen.

> As long as the different customer-facing parts of a company have different goals, you will not be able to create a cohesive customer experience. For example, sales and marketing are often focused on acquiring new business, and the goal of customer success and customer operations is to retain business. One of the biggest benefits in combining the operations functions is to be able to have an eye on both sides of the business in order to create unity. Ultimately, this pays off for the customer and for the business.
>
> **—ALEX SIMOES,** RevOps pioneer

SMOPS RESPONSIBILITIES

When I spoke with Mitch Diamond of McKesson about his combined function, he outlined three major areas of responsibility. "The first is that we manage the technology infrastructure to enable marketing functions," he explained. "This includes the marketing automation system, and in many cases, it's also the database and the database strategy."

The second component of MO that his team manages involves the analytics and metrics process for the department. "This is critical so we can benchmark our performance and can continuously improve," he said.

The third area consists of managing and optimizing key processes. Mitch and his team execute marketing automation campaigns for the marketing department, a function most often in the demand-generation team. But as Mitch pointed out, "In our case, that's part of MO."

In general, the key responsibility of a SMOPs organization is the optimization of technology, process and data to drive customer insights and revenue. You may think this sounds very much like something that is done by an MO organization. But there is a twist: in this case, SMOPs takes a holistic perspective and puts it into practice. By singular leadership and with fully integrated technology, processes and data across the entire customer life cycle, SMOPs can be effective in a way that will remain challenging for any MO organization. I'll describe each of these three areas briefly in the sections below.

TECHNOLOGY RESPONSIBILITIES

In addition to the broader approach, the way SMOPs executes on technology is unique. Consider that the number of technologies used by marketing has grown exponentially over the last few years. As I've stated previously, it's now common for a small marketing department to use over thirty different martech tools. Given this new tech reality, selecting, implementing, integrating, and optimizing the tech stack is a critical role of the SMOPs team. Of course, the same might be said for the separate sales and MO groups.

In this stage, the combined team is looking at the tech stack for marketing, sales and any other part of the organization that touches the customer. The tech stack is integrated and operationalized around a single and complete view of the customer life cycle. The result is the tech stack on steroids. In case you are wondering if you can reach the same state of goodness if the functions are siloed—no, you cannot.

PROCESS RESPONSIBILITIES

With one consolidated tech stack now in play, the SMOPs team becomes a master of process. The massive inefficiencies—most of which stem from trying to work across functions run by different leaders with different agendas and different goals—disappear (or are, at least, greatly minimized). Instead, a single function works under one charter and one leader to make quick and decisive changes. These result in vast improvements in efficiency and effectiveness. Rather than bickering and infighting over who owns what and when and how changes can be made, the SMOPs team serves as the neutral party, using data to make better process decisions.

DATA RESPONSIBILITIES

Another responsibility of a SMOPs team involves all things relating to good data and clear insights. Given the line of sight to the entire customer life cycle, the SMOPs team has access to data that creates a holistic picture of client behaviors, wants and needs. The insight, when provided in almost real time, helps the entire organization adopt a true customer focus and make better decisions.

CONSISTENCY, EFFICIENCY AND CREDIBILITY

In addition to carrying out the main responsibilities listed above, in this stage you'll want to work toward maintaining consistency, efficiency and credibility. When I talked with Kira Mondrus-Moyal, senior vice president of global marketing at Tricentis, she spoke of doing exactly that in her own organization. Regarding consistency, she said, "Whatever data is presented needs to be a single set of data. You're not going to have two different groups pulling two different reports and getting two different sets of data."

She also discussed the need to be efficient. "When I came in, we cut out a lot of technology," she noted. "Each group had its own set of technology that did the same thing yet produced two different sets of results. We streamlined our tech investments and aligned on process and definition."

Finally, she built a layer of credibility on top of this consistent and efficient foundation. "When I present to leadership and talk numbers, no one questions the accuracy," Kira said. "I had a centralized ops function to back up the data, and these folks had no skin in the game."

REVENUE OPERATIONS (REVOPS)

Revenue operations (RevOps) is a term we will be hearing a lot about. RevOps is the combination of the operations functions of sales, marketing, customer success and channel. In other words, it encompasses all the revenue-producing parts of the company.

"Revenue operations is a personal passion," Reuben Varella,

vice president of business systems at Veracode, told me recently. "I have a background in sales and now spend a good part of my career in marketing. I've seen the friction between these two groups in many organizations and in many different ways, depending on the culture."

After observing this tense environment, Reuben reflected on the root of the problem. "A lot of the time, it was challenging to run these two organizations in isolation," he told me.

When he paused to reflect on ways to create synergy between sales and marketing, Reuben came up with the solution of putting them together into one function. "For me, it just makes sense to combine the two," he explained. "At Veracode, we call this revenue operations."

I have seen a RevOps group include only sales ops and marketing ops, but most often it also contains customer success ops. By doing this, an organization can align sales, marketing and customer success operations across the customer life cycle to drive great customer experiences and revenue. A RevOps group might also include channel operations. While it may also include services in their responsibilities, the RevOps function now covers all facets of getting, keeping and growing customers.

One further note: The RevOps organization most often reports into the head of sales. I have also seen it report into the COO. While it may exist, I have not seen a RevOps organization report to a CMO.

MAKING THE LEAP

Like many innovations in business, most organizations that have a combined operations team are small and agile. Realizing that it's not the easiest thing in the world to break down well-established silos, what are a few things you can do to get started, given that you buy into the concept? If you want to position your organization to compete in today's customer-driven world by building a combined ops team, follow these five steps:

1. Make sure the customer-centric strategy is really important to your company by asking, "Where is the evidence?" Too many companies talk about being customer centric, but it's all talk. You do not want to start this kind of reorganization without a genuine passion for customer focus from all parts of the company.

2. Advocate for organizational change when times are good. While many org changes do occur as a response to poor business conditions or results, this kind of change works best when things are working well and when you can challenge the organization to go to the next level.

3. Select a strong leader to run the combined function. The person must have credibility with both sales and marketing, and great communication and collaboration skills.

4. Align your technology stack around the customer journey. Be intentional. Describe every stage of the customer journey around the key milestones. Assign roles, responsibilities, outcomes and the associated technology to support every desired outcome.

5. Share key data and customer insights with all parts of the organization. By doing this, everyone can do their job better and improve alignment and responsiveness to the customer.

I've now spent the last chapters (chapters 3 through 7) discussing the MOM model and going over an in-depth look of each stage.

NextGen, as the final stage, concludes our study of the model. You may be asking, "What's next?"

The short answer: Talent. When evolving into a strategic MO organization and then functioning as one, most leaders note an ongoing challenge. They need to gather the right talent to be able to build a strategic MO organization and then keep it running. The issue is so large that I've devoted the next chapter to talent. I'll show you what steps to take to find, hire and retain great minds.

CHAPTER SUMMARY
A QUICK GLANCE AT WHAT WE LEARNED

- NextGen is the final stage on the MOM model and is characterized by a major reorganization of functions.

- The reorganization to combine functions will lead to new names, definitions and reporting structures that make sense for the company.

- There is usually a visionary in this stage, along with a particular set of drivers and charter.

- SMOPs brings many benefits, chief of which is the line of sight to the end-to-end customer journey.

- The key responsibility of a SMOPs organization is the optimization of technology, process and data to drive customer insights and revenue.

- Follow these steps to make the leap to NextGen: make sure the customer-centric strategy is important; advocate for change during good times; choose a strong leader to run the function; align your technology stack around the customer journey and share key insights with all parts of the organization.

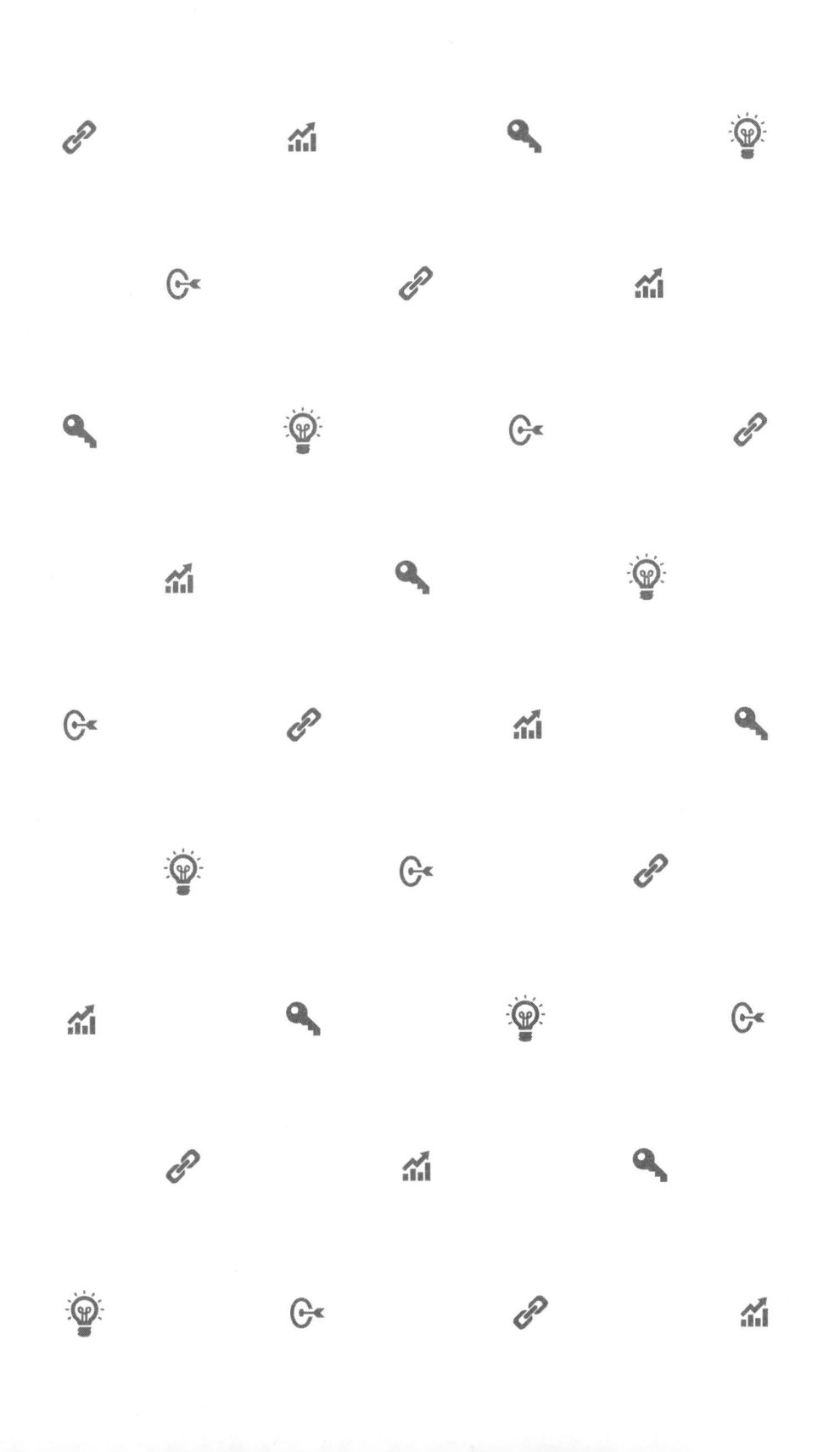

CHAPTER 8

GET, KEEP AND GROW TALENT

Once a year, I teach a class in the MBA program at the College of William and Mary in Virginia. For the past decade, my charter has been to introduce MBA students to the real world of revenue marketing. A few years ago, I began bringing other experts with me. In 2017, I added a section just for MO, and Dan Brown, vice president of marketing operations at Verint, joined us.

Dan did a beautiful job of sharing an overview of the MO function and his role as a leader. The class was highly engaged and fascinated with the scope of what Dan's group provided for the company. As Dan ended his presentation and asked for more questions, a hand went up. From the back of the lecture hall, a young man commented, "Wow, I didn't know this type of organization existed—it sounds exciting. How do we get jobs in this field?"

Dan looked the class over, smiled and responded, "I wouldn't hire any of you."

Silence followed. It was so quiet in that hall you could hear a pin drop.

Dan went on to explain to the stunned students, "You simply do not have the right mix of skills and experience. What I need in my MO group are people with solid technical skills, who exhibit a business mindset, have extensive marketing experience and who are excellent communicators and collaborators."

> **I wouldn't hire any of you.**

He later added that finding this kind of talent has been one of his top operational challenges as an MO leader.

Raise your hand with me if you just finished reading that last sentence and are nodding your head up and down. In every discussion I have with marketing and MO leaders, they always name talent management as one of their top two challenges. They also realize overcoming this obstacle is a must. They know that marketing executives who understand how to effectively source, train and keep talented digital marketers are the leaders of today and will rule tomorrow.

Let's explore how to get over this talent hurdle by delving into the main issues surrounding it. I'll lay out the skills gap that has arisen in digital marketing and the resulting painful process of looking for purple unicorns. I define a purple unicorn as an individual who has technical, analytical, marketing, communication and business skills and experience. From there, I'll outline a basic talent assessment process and four commonly used talent acquisition strategies. I'll also cover training and discuss ways to keep and manage talent in a millennial and virtual-focused world.

THE BIG SKILLS GAP IN DIGITAL MARKETING

As all aspects of digital marketing continue to explode and become part of the DNA of business, the requisite skills for marketers are evolving and expanding. Unfortunately, the digital marketing skills gap is growing, not contracting. The market reality is the crux of the talent challenge for the MO organization. Even if an MO organization has a budget to hire, finding talent can still be a challenge.

> Resources are always a constraint. Let's say you have the budget to get things done ... where do you find a talent pool to be able to do all the things that need to happen?
>
> **—KIRA MONDRUS-MOYAL,** senior vice president of global marketing at Tricentis

I see the digital marketing skills gap in two parts. The first part consists of a lack of singular skills and competencies. In a recent study measuring singular skill or competency areas such as SEO (search engine optimization), email marketing and social media, only 38 percent of participants tested as competent; however, 51 percent believed they were competent.[27] Given the rapid advancements in technology and the overall lack of training in companies, this is not a surprise. Yet this skills gap is the one most easily addressed. Just look at all the vendor training available on these singular topics. There really is no excuse not to have deep expertise in singular areas.

The second part of the skills gap issue concerns the need for multiple skills and competencies, which is much harder to address. In a recent study, more than two-thirds of all marketers reported feeling their overall digital skillset was deficient.[28] The largest skills gap involved basic business acumen: strategy and planning. Among participants, 63 percent said this item was a challenge. Given the scarcity of folks with multiple skill sets and competencies, we call them purple unicorns.

LOOKING FOR PURPLE UNICORNS

When I ask MO leaders the question, "What are you looking for?" they first respond with a pained expression. Then they begin to expound—a lot. They can easily describe what they want, yet it is almost impossible to find the optimal combination of talent. The process is akin to searching for a purple unicorn. While there is a need for deep competence in singular areas, every MO team member must bring more if they aim to be a strategic MO organization.

Many managers outside of marketing have a hard time understanding the purple unicorn concept so critical in MO. Jim Lefevere, an international business leader, shared with me, "If you're hiring a salesperson, it's very easy to find somebody with sales experience. If you're hiring a computer programmer, it's pretty straightforward to find somebody who has experience in this programming language. But it's hard to find somebody who's done modern B2B marketing with marketing technology and understands measurement, analytics, the funnel ... and the list goes on."

Let's delve more deeply into the core elements of a purple unicorn. Of course, there is usually a tech component involved, and being interested in new developments is a key attribute. "We're looking for somebody that is comfortable with technology," Ken Robinson, CMO of NetDocuments, explained to me. He went on to add, "Somebody who wants to understand new technology, how it works, how the pieces fit together and how it is additive to the business. We have people on the team that are really into technology, but they come from completely different backgrounds. These are the kind of people who get excited about the latest mobile phone; they can't wait to open it up and start to play with it. They should have a natural curiosity like this."

> **But it's hard to find somebody who's done modern B2B marketing with marketing technology and understands measurement, analytics, the funnel ... and the list goes on.**

But it's more than just the technical skills and curiosity that are in high demand. Purple unicorns have skills in technology, marketing and business, with a keen understanding of how they work together. "I think one of the things that I found really interesting is you can find highly technical folks, but they either don't have the skills or don't want the skills to be able to translate into business language or into nontechnical language," pointed out Abby Ryan, global director of marketing operations at SAP Concur. "I think people who can do both have to be who you look for. It can't just be, 'Oh I know how to use a tool.' *The most important thing is that they have to be able to connect the dots.*"

Add to this mix the desire to be forward thinking and ready to take strategic action, and you'll begin to get a fuller picture of the purple unicorn for an MO organization. Depending on what area of the country you live in, finding talent is even more challenging. "Finding that talent in the Seattle area is a challenge on its own, as we're competing with the big tech companies and a lot of tech start-ups," noted Aron Sweeney, senior marketing manager at Genie. "The other part of it is trying to find people that get it, that want to get the seat at the table versus go to market with how it's always been done—with low accountability and no skin in the game. I can't hire a traditional marketer and bring them into this environment when they are accustomed to cranking out flyers and going to trade shows. We need to have somebody with scars and dirt under their fingernails. Someone who has done the work and gets it."

> **The most important thing is that they have to be able to connect the dots.**

The marketing leaders I know and work with recognize that getting a fine-tuned, well-honed skill set is essential to transform into a strategic MO unit. Case in point: I recently worked with four CMOs preparing for a panel discussion at an upcoming MO conference. The panel discussion was (perhaps appropriately) named "The Good, the Bad, and the Ugly of Growing a Marketing Operations Capability." As we brainstormed topics for the panel to discuss, one CMO passionately expounded on the topic of talent and capabilities. The others quickly joined in and expressed a similar level of extreme frustration with talent acquisition and management in MO organizations—and this dissatisfaction went beyond finding the right skills and skills mix. They shared a strong sentiment that building an MO team that can evolve with the fast-changing technology landscape is a strategic imperative.

Their assessment seems logical. We live in a digital economy, and whether you work in a B2C or B2B company, having an effective digital engagement strategy is paramount to being competitive. Where does this leave us when marketing—the user of the digital skills—does not have the skills needed, a concise plan to get the skills or the budget to get the skills? In a losing position.

How do we get this incredibly diverse mix of skills? The place to begin is to define exactly what you need by role and across your organization. You do can this with a skills gap assessment.

THE SKILLS GAP ASSESSMENT

A critical leadership role is defining the skills needed, both for today and tomorrow, in the strategic MO function. Conducting a skills assessment allows you to define these skills. As a point of reference, take a moment and look at the MO Skills Chart (see Figure 4.1 in chapter 4). The figure outlines the skills needed for a strategic MO. You'll see there are a lot of skills required, and it can seem overwhelming to gather them all.

There is a practical way to begin a skills assessment. The following five steps provide a path to evaluate skills in your MO organization:

1. Determine your baseline for the assessment. While doing this, align the role of the MO organization to the goals of the company and to the goals of marketing over a one-to-three-year period.

2. With the baseline in place, determine the roles and the accompanying set of skills you will need to be able to execute successfully—for today and tomorrow. Use the MO Skills Chart (Figure 11.7 in the appendix) as guidance for both roles and skills.

3. Conduct a skills inventory across the entire MO group. MO managers can initially complete this step.

4. Follow up the manager assessment with a skills assessment by employee. Even if steps 3 and 4 are done qualitatively, it provides an excellent foundation. I like to have the employee

do a self-evaluation and marry that with the manager's evaluation. Use a simple 1–3 scale to indicate the skill level: 1 is "does not have the skill," 2 is "proficient in the skill," and 3 is "excels at the skill."

5. Determine the skills gap you need to address by role and for the organization.

The exercise will help you validate what you have and determine what you need for today and tomorrow. From here, you can better determine your talent acquisition strategies and the key leadership essentials you'll need to bring to the table.

FOUR TALENT ACQUISITION STRATEGIES

I see talent acquisition as the capability of defining, evaluating and securing MO talent to enable a high-performing MO team. As frustrating as talent acquisition may be, there are only a few ways to approach this challenge. There are no shortcuts. If you have one, call me.

Across the many companies I work with and talk to, four talent acquisition strategies stand out:

1. Rent the talent, and hit the ground running.
2. Hire outside experience, and hit the ground running.
3. Transfer talent from within and develop.
4. Hire young professionals and develop.

1. RENT THE SKILLS

The great thing about living in the digital economy is that virtually anything can be delivered as a service. From fractional CMOs to software development, we live in a world where we can define our needs and "rent" those services. MO skills can apply this concept as well. You can rent anything from singular skills such as SEO or managing a key part of the MO organization such as inbound. Some companies work best when having this kind of flexibility.

There are three primary benefits that come with renting the skills you need. First, by bringing in this talent, you can shorten the time it takes to reach the next level and produce tangible and credible results. You can immediately accelerate your growth as an MO function. Second, renting MO skills helps you train your current staff. Your team members learn from those who have done something many times in different types of environments. The third benefit is that there may be a lower risk in renting talent rather than buying expensive talent. Many organizations begin with some type of contract to bring in talent. Through this strategy, organizations can find out what they don't know and test the waters of a new direction. Companies that change direction frequently may find this type of arrangement particularly helpful.

One negative of renting, however, is that if you do it for too long and for the wrong skills, you might find yourself in an uncomfortable situation of not owning core competencies you need in MO. There is always a balance to strive for, although it can fluctuate over time as the needs of the business and corresponding technology change.

2. HIRE OUTSIDE EXPERIENCE

While renting is a solid option for getting quick results, training current employees and reducing risk, I find more and more MO leaders would rather buy or hire the right skill sets. Doing so gives them ultimate control over their group and allows them to move with speed and agility.

In this scenario, managers hire talent from outside the company. These new hires have experience and knowledge that do not currently exist in marketing. An advantage of this method is that the right hire is an expert in certain areas and does not need to undergo a vast amount of training. They can jump right in and make a difference. For certain situations, such as a critical business need, this strategy is the only appropriate strategy.

Rohit Prabhakar, vice president of digital marketing and e-commerce at Thomson Reuters, uses this technique of hiring experienced individuals. "I constantly build my network," he shared with me. "And I hire through my network or my network's network." Rohit has a highly sophisticated team with a huge set of responsibilities around digital transformation, so he needs more people who can hit the ground running.

The key drawback with hiring top talent lies in cost. I have yet to meet an MO leader with an unlimited budget, and real purple unicorns—required for strategic MO—can be pricey. To be mindful of the budget, MO leaders need to evaluate their situations and decide whether they can reap the most benefit for their organizations by paying a high price for experienced, cross-skilled experts who are ready to make immediate business impacts.

Before you brush off buying skills due to the high price tag, bear in mind that not everyone will be motivated solely by money. Millennials, for example, are highly driven by their social and capital consciousnesses. They tend to prefer working for companies with similar beliefs. With that in mind, rather than jumping to salary discussions when hiring millennials, first learn about their passions. If their passions line up with your company's goals, a potential match could be made. In such a case, the millennial's motivations may include money but will be moderated by social consciousness.

3. TRANSFER TALENT INTERNALLY

To start with, developing what you have is exactly what it implies. A typical path for this approach involves someone on a marketing team who is highly analytical, tech focused, and detail oriented. Over time, that person can grow into an MO role. They learn and develop through on-the-job experience and by being curious and interested. They bring a background in marketing and hopefully a bit of business acumen. For a company that's not in a big hurry or pressed by a major change initiative, this is an excellent "acquisition" strategy.

> I'm a big fan of building marketers with a lot in their tool belts. We have a process to train them ... I can have someone go from the social team over to the operations team, over to the relationship marketing team, and they grow every time they move. In most instances, I have the opportunity to keep growing their levels as they move.
>
> **—STEPHANIE FERGUSON,** corporate vice president at Microsoft

Not long ago, I worked with TraceLink, a company with headquarters in the Boston area, that used the internal talent transfer strategy. For their situation, it made perfect sense. They were building their first formal MO function with an offshore execution capability and needed someone to lead the initiative. An incredibly bright and motivated person was on their marketing team, and she was perfect for the job. She was curious, motivated, analytical and detail oriented.

When she became the director of marketing operations, I knew she was going to knock it out of the park. And she has!

4. HIRE YOUNG PROFESSIONALS

Hiring young professionals is the fourth commonly used talent strategy. Some companies begin with college interns. Kira Mondrus-Moyal, senior vice president of global marketing at Tricentis, has successfully implemented this tactic. "We bring in students in their last year or two of college, and we actually give them real work to do," she told me during an interview. "By the time they graduate, they are able to do some of the junior stuff that you always need in that team—things like data normalization, quality control, process optimization and some very basic automation or CMS stuff. *We love working with interns and then bringing them on board.*"

Other companies like to hire right out of college. Stephanie Ferguson, corporate vice president of Microsoft, explained the reasoning behind this method to me. She said, "What we realized is that there's just not enough talent out there. When we first started to scale our marketing technology platform, we were incredibly challenged to find people who had the right skills." Part of gathering those skills included reaching out to college students. "Now we have a great process with the college hiring team, where they bring people into a rotational program and work for two years in two one-year rotations," she said.

> **We love working with interns and then bringing them on board.**

Bear in mind that hiring young professionals still involves an initial skills assessment. "When we interview people right out of college, they will not get past the first step of the interview process if they can't talk about metrics," noted Randy Taylor, senior director of global marketing at Aderant. "They need to demonstrate they are interested in data and information and recognize that the role is not just creating pretty ads and doing social media."

Some companies prefer to hire individuals with several years of working experience. Jim Lefevere has often taken this approach. "For a large organization, I think it's easier to get somebody before they have hardened habits, are set in their ways, or have become too specialized," he said. "We look for more of a generalist—someone younger in their career who has passion and desire—and we train them."

A WORD ABOUT MILLENNIALS

In this category of generalists who have a few years of experience, you'll often find millennials. As marketers, they tend to be keenly interested in data, in analytics, and in looking at technology as a way to improve business. In other words, they have the potential to be a great hire. I have noticed in the MBA classes I teach at the College of William and Mary that there is a high level of interest in MO among the millennial students. I have found millennials to be a highly diverse population: they value family and community and have a passion for what they do. Recent global studies on millennials as a demographic show them to be well educated, civic oriented, conscious capitalists, global citizens, entrepreneurial, open to diversity, confident and results oriented.[29]

Millennials were estimated to make up 50 percent of the workforce in 2020.[30] Many of them are in marketing, and managers that I talk to share the following thoughts about millennials:

- "They are more flexible."
- "They are more tech savvy—they are true native technologists."
- "They provide a good balance on a team."

- "They are not mired down in past models."
- "They look for solutions that use technology."
- "They look for career opportunity, not just a job."
- "They motivate others to new ways of seeing things—they are like the energy charger for our team."

Embedded in these descriptions are a soft skill set and a hard skill set. The soft skills include the ability to collaborate, to be flexible and to be innovative in an ever-changing environment. The hard skills are the left-brain attributes of logic, analysis and solving puzzles. Furthermore, millennial marketers are more apt to see financial accountability as just another day at the office and nothing special. They are not mired down from legacy metrics because they are so new to the game. For many companies, this combination of skills is the right skill set that is coming along at just the right time.

TRAIN THE SKILLS

For two of the four talent acquisition strategies (internal transfer and young professionals), immediate and ongoing training is essential. In my many conversations with MO leaders, I find among them little patience for training and even less rigor. I have found this to be true across all parts of marketing. Only about 18 percent of companies have formalized training.[31] The rest do it piecemeal at best. Sure, they will see to it that the marketing automation administrator has the most current certification. After that, it's no-man's-land for training. Few companies have a formal MO training program that encompasses all the core competencies of tech, analytics, marketing, communication, teaming and business. By the way, if you do have one, please let me know!

Instead, most of the training I see is informal and on the job. While on-the-job training is very valuable, be aware that when it happens, it is usually haphazard. Unfortunately, what folks in the MO group get exposed to determines what they learn and what they can contribute. The latest project they worked on or the latest white paper they read determines their skill set—not the needs of the business.

MO leaders need to address this gap in process and skills immediately. I'll go into more details about training in the following section. For now, here are five tricks to use to implement training for all MO employees:

1. Create specific role descriptions and career paths based on specific skill sets—both soft and hard.
2. Create a development plan that includes rotations in all parts of marketing with certifications in communications, consulting and the core aspects of technology and analysis.
3. Hire a technical skill set, and have them take a rotation in marketing. Add a basic marketing training curriculum.
4. Hire someone with marketing or business acumen (or both), and have them take a rotation in some aspects of technology and analysis. Add levels of technical training to the curriculum that can be achieved over time.
5. Award badges and certifications. Gamify where you can.

TRAINING SUCCESSFULLY: A PLAYBOOK APPROACH

In the previous sections, I mentioned training as a key component in honing talent. I also observed that many companies don't have a formal training program for marketing in place. If you're thinking of implementing more training in your organization, it can be helpful to see what others are doing.

Let me share an example of an approach that's very familiar to me. I'm a partner at The Pedowitz Group, and as a consulting company for marketing and MO, we have to bring A+ talent to the table. Since our beginning in 2007, we have always provided a lot of training—specifically in systems, communication skills, consulting skills, and project management skills. Several years ago, we knew we had to do more. In 2017, we introduced our eighteen-month playbook.

We decided to make it eighteen months for a reason. We realized that you can't have the best consultants if all they get is a half-day onboarding process with the odd class or two thrown in and some technical certifications. After much trial and error, we learned it takes us eighteen months to get a consultant to their top potential. Following this strategy allows us to have our consultants work across many different projects, customers and situations in a very short period of time.

Now everyone who comes on board gets an eighteen-month customized playbook. The playbook includes the general training everyone needs, as well as training specific to their role. The training might be in technology, project management, management or advanced consulting. All their required activities for an eighteen-month period are loaded into Workfront, and their activity is tracked and reviewed. The method used might be digital, live, one on one or team based.

Regardless of what their playbook looks like, everyone begins with our in-person new-hire orientation. My business partner and our CEO, Jeff Pedowitz, always does this step. The orientation is a two-day event, and every manager presents part of the program. We begin to create working and personal relationships, which is helpful because we have a virtual work arrangement. For those of us on site, we always have a team dinner with the new hires. These activities are a great way to introduce people to the company. From this point, they begin with their digital playbook, which is arranged in three general stages. I'll walk you through each stage briefly here.

Stage 1: Where Are My Office Supplies?

Anyone's first day on a new job includes learning about the tools they need to do their job. They must know where those tools are located and how they are used. For us, this learning exercise consists of a set of prerecorded audio and video learning modules. These modules include testing and equip employees with the information they need to do their jobs. We not only provide training on all the different work tools we use, but we go beyond the basics and explain the purpose as well. For example, the learning module on Microsoft Teams is not just about the technology; it also lays out our set of best practices in how we use it. We have approximately fifteen general work technologies that we use consistently.

One fun learning module we have in this stage is how to set up a home office environment. In this section, new hires get to see videos done by other staff members on how they have set up their offices. Some employees go way out and "produce" these short videos. In the end, each employee reviews their home setup with their manager. And while it can be enjoyable, this module is also vital: we have grown as a virtual company, and ensuring everyone has an optimized home office set up is critical to their success.

Stage 2: Consulting Basics

Since our employees, regardless of the level they begin at in our company, work with clients every day, they need some level of consulting training. In this stage of the learning journey, we introduce them to communications training, which is the most essential ingredient for effective consulting. The training consists of a two-day live class or a twenty-hour digital class that is required for everyone. In it, we teach the basics of listening and asking questions, as well as oral and written communication. We do a lot of customized role-plays in this course to bring these critical skills to life.

In this stage, we also introduce a set of training modules around our solutions—and we have a lot of them. The training modules give an overview of the services the company can provide. Furthermore, we discuss the part their specific role-plays in delivering that solution. Employees can then internalize and apply skills to their unique situations.

At this point, role-specific training begins. Since we have more than six hundred different certifications across our team, many employees require technology-specific training or certification updates for their role. Our employees love keeping up to speed on key technologies, and that, of course, benefits our customers too. For example, for our strategists, they need to learn how to deliver our workshops. Their training involves attending a workshop. After that, the workshop trainer shows them how to deliver the workshop. Following this, they codeliver the workshop and then go solo. In 2020, we had to retrain our team with new tools and processes to do virtual workshops.

The specific role training and experience takes a good amount of time, but it's a solid investment. Each consultant has their own career path, and we endeavor to give them client experiences that will accelerate the employee's learning journey.

We also begin cross-functional training at this stage to introduce them to the other specialists in their midst. Employees can see what other parts of the company are doing. At some point, they may be working with someone from a different team or even decide to join another team.

Stage 3: Advanced Consulting

High-level consulting must be based on experience, and it takes a lot of hours working with clients to get to this stage. Once employees reach this level, we introduce them to advanced skills, which might include getting some high-level certifications. One such certification involves a rigorous two-day course on advanced consulting skills and critical thinking. We also look for employees to become player-coaches. Many of our "teachers" are simply our more experienced employees.

Benefits of an Eighteen-Month Playbook

The playbook isn't simply a handbook to get an employee started off on the right foot. Rather, it is a device to provide ROI across the board. In our company, we see playbook benefits for three different groups: our customers, our employees and our business.

The benefits for clients include the following:

- Well-trained and knowledgeable consultants who work as partners with the client
- High-quality communication
- Fewer project issues
- Consistency across all our consultants

Some of the main perks for employees include the following:

- A guided and defined plan that helps new hires acclimate into the company while improving their knowledge of the company and their consulting skills
- A tangible and visible set of milestones

- More touch points to ensure success
- A sense of accomplishment

For our business, a few of the benefits are as follows:

- A chance to save time and money in the field
- The chance to provide a standardized education for employees, which allows us to attract more talent and have employees perform better and stay longer
- Early check-ins by multiple people to assess new-hire progress and potential
- Reduction of costly client issues

The training process we've established pays off for everyone involved. As you think about a development program for your own organization, consider all the stakeholders involved. While employees might benefit from a training program, you'll also want to see strategic gains for the MO group and the company.

Running an MO organization is one of the coolest places to be in marketing today. Gathering the right skills can enable marketing to step up in terms of business accountability and leadership, which is both exciting and inspiring. The forward-thinking MO leader will address the talent acquisition challenge with a fluid combination of the four strategies discussed. As Stephanie Ferguson of Microsoft shared with me, "What we found was that we needed to both acquire experienced talent and invest in developing early in career talent." A multistrategy talent approach ensures success for current and future MO teams.

MANAGING TALENT

In addition to acquiring skills and training new hires, managing team members is key to retaining talent. I see talent management as the capability of aligning employees with strategic goals and objectives, implementing learning and development programs, developing career paths, providing opportunities for professional growth and development and rewarding and recognizing achievement. As the MO organization grows and evolves, establishing formal talent management processes is essential.

Team members will naturally be curious about how they can advance. In fact, many employees will expect this type of opportunity. "Providing training as a way to help people advance in their careers is almost a requirement in today's world," stated Jim Lefevere. "*Millennials, in particular, have an expectation that we will invest in them.* They want frequent and different assignments, and they want to be challenged."

MO team members will also be seeking a growth process they can follow.

> **Millennials, in particular, have an expectation that we will invest in them.**

"We really have to have career paths," noted Stephanie Ferguson of Microsoft. "If somebody comes into an MO role, we need to show them the possibility and the paths—and the proof, frankly—that they can move from an MO role over to be a global engagement program leader or a platform operations leader."

INCORPORATING NEW TALENT WITH CURRENT TALENT

One aspect of talent management that is often neglected is aligning MO talent with all the parts of marketing. I've seen companies bring in MO talent, and these new roles totally upset the equilibrium of marketing. Employees who have already been working at the company wonder, "What is the role of the new hire (or hires), and how does that affect my role?" They might also worry and ask questions such as "What will happen to my job? Why are these new workers paid more? Will the reporting structure change?"

Remember that employees—both current and new—have a need to know where and how they fit into the ecosystem. New roles bring change. As a manager, be very aware of these dynamics, and have a plan for managing this shift.

Part of this incorporation involves properly identifying the new roles and their expectations and then weaving this into the established workforce. In addition to roles, bringing on board marketers with a different mindset can also be tricky. For instance, adding millennials to a nonmillennial team can be a challenge. Millennials tend to view technology as a useful and practical tool, while nonmillennials may see technology as something scary and over-

> I think that everybody should make the time to be able to tweak and find the right fit for every role that they have and for the people that they have. I think it's on us as people managers to make that a priority.
>
> **—ABBY RYAN,** global director of marketing operations at SAP Concur

whelming. I remember when I bought my first marketing automation system. At that time, there was a stark contrast between two marketers on my team. The older one had a difficult time adjusting to both the use of the technology and the changes it was driving in marketing. The younger one, who had a degree in marketing, welcomed the technology with relish and has since gone on to have a wonderful career as a marketing consultant.

To retain both millennials and nonmillennials, consider everyone's interests. In general, millennials want clarity on upward mobility. They often have less loyalty and more goals for career building than the prior generation. They also tend to be lifelong learners and want to learn at their own pace and in a way that is 100 percent applicable to their job. With that in mind, by having clear responsibilities and guidelines for training and advancement, you'll give millennials a blueprint they can follow. At the same time, you'll want to avoid overlooking your nonmillennial team members. Proactively listening to their concerns can help you understand what they need, and then lay out a path that provides a solution and overall team balance.

THE MARKETING ENABLEMENT FUNCTION

I will admit right up front that marketing enablement is a bit of a soapbox issue for me. Companies spend an inordinate amount of money on sales enablement and training salespeople. Firms typically view salespeople as the "moneymakers." In contrast, the overwhelming majority of companies do not have a corollary training focus on marketing—even as marketing is now also responsible for revenue. Instead, most marketers search for training nuggets by attending conferences or webinars on an ad hoc basis. Universities aren't helping, either, as their curricula are woefully outdated.

The madness cannot continue. The pace of change requires dedicated training, career paths, and experience. I see this training formula for marketers in only a handful of companies, but it will be these companies who win in the digital economy.

Allow me, then, to address the elephant in the room: Why isn't there a marketing enablement team that is an equivalent of sales enablement?

Keep in mind that marketing enablement is hardly a new concept. But it's important to understand why it's crucial now and how it can be put into place in your organization. Ultimately, it can give you a chance to lead on many levels and have a bigger say at the table.

WHY NOW?

I've heard the term "marketing enablement" (or ME) being tossed around for years. In the past, it never caught on as a buzzword for marketers. The difference between a few years ago and today is substantial, and the need for a dedicated marketing enablement function is now at a critical level. Marketing and MO will not succeed in responding to current and future challenges without this function.

To fully understand the need for a marketing enablement function now, let's start by considering the scenario marketers face today. Only one-third of B2B marketing organizations report credible financial results. The average marketing team is juggling more than thirty different technologies. Fewer than 58 percent say they have an optimized martech stack.[32] Less than half of B2B marketing organizations have an actionable customer journey map that they can use effectively.[33]

One of my favorite ancient Chinese proverbs states, "The beginning of wisdom is to call things by their right names." As marketing has struggled to constantly transform to keep up with massive market changes, we've never really given a name to the idea that marketing must now be enabled in a new way. Let's name what's needed, which is a marketing enablement function. The pioneering method is one that is overarching, deliberate, and orchestrated. The new way is to *operationalize* a marketing enablement capability.

THE MARKETING ENABLEMENT CHARTER

First, it's necessary to recognize that ME is an *organizational* capability. An organizational capability is derived from a strategy, is continuous and consists of a bundle of people, processes and technology. Together, this bundle drives a business result. Having ME as an organizational capability, then, means that if one person, or even several people, leave the marketing team, this capability will persist. The organization will be as successful as it was prior to their departure.

The charter, then, of a ME function is to enable the entire marketing organization with the skills and competencies required to optimize the performance of a modern-day marketing organization. The charter is no different from a sales charter and certainly no less important in today's digital world.

STRATEGIC MARKETING OPERATIONS AS EARLY MARKETING ENABLEMENT

I have found it interesting to watch how the MO team evolved into being an educator for the rest of the marketing team. Quite often, the MO team is helping marketing learn about data. They might show the marketing team how to access data, how to analyze it and how to use it to make better decisions. The MO team creates data-based dashboards and KPIs for overall team performance. By providing education and the tools for access and use of data, the MO team helps to drive the transformation of marketing from the pens-and-mugs department to an ROI-driven business group. MO also brings in project management practices (e.g., formal processes for campaigns and other work activities) and technology education (at different levels). Most of this learning has been on the job and highly valuable for the marketing team. However, it's not enough.

In my opinion, we will soon see more organizations develop a marketing enablement function that parallels the sales enablement function. There will be curricula that are general, along with those that are specific for certain roles. There will be a progression of training that enables careers in deliberate rather than sporadic paths. The MO group may lead this, or at the very least, the MO group will be a major contributor to curriculum development and delivery. Just consider how valuable such a development would be for your organization!

PUTTING IT IN ACTION

When I sat down with Tom DelMonte, head of North America marketing operations at SAP, he told me how his team developed and led critical training for his organization at a key time. "We had to enable a training workstream to support a huge technology shift in marketing," he recalled. "Our partners across MO started with an analysis."

Specifically, they asked these questions:

- What do your marketers need to know?

- If we now have access to this new technology, which provides access to new data, and I can write these new types of reports, how would a marketer use that report?

- What does a report need to look like? What questions would the report answer?

- On the flip side, are marketers asking questions that previous reports could answer but now, with the new technology that provides new data models, it isn't possible to answer?

In addition, "we built personas for all the different types of marketers we have," Tom explained. Once they had defined the different roles involved, Tom and his team considered what parts of the system each position would need to know and understand. They then built out an enablement plan for each of the roles.

By applying this logic, Tom and his partners created a college-based training approach. They developed a 100-level course in marketing automation for everyone to take. Then they made a 200-level course for specific marketing disciplines, followed by a 300-level course focused on becoming an expert in certain areas.

"We recorded sessions using ON24 to build that virtual event platform where it looks like you're in a conference hall and you walk in and you see the keynotes," Tom explained. "From an education perspective, we put a lot of thought into it, and we built that out, and then we built in learning days. You know, like Amazon Prime Day—everyone knows when that day is."

Moving forward, to help everyone plan for learning days, Tom and his team communicate the date in advance. "Then we tease out the agenda items," he said. "Marketers hold their people accountable to be 100 percent focused on whatever the learning curriculum is for that day."

MANAGING IN A VIRTUAL WORLD

Another twist in talent management is managing in a virtual world. The situation is similar to managing in the perfect storm, which is a combination of events that usually does not happen at the same time. For the MO organization, the perfect storm elements are being virtual, having increasing responsibility in a virtual world and having to team up with cross-functional stakeholders in a virtual environment. The perfect storm has strong implications on any talent strategy.

Given this, it would be remiss to discuss talent in this chapter and not point out that you may not see your team members on a day-to-day basis. Increasingly, talent management occurs virtually, as more employees work from home. Some companies have been operating on a remote basis for a while, and others made the shift during the 2020 pandemic.

The online working environment is much different than an office where in-person interaction takes place every day. Yet the virtual team is quickly replacing the previous norm, and that holds true in marketing. In 2020, 87 percent of marketers reported they were working 100 percent remotely.[34] Furthermore, the pandemic spurred many companies to start down a virtual path with no return. I watched companies shift their entire marketing organizations from onsite to online during the pandemic. These days, I work with and see many MO teams that are distributed over states, countries, and time zones. I have to tell you, it is much more common to see a virtual team than a team all in one office.

Let's recognize that this move is leading marketing to change forever, and we shouldn't have expectations of things going back to exactly the way they were before. From an employee perspective, this makes sense. Here's why: letting workers carry out their roles from home is a bit like letting the genie out of the bottle. By that, I mean employees are learning how great it is to work from home, and many will seek opportunities to continue to do so. And if those workers have the skill sets so sought after by marketing, they can call the shots.

In addition, companies are learning they can have a better chance at sourcing and keeping talent if they offer a virtual work environment.

At the same time, MO teams are under a lot of pressure and have expanded responsibilities. In 2020, more than 60 percent of respondents to a CMO survey stated that the marketing function had increased in importance during the pandemic.[35] Now MO teams have to do more than just keep up with technology, buy it, integrate it and optimize it; they also have to ensure data quality and data access. They have to conduct ongoing analysis of data to help improve and report on marketing performance. They are responsible for rearchitecting core processes. They have to understand the business of marketing while helping marketing become a data-driven and revenue-oriented organization. And they must be proactive. Need I go on?

With these new responsibilities comes the need to effectively team with other functions and stakeholders. In this new world, things get done by taking a team approach. To see this cross-functional collaboration at play, consider the teaming dynamics that are needed to carry out the following tasks. Think about who else is affected and whom you need to work with for each of the following:

- Making the decision to buy or replace your marketing automation system (and then implementing it)
- Creating an optimal martech stack
- Developing a new reporting process and dashboards
- Rearchitecting a new lead management process

None of these activities can be done in a marketing silo. Instead, they all require a high degree of collaboration and communication across other functions to be successful. Taking the time to develop teamwork skills will result in more successful projects and improved overall team performance. Trust me, it's worth the effort. Research indicates that over 70 percent of organizations that are focused on building and supporting cross-functional teams also report improvement in productivity, efficiency and profitability.[36] These three key metrics are near and dear to marketing ops. Given the importance of teamwork to achieve expanded responsibilities in a virtual environment, let's discuss what teamwork skills are important.

TEAMWORK IN A VIRTUAL ENVIRONMENT

Teamwork can be broken down into a very specific set of skills that, when used appropriately, result in improved performance. Since books have been written on this topic, for the sake of brevity and relevance, let's look at three core skills that directly relate to a virtual marketing ops team. They are communicating, listening/asking questions and resolving conflict.

Communicating

Communication is the cornerstone of an effective team and is especially important on a virtual team working across functions. If you just read this sentence and rolled your eyes, don't. We talk about this constantly yet do very little to improve communication skills. The ability to communicate, to get your point across and to fully understand the other person, is probably the most overlooked skill in strategic MO today (and in marketing). How we communicate, when we communicate and what channels we use for communication must all be considered. In a virtual environment, the need for effective communication is even stronger.

"I need somebody that has very strong communication skills, because in many cases, they're working across functions," Ken

Robinson of NetDocuments told me in a recent conversation. "And in a lot of cases, and certainly with my team today, they're engaging at the highest levels of the organization. My MO person has dedicated time on a monthly basis to work through KPIs, data, and analysis about the performance of the business with the CEO and the head of sales. They have to be able to convey their perspective with some conviction and potentially work through a debate. Presentation skills and communication skills are going to be hugely important."

In my company (and we are a virtual company), we place a very high value on communication skills. In 2015, I developed a virtual communications class that is required for everyone in our company. The course includes subjects such as recognizing your own communication style, listening actively, asking questions, and handling difficult conversations both in person and in a virtual environment. As such, we do a lot of role-play. We also created a rubric for when to communicate (response time), in what format (phone, email, text, Skype), and whom to include in the communication. The rubric is particularly helpful when we start a new project, as it helps to establish in-person and virtual communication protocols for the team and with our customers.

For a virtual team, the following two areas are key for effective communication:

- Internal communication system: You might communicate through Skype, Microsoft Teams, Slack and so on. The goal is to enhance the communication and productivity of your MO team. Consider setting standards that indicate when to use which communication channel, how to send attachments or links to where they are stored, naming conventions for subject lines and length of the email. Whatever your primary communication channel, review how it is being used and look for opportunities to improve its use. Make this a special project, and don't trust that it will happen organically.

- Responsiveness: In the world of remote teamwork, the number one strategy for improvement is how long you take to respond to a virtual communication. Consider this scenario: you send out a message to two team members with a call to action that gives a two-day timeframe. One responds within fifteen minutes, acknowledges the action item and promises it in two days, while the other responds with the action item completed a full two days later. In both cases you get what you asked for, but the experience feels very different. To avoid this prolonged return, create a protocol for response time.

Listening and Asking Questions

A second critical teamwork skill in a virtual MO environment is listening and asking great questions. As basic as these skills sound, I cannot express how important they are for an MO team to be effective. In my experience, I have found MO teams full of very smart people who are ready to get things done. Yet this doer type of mentality can often result in thinking ahead to what has to get done, rather than listening to the problem, project or issue and then asking questions for clarity. Miscommunication often occurs, which then leads to rework and delays in projects.

As busy as a marketing operations team can be, trying to multitask (like writing an email while you are in a virtual meeting) does not work. Scientists have demonstrated that the brain cannot effectively or efficiently switch between tasks, as noted by Julie Morgenstern.[37] In the end you lose time. Recognizing new things takes four times longer, so you're not really saving time: multitasking actually costs time. Furthermore, you also lose time because you will often make more mistakes. Work to listen actively and ask more questions—your projects will love you for it. In a world of constant Zoom meetings, this can be a struggle, but you will see an increase in productivity if you apply this rule of thumb.

Conflict Resolution

Many people are challenged with conflict resolution, and this issue is amplified in a virtual environment. In addition, conflict resolution training is typically only done for salespeople. Many marketers shy away from any conflict and flounder in any kind of response. For the MO team, finding a way to immediately address conflict before it escalates is key to acting as an effective team. The first step to do this is to decide when and how conflict resolution should occur. For example, if you have a team member who disagrees on the best way to integrate two important systems, you need to address this immediately. In a case such as this, picking up the phone is the best way to handle the conflict. On the phone, fully explore the other person's perspective before you present your preferred method. By listening first and clarifying you understand their position, you build an environment of respect, which can ease the way to solving the conflict.

I would also recommend providing training on resolving conflict and creating an environment for almost immediate 360-degree feedback. You'll avoid "stewing" from a home office, which is very easy to do. Other areas that are especially important for improving teamwork include rapport building, problem-solving, planning, influencing, being reliable and being respectful.

LEADING IN THE VIRTUAL WORLD

I have highlighted a few of the skills needed for a virtual team to be more efficient, productive and profitable, but the job of the MO leader is to organize people into the right teams and to create an environment for virtual team success. In addition to considering particular skill sets, managers need to think about how people behave in teams. For more information on this, you can study the Belbin Team Roles (see www.belbin.com/about/belbin-team-roles/), which is a widely used model. The essence of this model is that out of nine roles, people serve different roles on a team such as a coordinator, an implementor or a team driver. The most successful team compositions include all nine roles.

Additionally, an MO manager needs to establish an environment for virtual team success. Sometimes a manager can get lucky and this happens organically. In my experience, however, this is rare. Recognizing the unique challenges of an MO team working in a virtual environment is the first step. The second step is to engage the entire team in a dialogue around how you can improve teamwork, efficiency, effectiveness and productivity in a virtual environment. The third step is to institutionalize the processes and train for the skills. If your company plans to continue to do more work in a virtual environment, pay special attention to these dynamics, as they are much harder to identify in situations where everyone works remotely. Make this a dedicated effort.

Finally, MO leadership must provide the tools required for a home office environment. The ability to connect and to have optimal access to systems and tools is a ground-level requirement for success. While it may seem complicated, it doesn't have to be. In the spring of 2020, during the onset of the pandemic, I heard of one company that resourced their MO team for home offices over a single weekend. It can be done.

The MO team is often the central hub for important projects for marketing and the company. While it is easy to focus on technical skills, don't forget or ignore other key skills that can improve overall team performance. Learning how to work as a team—especially a virtual team—requires effort but can produce great rewards. Take the time to make communications training a requirement, and ensure that managers support and coach to these skills.

A WORD ABOUT PAY

When we think about acquiring talent, training, and managing team members, there are always dollars involved. In any profession, you'll pay top dollar for top talent. As I stated earlier in this chapter, MO as top talent can be very pricey. The rate is especially high in terms of current marketing salaries. For this reason, many hire young and train on the job. Most organizations that I see have a mixture of top talent and talent that they are growing.

The pressure on budgets from hiring skilled MO employees will continue. For this reason, thinking about other perks can help attract and retain talent. For some companies, a key benefit can be the freedom for employees to work from home. Millennials, whom I have highlighted as a rising force of talent, especially appreciate this perk. Other companies dole out great benefits such as unlimited vacations.

Besides the perks associated with the job, some organizations are paying bonuses based on performance. For instance, just like a sales organization, marketing might receive additional pay for achieving and overachieving revenue goals. I like this approach because it gets everyone on the same page.

In summary, getting and managing talent will continue to be a topic of conversation in our industry. I've presented various strategies to gather the right skill set, along with ways to implement solid training programs. I also gave an overview of the methods used to help employees grow in their careers. I shared ideas to help you build a productive team while working in a virtual environment. The icing on the cake for a strong talent base that is strategically aligned with the company is to offer a competitive package that encompasses more than just pay. Get creative. Your staff will thank you for it, and so will your boss.

> You need a visionary group to really help move plans forward.
>
> **—HEATHER COLE,** vice president of enterprise marketing products and solutions at AMEX

CHAPTER SUMMARY
A QUICK GLANCE AT WHAT WE LEARNED

- Recent advancements and trends in technology have created a significant skills gap in MO.

- Purple unicorns are those rare individuals who possess multiple and diverse skill sets needed for a strategic MO organization.

- Fast-growing companies often rent talent or hire experience.

- Companies with a slower growth plan and less urgency typically transfer internal talent or hire young professionals and develop them.

- The right training program can take MO to the next level.

- A marketing enabling function creates strategic and leadership opportunities.

- Managing in a virtual world requires a focus on core soft skills and systems as well as the ability to effectively lead from afar.

- While top talent can come with a high price tag, today's employees may be attracted to other benefits like working from home, unlimited vacations or performance-based bonuses.

CHAPTER 9

THE VALUE OF STRATEGIC MO TO KEY STAKEHOLDERS

How does a strategic MO organization act within and across a company? The reality is that other stakeholders may be oblivious to the potential MO brings to the business. Old perceptions of what marketing is and what it can deliver act as highly effective blinders.

Breaking down these barriers begins with a new approach. As you transform the role of MO, you must also transform current relationships and perceptions of marketing. The move is a must for today's strategic MO function. By doing so, MO can help reorient the company to see the real value that marketing can and should bring to the business.

Moreover, partnering with other key stakeholders enables a tighter and more productive working relationship that results in improved business performance. When I sat down to chat with Heather Cole, vice president of enterprise marketing products and solutions at AMEX, she discussed what happened when her own MO organization grew to be strategic and started interacting with other stakeholders. "One seemingly small but important tactic we took was to implement shared goals with key internal partners," she said.

Establishing common goals made a significant difference in two areas. First, "it helped our partners appreciate that we are in this together," Heather noted. Second, "it resulted in the team needing to better understand our partners' strategies and the desired outcomes." As a result, she and her team could start thinking about ways to help partners better achieve their targets.

Because of the potential that is at stake, I believe a key element of the mission statement for the MO function should be to reeducate executives and key stakeholders on new marketing possibilities. Don't get me wrong; all the other tasks the MO organization carries out are important. If stakeholders can't "see" marketing in a new light, trying to make changes will be like swimming through peanut butter.

Before we can "sell" this new vision, however, we must concretely define the real value that a strategic MO group brings to key stakeholders. In the following sections, I'll lay out how being strategic creates a new relationship between MO and sales. I'll also identify the benefits a strategic MO group provides for the CEO and the CFO. I discussed how the MO organization is tied to the CMO in chapter 2. In this chapter, I'll touch on the CMO again briefly, with the intent of demonstrating how MO can propel the CMO forward once the strategic function is fully integrated and running at top speed. I'll close with showing the value strategic MO creates for marketing and IT.

BECOMING A REVENUE PARTNER WITH SALES

My doctoral dissertation research revealed strategies CMOs consider to be important in adopting financial accountability (for more on this topic, see page 42). Among all the strategies identified, the one that had the highest level of agreement among the CMOs in the study was achieving sales and marketing alignment. For marketing to be successful, they must have a peer- and revenue-oriented relationship with sales.

To accomplish this, they must have a strategic MO organization.

> 💡 When it came to the sales organization, they were begging for a relationship with marketing. They were just looking for how we get things aligned.
>
> **—RANDY TAYLOR,** senior director of marketing operations at Aderant

Given this, it still baffles me why marketing has such a hard time understanding sales. The solution is quite simple: give them leads that convert to opportunities and closed business, and give them real-time digital insights that better prepare them for conversations. Yet marketing continues to not address these needs. A hallmark of the strategic MO organization is how they create a joint revenue relationship with sales. Let's see what that might look like and the role strategic MO plays.

CHANGE IS A TWO-WAY STREET

Marketing is not the only culprit in blocking a new and better way to drive revenue. Sales is just as guilty. For the modern revenue machine to work, both sales and marketing need to make significant changes. By looking at how sales needs to change, marketing will be better informed on the actions they need to take to become partners in revenue. Let's begin with an optimal view of what sales should be doing, outline what they are doing wrong, and bring it all together through market forces.

Imagine a sales process nearly devoid of guesswork: one where salespeople track what their prospects are researching—and thinking—without having a conversation or meeting.

In this new world, cold calls have become obsolete. They have been replaced by technology that provides salespeople with a real-time view into the prospect's digital body language.

What if, at a critical point in the buyer's evaluation, but before they engage with a competitor, an alert is sent to the salesperson's inbox or phone telling them it's time to engage?

Salespeople really want this, and in today's competitive arena, it's what they must have to survive. These new capabilities are causing a seismic shift in the traditional sales cycle. They are ultimately changing how leads are managed and opportunities are converted into sales.

> 💡 I've built a relationship with sales leadership ... when we think about some of the strategic initiatives of an organization, we're brought in early to those discussions, not kind of as an afterthought to make sure the fit and finish looks good.
>
> **—KEN ROBINSON,** chief marketing officer at ProSites

Salespeople who don't have it want it. Those who have it say they couldn't live without it.

I recently spoke with an office equipment salesperson who used this exact type of process I just described. The person explained to me what it was like: *Once you have this kind of insight at your fingertips, you simply can't go back to not knowing.*

THE DEFINITION OF INSANITY

Like marketing, sales needs to adopt new thinking and new processes to be successful in the digital age. Sales must recognize marketing as part of the revenue team and, in doing so, change how they operate. Yet too often I see sales "doing the same thing in the same way and expecting a different result." Yep, the definition of insanity.

At the beginning of every year, I see lots of sales leaders deploy what I call the *re* strategy. They are *re*thinking, *re*organizing, *re*doing and *re*aligning all the same things they have done before. They expect a new result in what has become a dramatically different selling game. I see this happen from the beginning of lead generation to the opportunity pursuit and the final closing of business. Let's analyze this further and see how MO can help stop this vicious and unproductive *re* cycle.

For companies today, the lead-production process occurs in three different ways:

1. Sales scratches out leads by prospecting their personal networks, cold calling and sending one-off or batch emails.

2. The marketing departments turn over long lists of leads, which are typically no more than contacts with pulses.

3. The marketing department is a revenue marketing machine powered by a strategic MO group.

In the first two cases, the essence of effort is thick-skinned people trying to overcome the telephone rejection. For the most part, they blindly cold call and email contacts for months, hoping to set up a meeting and begin a sales cycle. When they finally have a genuinely interested prospect, they are smart enough to stay out of their own way. Eventually they move on to a fresh list and classify previous prospecting failures as disqualified leads.

Once disqualified, the leads fall into a zombie lobby. There they wait for the "new guy" assigned to begin the blind cold-call/email process all over again. Or worse, they're never actually contacted again. And then there's the cruelest outcome of all: marketing repurchases the zombies for the third, fourth, or fifth time. The nightmare recycles, and you can't wake up!

In this traditional sales landscape, it's difficult to get a sense of what is (or isn't) working. What are your salespeople really doing, how are prospects really acting, and how hot are the opportunities they are chasing? Most sales leaders just keep coming up with the next *re* strategy, simply because they have no better way to attack these age-old challenges.

THE IMPACT OF DIGITAL

You see it every day: technology is changing at warp speed. Some of it annoys; some amazes. As sales leaders and professionals, it's up to us to recognize which changes and which advances can have a profound impact on our selling efforts and competitive position.

The use of the internet for research has produced a radical break in the mode of how individuals and companies buy. Even so, there's been little corresponding response in the way most companies sell. There are exceptions, though. New technologies—especially automated sales enablement tools—provide sales leaders with a way to rapidly respond to this new buyer behavior. They align the sales process to the customer's buy process, which translates to more revenue and a stronger competitive position.

In chapter 3, I introduced the Marketing Operations Maturity (MOM) model (see Figure 3.2 on page 67) and highlighted the role of MO in revenue management. Engineering a flawless revenue management process that is repeatable, scalable and predictable (RPS) is the number one benefit sales accrues from MO. For full detail on the role of MO in lead management (which I have noted should now be referred to as revenue management), see page 119.

Sales is a key stakeholder in marketing becoming a revenue partner. Through the unique advantage of a strategic MO, marketing can successfully assume this role.

DRIVING BUSINESS RESULTS FOR THE CEO

CEOs are uniquely responsible for driving shareholder value. Of course, there are other important initiatives, but this is the reason they are hired. As such, CEOs spend their days working to maximize every asset at their disposal to make better decisions for the company, resulting in improved shareholder value.

As these assets are evaluated, it isn't uncommon to see marketing overlooked and certainly undervalued. CEOs may simply be unaware of what marketing has the capability of doing today. Traditional views or legacy thinking can create a perception that marketing is merely a money pit. A CEO might not understand that marketing is a critical lever that can be pulled to drive the business forward.

An example I've seen multiple times involves mergers and acquisitions. In these scenarios, I've seen marketing cut to the bone because there was no perceived business value. The powers that be were focused on the more traditional revenue-generating parts of the company and saw marketing as only an expense. They didn't fully recognize the tools, technology and data that marketing can bring to the table.

To reverse this thinking, a strategic MO function can work to inform a CEO about the opportunities at hand. To carry this out, we must go back to the three challenges of the CMO I first laid out earlier (see page 31). They are driving revenue, driving digital transformation and being the customer expert. All of these are shareholder value-creating initiatives that can only succeed with a strategic MO in place.

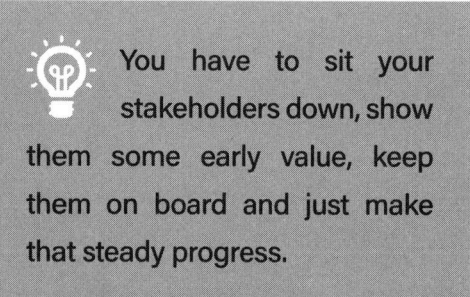

> You have to sit your stakeholders down, show them some early value, keep them on board and just make that steady progress.
>
> **—STEPHANIE FERGUSON,** corporate vice president at Microsoft

By focusing on the three big challenges of the CMO—all of which are tied to company goals that are tied to shareholder value—the strategic MO organization becomes essential. Operationalizing strategies for the company is the core value of strategic MO. Delivering insights related to these objectives enables the CEO to view marketing as an important cog in the revenue-generating, digitally transforming and customer-centric machine.

DEMONSTRATING ROI FOR THE CFO

In many companies, the relationship between the CMO and CFO narrows down to the annual budget brawl. The CMO asks for more money, and the CFO wants to know the return on investment (ROI) to expect from the funds. In the end, they reach a stalemate.

For years, the CFO has been frustrated by the inability of marketing to show an ROI on any of the very substantial investments in marketing. In this scenario, the marketing budget is the bane of the CFO's existence. The CFO views marketing as a pure cost center, and as such, just tries to make sure marketing spend is kept within budget parameters.

A recent study correlated this view. From a pool of over two hundred participating marketing organizations, only 14 percent viewed finance as a strategic partner. Among participants, 20 percent either had no relationship with finance or spoke with finance only when forced. In contrast, the study also revealed strong correlations that underscore the importance of obtaining the CMO/CFO alliance. The study reported that high-growth organizations were three times more likely to align marketing and finance.[38]

ENTER STRATEGIC MARKETING OPERATIONS

The strategic MO organization is the solution to the CFO's sleepless nights for two reasons. First, the strategic MO organization is frequently responsible for professionally managing the budgeting process and tracking for marketing. Second, they enable ROI and revenue contribution from marketing.

I've worked with many marketing organizations, and no one has ever told me how much they love the budget-planning and management process. In fact, it's usually quite the opposite. They often do the minimum and hope it doesn't come back to harm them later. The opposition occurs sometimes because they don't have the skills or the time to do it well. The strategic MO group has both.

A strategic MO organization provides marketing with professional project management skills, analytical skills and dedication to the effort. All of these are required for the budgeting process. As professional project managers, the MO organization is not afraid of a spreadsheet and understands how the pieces fit together across the many parts of marketing. I often see MO working with, collaborating with and integrating all the different budget requests across marketing. The task is huge and one that greatly benefits marketing. The end results are saved time and a budget that is most often realistic and focused on spending money to drive results.

The dedication to both the process and the management of the budget is also highly valuable to the marketing team. Looking at, calibrating, and forecasting spend ensures marketing has what they need at the right time. The strategic MO group proactively looks at the spend and compares it to the constant evaluation of results. The activity is not a drop-in kind of task. The continuous monitoring and application to changes in the business requires a dedicated resource.

The strategic MO understands how the CFO approaches budgeting, and that's a significant benefit. Working with the CFO to adopt their processes so everything can be expressed in CFO terms creates transparency. These steps foster a better working relationship with the CFO. After all, the closer the CFO is to understanding the business of marketing, the more credibility marketing will earn.

> 💡 If you do find something that works and you have the data to support it, all of a sudden, you have a credible case to take to your CEO or CFO to get additional funding to support those things that are really working. Any smart CEO, if he sees that something is actually generating more revenue, is going to continue to invest in that.
>
> —**CLAUDINE BIANCHI,** chief marketing officer at LeanIX

ELEVATING THE CMO TO THE CORNER OFFICE

The value of MO to the CMO can be expressed in terms of the CMO's current position—or it can be expressed in terms of their future job. Earlier, I explained that through strategic MO, the CMO can become a business leader, a customer expert and a digital transformation trailblazer (for more information, see page 29). This connection can help marketing earn that sought-after seat at the table.

But it doesn't end there. The attributes that help the CMO enter the boardroom can move the position even more. A board of directors will want a CEO of the future to have the skills the CMO develops through strategic MO. In other words, the CMO moves up to the board meeting—and then she runs it.

As MO continues to mature and focus on solving business problems, we will see more CMOs at the table representing all of marketing. We will also see more CMOs move to the corner office with a CEO sign on the door. And what happens to the open CMO spot? Well, it's taken by the strategic MO leader.

UP-LEVELING MARKETING'S GAME

Beyond providing benefits to the CMO, the strategic MO function delivers advantages for the marketing team. I'll point out the main areas where I typically see MO drive value for marketing. These involve meeting goals and enabling marketing to see and utilize the power of data.

> We've worked hard to develop a reputation of being strategic partners and to show the value that we bring to the business. I have a lot of passion for the role that MO plays and the transformation we can help drive for marketing.
>
> **—HEATHER COLE,** vice president of enterprise marketing products and solutions at AMEX

To meet goals, MO engineers technology, people, process and data. A strategic MO function carries out these tasks in a way that drives business results. Through these efforts, marketing is able to better achieve its objectives.

The MO function is also essential in aiding all of marketing to understand and adopt data-driven decision-making. In organizations that do not have a vibrant MO organization, I find they operate more on "gut feel" rather than data. I am also seeing more and more marketers beginning to understand the power of data. They seem to evolve over time, and MO vastly speeds up that evolution. I believe that a key role of MO is to understand the level of data knowledge across the marketing group as a whole and then help them improve that knowledge. Having everyone in marketing making data-driven decisions is a fast track to achieving results.

> It's being able to understand what the key questions are that need to be answered by the business stakeholders and being able to address that with data-driven conversation.
>
> **—KIRA MONDRUS-MOYAL,** senior vice president of global marketing at Tricentis

REAL DATA WITH REAL VALUE

A few years ago, I began to use the term *datanista* as a moniker for team members who were being introduced to the power of data. The MO function can use this model to assess and work with marketing. I'll explain three types of datanistas: rookie, analytic and predictor.

The Rookie Datanista

Rookie datanistas work based on their gut feelings. They talk to people, hear things and then make decisions. They are focused on activities and not results. Their success metric is getting something done. They don't lean in and dig out data on their own—either pre- or postinitiative. In many cases, they have spent careers as more traditional marketers, and they just have not been shown a better way.

In this kind of marketing organization, the key for MO is to begin with quantitative data the marketing team can understand and act upon. For example, MO could provide a report on campaign performance with basic metrics for twenty-four, forty-eight and seventy-two hours after the launch. The report will help rookie datanistas adopt the behavior of looking at the early data and making adjustments as needed. Another example is creating and sharing marketing dashboards in marketing meetings. I recently worked with a marketing team that was newly accountable for the number of MQLs sent to sales. Once the MO team crafted the dashboard, they began weekly team meetings to go over the numbers. The new conversation cadence helped the marketing team embrace making data-driven decisions.

The Analytic Datanista

Analytic datanistas have access to data that gives them visibility into digital body language. The information allows them to make real-time, data-driven decisions about their interactions with the customer. They can also provide key customer insights to a larger stakeholder group.

The analytic datanista is the MO group's best friend for several reasons. First, they want and appreciate data. Second, they know what to do with the data. Third, they go get their data. Fourth, they pride themselves on making data-driven decisions.

Analytic datanistas bring skill sets that can be applied to customer data. The data is available from different systems and in various formats. For instance, it might be digital body language from the marketing automation system, or it might be composite data from Google. Marketers are interested in a better understanding of prospects and customers—more than word of mouth. The data, which is collected and responded to in real time, is used by a wider stakeholder group, including the digital marketing team, product marketers, marketing/program managers and MO. These groups leverage the data to optimize every customer touch to improve effectiveness, boost efficiency and drive revenue.

As the MO organization, you now need to up your data game. The data must be clean, it must be normalized, it must be accessible and it must be usable. I typically see at least one data scientist or analyst on the MO team to support the data appetite.

The Predictor Datanista

Predictor datanistas may not be the MO group's best friends because they constantly push for more in terms of sophisticated tools and technology. Predictor datanistas require a wide network of data sources, including digital body language, demographic data, CRM, back-end systems, web, intent data and third parties. They expect data to be available in real time. and they expect it to be of high quality. They want in-depth data analysis and the ability to do data modeling. Only then can they fully leverage the power of the more sophisticated tools to predict behavior. These predictions provide powerful and actionable insights to sales and other key stakeholders.

SPEAKING THE SAME LANGUAGE AS IT

From my experience, working with IT is a double-edged sword. IT sometimes owns all the technology that is being used by marketing. If they don't own all of it, they might own parts of the technology that need to integrate with the marketing technology. While marketing often must work with IT, the needs of marketing are often very low on IT's priority scale. Sales or other parts of the company often get preference over marketing.

The strategic MO function has the chance to redefine and significantly improve this relationship with IT. Since MO teams understand technology and can speak the same language as IT, they share more in common with IT than marketing does. At the same time, MO teams grasp marketing's specific needs. Thus, the strategic MO function can become a mediator and a translator between marketing and IT. In this interpreter role, strategic MO can work with IT to stress the importance of the marketing requirements and move them from the graveyard to the VIP list.

Consider this: I worked with a company in which the IT department owned the CRM system. The marketing department didn't know enough about how the technology of the system worked to put in the right kind of request. Due to this, their requests were always given low priority. When they began to use strategic MO, however, everything changed. Given MO's deep technology insight, they understood how the IT department worked. MO put in requests and worked within IT's processes to get marketing the priority it deserved.

In this way, MO can help IT become a more effective partner for marketing. Recognizing limits is also important. In my opinion, MO should never report to IT. Doing so is a recipe for disaster, and I've never seen it done successfully.

Throughout this book, I've revealed how MO can identify where they are in terms of maturity and where they need to go. I've laid out the steps of building a strategic MO and embodying it with top talent. In this chapter, I showed you how once that strategic MO function is running at full speed, others will notice. Not only that, but they'll be ready to partner with MO and work together to accomplish goals, drive revenue, optimize processes and make data-driven decisions.

What's left? Nothing more than to get started on your journey toward building a strategic MO function. And that step, in reality, is often harder than it first appears. Where exactly do we begin to put all these pieces into place? I'll show you how to initiate the process of becoming a strategic MO organization in the next chapter.

CHAPTER SUMMARY
A QUICK GLANCE AT WHAT WE LEARNED

- The strategic MO function partners with executive team members and key stakeholders to deliver value and drive results.

- Once MO masters revenue management, sales considers them a must-have, invaluable resource—a true partner in revenue.

- For the CEO, a strategic MO function helps carry out shareholder, value-creating initiatives like driving revenue, digital transformation and being the customer expert.

- The CFO appreciates a strategic MO function's ability to understand budgeting and the processes related to monitoring budgets.

- A strategic MO organization provides a way for the CMO to become a future CEO, and in doing so, the strategic MO leader moves up to the CMO position.

- The strategic MO function helps marketing meet goals and understand the power of data to make decisions.

- MO can work within the IT processes to help IT become a more effective partner for marketing.

CHAPTER 10

SETTING IT IN MOTION: NEXT STEPS TO BUILDING A STRATEGIC MO FUNCTION

I started this book by reassuring you that MO is so much more than the misdirected "button pushers" image. Then I walked you through looking at what MO leadership entails, the challenges of today's CMO and how strategic MO is the secret sauce to getting that seat at the table. I spent a considerable amount of time explaining the Marketing Operations Maturity (MOM) model (see Figure 3.2 on page 67), an essential tool to help you build a *strategic* MO organization. Within the MOM discussion, I also included information on key skills and key roles. I touched on the complex art of gathering, shaping, and keeping top talent today. Finally, I showed you how that all-important strategic MO function enables you to build bridges and partner with key stakeholders and executive team members.

Is that it? Yes and no. While we have covered the basics, I want to leave you with a set of practical action steps. These are real-world tips that I've gathered from my own research and experience, coupled with input I've received from experts and top players in the field.

As we cover this process, I'll point out three different areas where you can get started right away. They are discovery, vision/mission/brand and change management. I'll explain how you can move forward in each of these. Collectively, the steps detailed in the following sections will help you get started on your journey and/or accelerate your journey to building a strategic MO function. In addition, I've created an online workbook with more detail at www.pedowitzgroup.com/offers/backroom-to-boardroom-workbook.

DISCOVERY

Discovery is the activity of gathering and processing data from multiple sources required to develop the key strategies and tactics for building, executing and institutionalizing a strategic MO function. The activity is also a phenomenal exercise for involving key stakeholders and making them part of the upcoming change. The discovery process signals to the stakeholders that the role of MO is shifting.

During discovery, put on your consulting hat, and think like an unemotional third party. The process should be formal, not one drafted on the back of a napkin and executed carelessly. Discovery should be planned and coordinated, and allow for data-driven decisions regarding the future of MO.

To make it straightforward, I break the discovery process into eight different areas for MO. I'm listing them here; then in the following sections, I'll lay out details for each of these areas.

1. Company goals and initiatives
2. Marketing/MO goals and initiatives
3. The Marketing Operations Maturity (MOM) model—Where are you?
4. MarTech ecosystem
5. Marketing operations skills and talent assessment
6. Key stakeholder interviews
7. Challenges and accelerators
8. Metrics

AREAS 1 AND 2: COMPANY AND MARKETING/MO GOALS AND INITIATIVES

The first two items on the list are so interrelated that I'll discuss them together. Company and marketing goals and initiatives are foundational to what you will become as a strategic MO organization.

Understanding company goals and creating the case for how MO plays a role in achieving those goals are where it all begins. If you can't tie to a company strategic initiative or set of goals to demonstrate how strategic MO can better enable that effort, it will be challenging for you to mature. Most of the time, you can't grow a plant in sand; it needs fertile soil to flourish.

Marketing goals are next. They should be fully aligned to company goals and help drive achievement of those goals. If marketing goals and company goals are not aligned, MO cannot be successful. An

MO leader must understand this alignment and ensure its creation.

I find that when MO begins to mature as a capability, most marketing groups are relieved. They understand that with MO on their team, they have a much better chance at achieving goals that may feel out of reach. I share this observation because part of your discovery process may include helping marketing evolve in how they view themselves and how they align to company goals.

The deliverable from this part of the discovery process is an integrated set of initiatives and goals between marketing and the company that is shaped and enabled by MO. These initiatives and goals might be in terms of accelerating current actions or helping to drive something new. In addition, the role that MO plays in achieving company goals is highlighted, is shared and remains transparent to all key stakeholders. The important thing is that everyone comes to agreement on the goals and who is doing what.

AREA 3: THE MARKETING OPERATIONS MATURITY (MOM) MODEL

While you are still working at a fairly high level in the discovery process, take the time to assess where you are on the MOM model. (You can take the MO assessment here: www.pedowitzgroup.com/offers/marketing-operations-assessment.)

Are you in the early stage of efficient/effective? Are you in the middle of operationalizing the NextGen stage? Where you are today determines your starting point and predicates your journey. Using an easy, third-party assessment provides you with one more set of data to build your business case for change.

The deliverable from this part of the discovery process is an identification and description of where you are on a validated, third-party model. Carrying out this assessment helps you gain credibility.

AREA 4: MARTECH ECOSYSTEM

While the prior activities are high level and help you directionally, the martech assessment begins to get into the details—defining the backbone of your MO stack. Once you understand company and marketing goals, you can use that knowledge as the lens through which to review, evaluate, and remediate your current martech stack. Without this lens, you are reviewing tech and systems just for the sake of tech and systems—not for driving business results.

Understanding what you have, how it is used, the integration points, and the gaps is a big part of your discovery process. In many of the companies I work with, I find they have most of the actual technology they need. Yet they aren't optimizing what they have and ensuring that the technology has integrations to drive the right business results.

Fortunately, there are many ways to conduct a martech assessment. If you are part of a small company, you can gather this data based on what you know. For larger companies you can use surveys, one-on-one interviews or both.

Regardless of your approach, there are key questions to ask along the way. Here is a sample set of questions you might use to guide your own martech assessment in Figure 10.1:

CREATE A MARTECH CATALOG

SYSTEMS 101:

What systems do you have?

Who is using each one, why and how?

Who else could be using a system (anywhere in the company, not just in marketing)—for what and why?

How aware is everyone of all the tools available in the stack?

PLAYING NICELY TOGETHER:

What is the state of integrations?

What is the state of optimization for each system used?

What is the state of relevance (do you have the right tool for the job)?

DECISION-MAKING:

How are martech purchase decisions made?

DATA:

What is the state of your data?

How is data used, by whom and for what?

Where are the gaps?

COST STRUCTURE:

What are the martech costs?

Where are there system redundancies?

How effectively are the martech contracts managed?

How effectively are martech vendors managed?

ALIGNMENT TO GOALS:

How aligned is the martech ecosystem to goal and initiative attainment?

FIGURE 10.1

The deliverable of your martech assessment is a clear and communicable understanding of what you have to work with. You also should have a graphical rendering of your current and future martech stack. The deliverable is a key part of your road map for change.

AREA 5: MARKETING OPERATIONS SKILLS AND TALENT ASSESSMENT

Much like you need to do a systems and platforms assessment, you also must conduct a skills and talent inventory. After all, what's the good of trying to build a strategic MO organization if you don't have the right skills or can't get enough people to do the work? Quite often, a big part of the MO budget is designated for talent.

At this point, you just need to build a simple skills inventory. Use the MO Skills Chart, which is Figure 11.7 in the appendix, to help you baseline your current skillset. The exercise will help you assess what you already have in place.

The deliverable from this stage of discovery is a skills inventory document. The document outlines the current skill base you have today and the gaps you need to fill for the future.

AREA 6: KEY STAKEHOLDER INTERVIEWS

I recently worked with a company that was transitioning to have all campaigns built and executed in the new MO organization. During the key stakeholder interview process, MO leaders asked questions about challenges with the current campaign process. The answers gave them ideas for how to consolidate efforts in a way that would benefit every part of the organization.

The story reinforces the fact that one of the most vital parts of the discovery process is to interview key MO stakeholders both in marketing and outside of marketing. You can find out what they need and what they are not getting that you might be able to provide. In these interviews, you also begin to set the stage for change.

The deliverable from this discovery effort is a set of What's in It for Me (WIIFM) statements for each key stakeholder group. These statements are baked into your messaging about what you are changing in MO. The wording will help communicate how the change will benefit different constituents, which is essential to the communication plan.

AREA 7: CHALLENGES AND ACCELERATORS

I've always asked marketers about their challenges. They usually share a data dump. I have never trivialized this information: it is important to be very realistic about the challenges in transforming into a strategic MO organization.

However, in the past I always felt like something was missing, and it was the accelerators. If there were challenges that were getting in the way, surely there must be some accelerators that would speed things up. A few years ago, I began incorporating accelerators into my discussions. Accelerators are any key initiatives in the company that the MO team might associate with and, as a result, accelerate their journey to strategic MO.

An example might be when a company is pivoting from a product-first to a customer-first strategy. Strategic MO is often in a position to greatly influence this change, as they have a treasure trove of behavioral customer data and can get data more quickly using a variety of marketing tactics. The key to determining your accelerators is to simply look around your company for any key business initiative to which you might attach.

The deliverable from this stage of the discovery is a set of challenges you will need to tackle and a set of accelerators to which you might attach. The accelerators form a good part of the business case you are building for a strategic MO.

AREA 8: METRICS

Metrics flavor everything in marketing today. There are metrics a strategic MO group can drive that may be net-new to marketing, such as contribution to pipeline. There are also metrics that a strategic MO organization can use to benchmark their own journey, like the percent of integrations complete and optimized in the martech stack, or the number of key processes mapped and operationalized through systems and data. There is no favorite here—both types of metrics are important.

The deliverable from this stage of discovery includes metrics that matter to the business, such as pipeline contribution or a set of customer engagement metrics. They also include metrics for how the MO function is growing and improving.

CREATING A VISION, MISSION AND BRAND

Starting with your corporate vision and mission statements not only puts you on the right track; it also helps keep you there. A vision statement is an aspirational statement for what you want to become or what you want to affect. A mission statement is how you aim to get there. A brand identifies who you are and why you are better. All three are particularly important when you make big changes in MO—they become foundational to your stump speech and serve as a guiding light for your team.

I always suggest to an MO organization that wants to change and become more strategic to begin with a vision statement and a mission statement. After all, if you are not vividly clear on who you are, what you stand for and where you are going as an organization, neither will anyone else. You will continue to be viewed as the button pushers. For many MO teams, this exercise may feel out of their comfort level. However, I've seen this exercise make a huge impact on the team. They feel proud to be a part of something that has direction and meaning. They feel energized, motivated, and inspired. The exercise is essential to the rebranding of who you are as a team.

BRANDING

Your MO brand within your company must establish a significant and differentiated identity that attracts, aligns and retains your stakeholders. What is your brand right now? Is it the tech geeks, the marketing automation team or the button pushers? Using the vision and mission along with other elements included in change management, you have the opportunity to create your strategic MO brand.

A few years ago, I worked with a large financial services organization, and specifically with the marketing automation platform team. They were frustrated because they were seen as only campaign

> The reason for MO is to get marketing a seat at the table. In a lot of ways we're back to the three Ts of marketing (trinkets, trash and trade shows) and the sales team treating marketing like their admin assistants. Changing that perception to one of marketing can generate revenue, we can track performance, we can benchmark and we can improve. That's the mandate: to get marketing a seat at the table.
>
> **—ARON SWEENEY,** senior marketing manager at Genie

builders who did not add any strategic value. Because this group held an astounding amount of talent and knowledge around campaign best practices, we conducted a branding exercise to give them a new identity. We created a new name for the group, a charter and even an elevator pitch. We had every person on the team practice the elevator pitch and give it as many times possible during the next thirty days.

As part of the rebranding, we included the benefits to using the group as a best practices consultant for campaign performance. We set up monthly forums to highlight best practices and results. We even created a "Would you like fries with that?" type of upsell dialogue with groups using their services.

As a result of this rebranding, the team became actively engaged with multiple parts of the organization to help them develop best practices and improve campaign performance.

CHANGE MANAGEMENT

Change management is one of my favorite topics for two reasons. First, change management is necessary to become a strategic MO organization. Second, it is a straightforward and well-documented process—you just have to do it.

Let's begin with a definition: change management is a systematic approach to dealing with the transition or transformation of an organization's goals, processes or technologies, the discipline that guides how to prepare, equip and support individuals to successfully adopt change in order to drive organizational success and outcomes.[39]

It sounds pretty straightforward, but change management continues to be an afterthought, if a thought at all. Here is an example. In 2019 I attended a session at MarTech where the presenter discussed how she built an MO team from scratch. She expounded on all the elements of change management they used to ensure the success of the new organization. What struck me most about this talk was her emphasis on change management, not systems or data. I thought it was interesting that when building an MO team from scratch, change management was identified as a critical success factor, yet when transforming a current team, change management is often not on the menu.

For the MO organization in transition, change management has two primary elements: what to communicate and how to communicate. The *what* is a road map, and the *how* is a communications plan.

A ROAD MAP

To put substance behind the vision, you must have a road map. The road map includes a high-level view of how change will happen in stages and over time. The road map gives team members a sense of direction and a way to provide invaluable input on the journey. People can then feel like they are participating in the change. The road map is also your main document for communicating change in MO to every part of the organization.

I recently worked with a group that was just coming together as an MO team. They set their ninety-day goals and then proceeded to create a road map for the next twenty-four months. The road map included a list of required MO capabilities, roles, responsibilities, and technologies. They chose to measure progress in six-month increments against goals in each of these categories.

For example, one capability identified was data analytics. In the first stage of the road map, data analytics included analyzing campaign performance. In the second stage, it involved analyzing prospect and customer behavior specific to campaigns and to web visits. In the third stage, it included analyzing a larger set of customer data to help inform cross-sell and upsell opportunities. In the fourth and final stage, the capability evolved to providing customer insights to sales and executives.

For this company, given their resources and future goals, this road map made sense. Team members could use the road map to see the evolution of the data analysis capability and to participate in achieving the future vision. Rather than being exclusive and secret, it became inclusive and participative.

THE COMMUNICATION PLAN

Inherent in this discussion so far is the importance of communication to help drive change. The powerful change tactic involves building an intentional and multichannel communication plan that is based on individual stakeholder personas. If this sounds like how you build a campaign, that's because it is! Begin by identifying all the key stakeholders that will be affected by the change—both inside and outside of marketing. Then create value statements for each persona that you can use in messaging the change.

Consider, too, the channels of communication you will use. The channels can be internal company sites, email, company meetings, sales meetings or watercooler meetings. As much as possible, try to use your marketing automation system as one of your channels of communication so you can see and track engagement with your messages. Even though this change management tactic seems so practical, it is very underutilized by marketing.

Another way to reinforce change is to copy political campaign best practices. From a practical perspective, you should write a stump speech and then present it at every possible meeting and event.

A few years ago, I worked with a technology company that had a marketing team that was experiencing tremendous change. To help inform this large company of all the changes, we actually wrote a positioning paper and created a stump speech. We made a slide deck so others could articulate the vision and produced a video of the slide deck.

We created messaging for each stakeholder group and then identified all the communication channels most effective for the delivery of the message. We also identified peer influencers and had them help spread the message. Promoting the change this way helped both the marketing teams and other groups affected by the change more readily engage, work with and validate the changes.

I have worked with several organizations that have assigned a change management role to marketing transformation. I really like this role, as they are the one proactively looking at how to manage and communicate change to all affected parties. Having this role in place highlights the importance of revamping MO. The role also sets the tone for organizational support.

TRAINING

I recently consulted for a US-based company that was moving to a new organizational structure in marketing. They were doing this so they could better implement the Agile methodology. The initiative took place company-wide, and marketing was struggling to execute the move. While the reporting structure remained similar, the work structure was becoming very different.

To address this huge change, this company created a series of "A Day in the Life" scenarios for the broad marketing teams. They also made more specific "A Day in the Life" scenarios for specialized teams. Everyone was required to go through the scenarios, take a series of tests, and get certified in the new work approach. While it was difficult to make the time for this training, the end results were twofold: improved cross-functional team interactions and higher productivity.

The point is, don't forget about training—not just on technology, but in other softer areas around change. For your company, that might be improved communication skills, how to work on a cross-functional team, or how to act like a consultant to other parts of the business.

Change is no longer a dirty word for marketers and is now becoming a more common capability. By taking a practical approach to change by being intentional about change, and by learning a few techniques, marketers are driving change in new ways in their organizations.

Don't let change happen to you. Take control and make it happen.

BON VOYAGE

In the foreword of this book, Scott Brinker wrote, "Let's face it: marketing operations has been the island of misfit toys." His words are true. The less-than-flattering perception combined with the unleashed potential of marketing operations inspired me to write this book. I wanted a book that provided frustrated marketers with inspiration, a vision for what can be, the value of a new approach and a practical path forward to becoming a strategic marketing operations organization. I wanted a book that highlighted the role of strategic marketing operations as a game changer. I wanted a book that provided guidance on how to move from the backroom to the boardroom.

As a forward-thinking and acting marketing leader, it is now up to you to take the ideas, models, charts, stories, and best practices presented in this book and use them to plot your journey. You can use this to help accelerate your current journey or to begin your journey for the first time. Now you have the framework, and it's time to put strategy into action. Is it hard? Yes. Does it happen overnight? No. Is it worth it? Absolutely.

CHAPTER SUMMARY
A QUICK GLANCE AT WHAT WE LEARNED

- There are steps you can take right away to start building a strategic MO function.

- Carrying out a discovery process will help you evaluate your current position.

- Developing a vision/mission/brand begins the change process required for transformation.

- Change management has two elements: the MO road map details what you communicate, and the communications plan dictates how you communicate.

- Training is key when implementing changes and often covers areas like technology and communication.

- Now that you have the framework to build a strategic MO organization, it's time to put these steps into action!

APPENDIX

SIX BEHAVIORS FOR THE SUCCESSFUL STRATEGIC MARKETING OPERATIONS LEADER

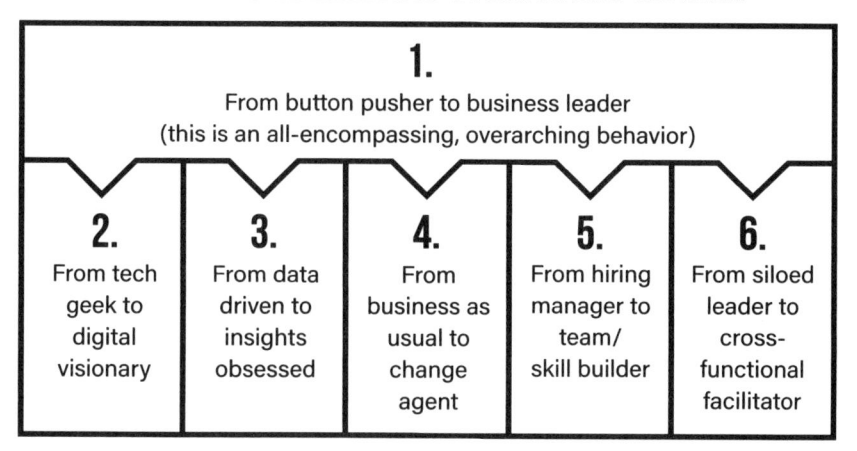

1. From button pusher to business leader (this is an all-encompassing, overarching behavior)				
2. From tech geek to digital visionary	3. From data driven to insights obsessed	4. From business as usual to change agent	5. From hiring manager to team/ skill builder	6. From siloed leader to cross-functional facilitator

FIGURE 1.1

THREE CMO CHALLENGES

FIGURE 2.1

269

14 FORWARD-LOOKING STRATEGIES FOR HOW FUTURE B2B CMOS MIGHT ADOPT FINANCIAL ACCOUNTABILITY

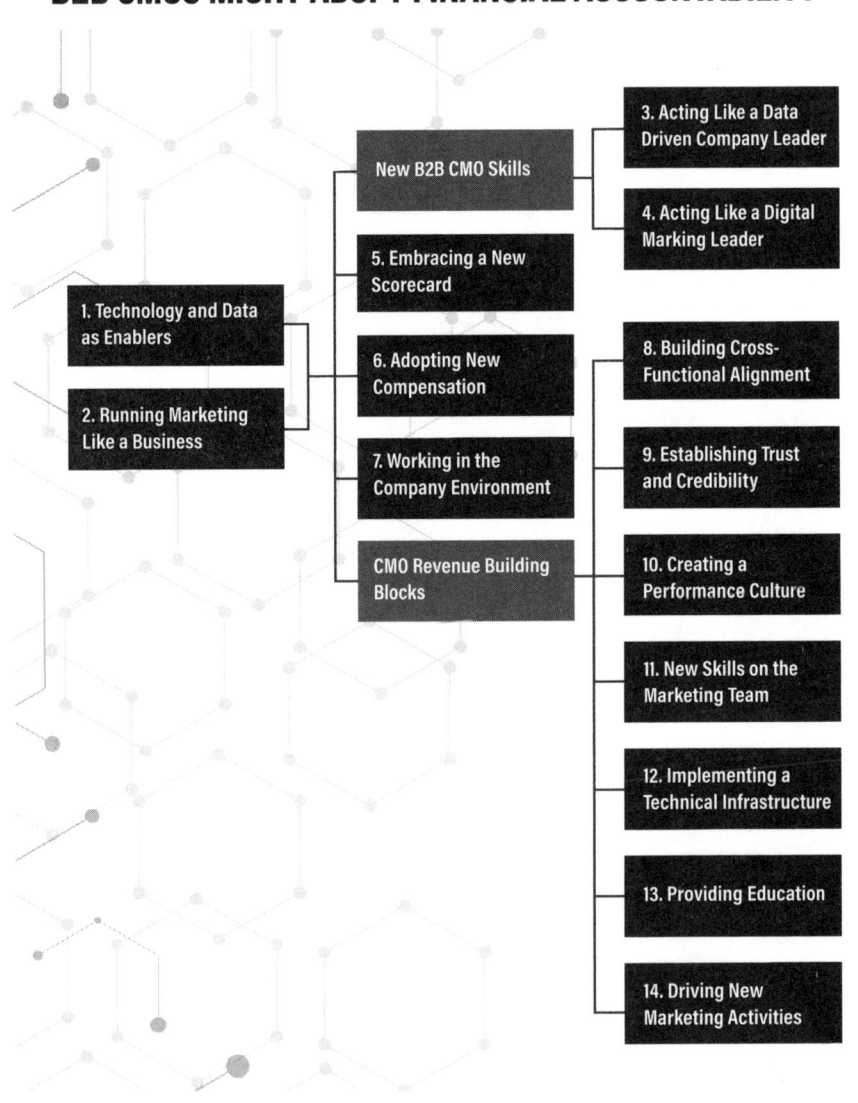

- 1. Technology and Data as Enablers
- 2. Running Marketing Like a Business
  - New B2B CMO Skills
    - 3. Acting Like a Data Driven Company Leader
    - 4. Acting Like a Digital Marking Leader
  - 5. Embracing a New Scorecard
  - 6. Adopting New Compensation
  - 7. Working in the Company Environment
  - CMO Revenue Building Blocks
    - 8. Building Cross-Functional Alignment
    - 9. Establishing Trust and Credibility
    - 10. Creating a Performance Culture
    - 11. New Skills on the Marketing Team
    - 12. Implementing a Technical Infrastructure
    - 13. Providing Education
    - 14. Driving New Marketing Activities

FIGURE 2.2

APPENDIX

A DECADE OF GROWTH:
TIMETABLE OUTLINING THE EVOLUTION OF MARTECH AND MARKETING OPERATIONS

- 2011 — ~150 Solutions
- 2012 — ~350 Solutions
- 2014 — ~1,000 Solutions
- 2015 — ~2,000 Solutions
- 2016 — ~3,500 Solutions
- 2017 — ~5,000 Solutions
- 2018 — ~6,800 Solutions
- 2019 — ~7,000 Solutions
- 2020 — ~8,000 Solutions

REACTIVE: 2011–2012
PROACTIVE, DECENTRALIZED: 2014–2015
PROACTIVE, CENTRALIZED: 2016–2017
STRATEGIC: 2018–2020

FIGURE 3.1

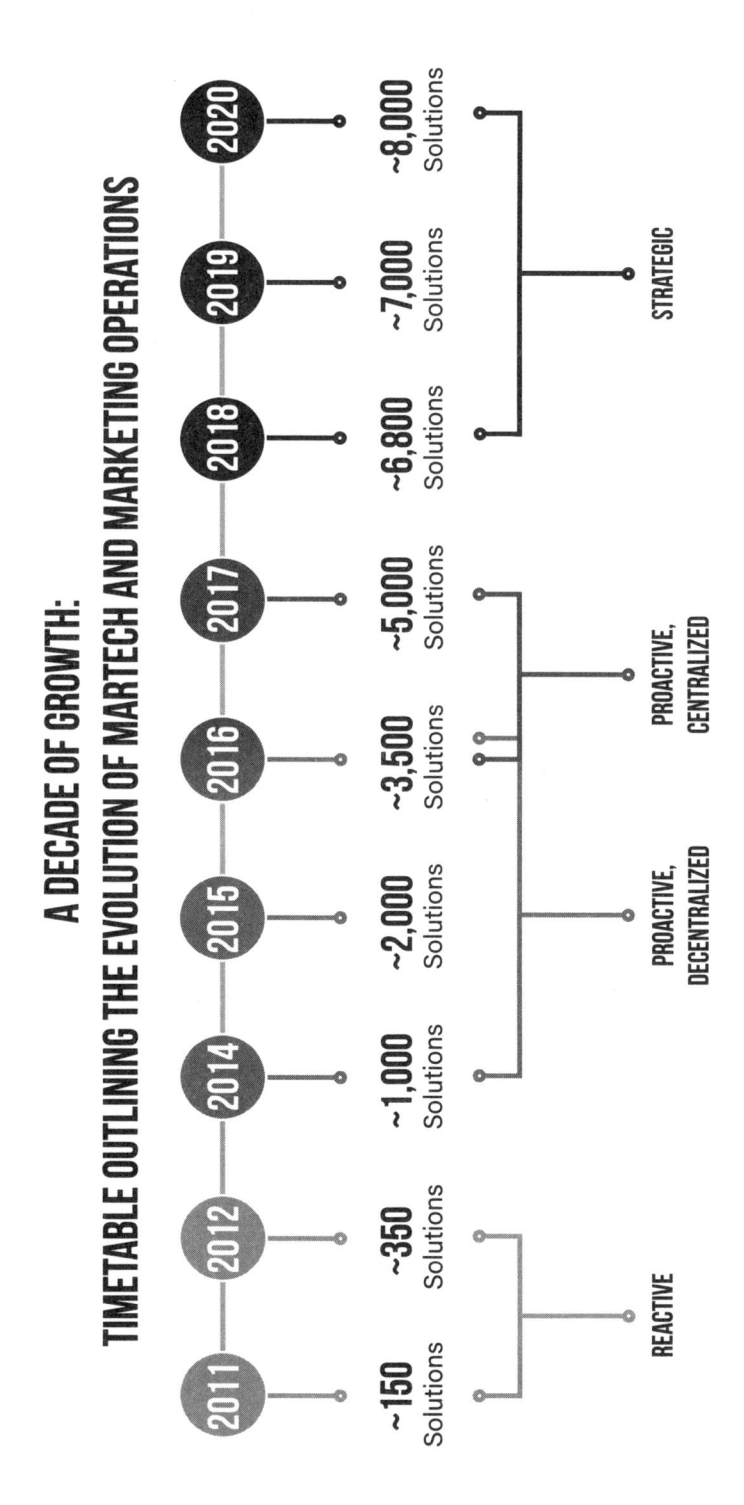

271

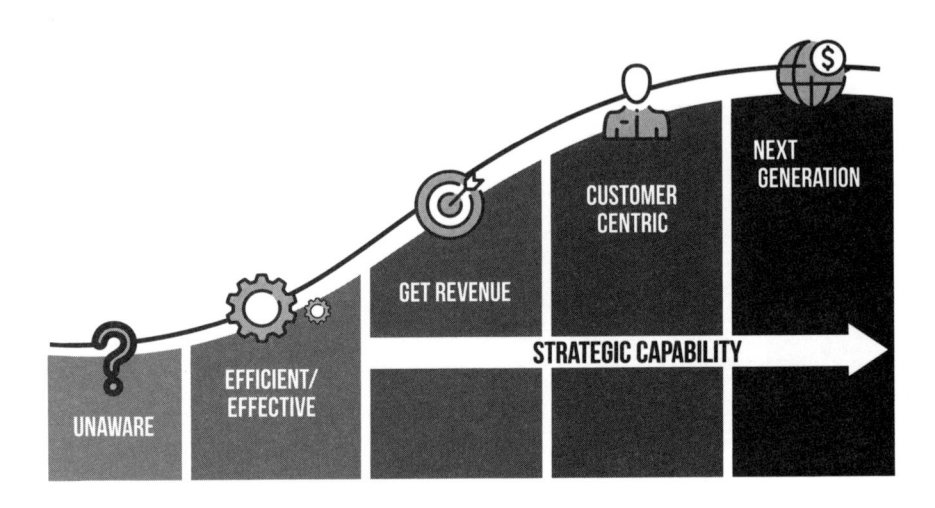

FIGURE 3.2

APPENDIX

MARKETING OPERATIONS SKILLS CHART

INTERPRET AND DRIVE BUSINESS GOALS

TECHNOLOGY, DATA & ANALYTICS

MarTech Stack
- Cross-Functional Strategy
- Cross-Functional Road map
- Vision
- Interpreter
- Selection
- Integration
- Optimization
- Manage
- Infrastructure
- Admin
- Vendor Management
- Scanning

Data
- Cross-Functional Strategy
- Cross-Functional Road map
- Strategy
- Governance
- Insights
- Quality
- Cleanliness
- Optimization
- DB Management
- Data Management
- Predictive
- Warehouse
- BI

Performance Management
- Reporting
- Analytics
- Insights
- Metrics & KPIs
- Dashboards
- Funnel Management
- Operational Insights
- Customer Intelligence

PROCESS ENGINEERING

Across Functions
- Funnel Management
- Lead Management
- Lead Life Cycle
- Lead Conversion
- Customer Buyer Journey
- Personas
- Campaign Operations
- Segmentation
- Content Operations
- Shared Services Ops
- Ticketing System
- Insights
- Optimization
- Consulting
- Best Practices
- Performance Management

PROJECT MANAGEMENT & TRAINING

Project Management & Budget
- Professional Project Management
- Budget & Budget Tracking
- Financial Compliance

Training and Education
- Training on New Systems
- Training on New Processes
- Training on Marketing Operations Skills
- Marketing Enablement in Tech and Data

CHANGE MANAGEMENT & CUSTOMER INSIGHTS

Across Functions
- Change Agent
- Visionary
- Strategy to Action
- Collaboration, Communication & Influence with Key Stakeholders
- Empower Accountability
- Dive innovation
- Create Actionable Customer Insights for All Key Stakeholders

FIGURE 4.1

FROM BACKROOM TO BOARDROOM

SAMPLE MARTECH ROAD MAP

PHASE 1 — MONTHS 1-3

PHASE 1

UP-LEVEL INFRASTRUCTURE AND MARKETING OPERATIONS CAPABILITIES

Marketing Operations - Tech
- Across functions, consolidate overlapping functionality in data analytics and management.
- Audit and remediate Marketo Engage/SFDC integration deficiencies to amplify lead management.
- Implement Jira for ticketing system.

Marketing Operations - Process
- Up-Level the Marketing Operations function that meets current needs.
- Design processes for development of content and campaign execution including all relevant engagement channels.
- Create intake process for shared services for campaign building and execution.
- Collaborate and build Personas and Customer Journeys for new market.

PHASE 2 — MONTHS 4-6

PHASE 2

SCALE CONTENT AND CAMPAIGNS TO OPTIMIZE NEW CUSTOMER INTERACTIONS

Marketing Operations - Tech
- Implement web personalization in CMS.
- Expand email personalization in MAP.
- Consistent utilization of A/B testing in MAP to optimize email engagement.
- Evaluate additional platforms for web personalization, video engagement and chat capabilities.

Marketing Operations - Data and Analytics
- Enable a centralized customer data repository.
- Identify and adopt a middleware for data integrations in support of segmentation, personalization and data analytics.
- Ongoing maintenance of data architecture and data quality.
- Development of standard dashboards for Operational, Management and Executive reporting.
- Consider implementing Data Science capabilities.

PHASE 3 — MONTHS 7-9

PHASE 3

GET REVENUE

Marketing Operations - Technology
- Identify and evaluate additional platforms or services to meet evolving business demands.
- Optimize what you have.

Marketing Operations - Process
- Optimize lead scoring.
- Optimize lead management.
- Empower ownership of platforms and responsibility for documentation and enhancements to continue to meet changing demands of the business.
- Develop internal processes using resourcing platform to better predict realistic project timelines and resource allocation and increase campaign creation velocity.

Marketing Operations - Data and Analytics
- Improve adoption of Domo or select and implement an alternative platform for data visualization and self-serve data analytics.
- Continue improving integrations to enable a better 360-degree view of customers and prospects.

FIGURE 4.2

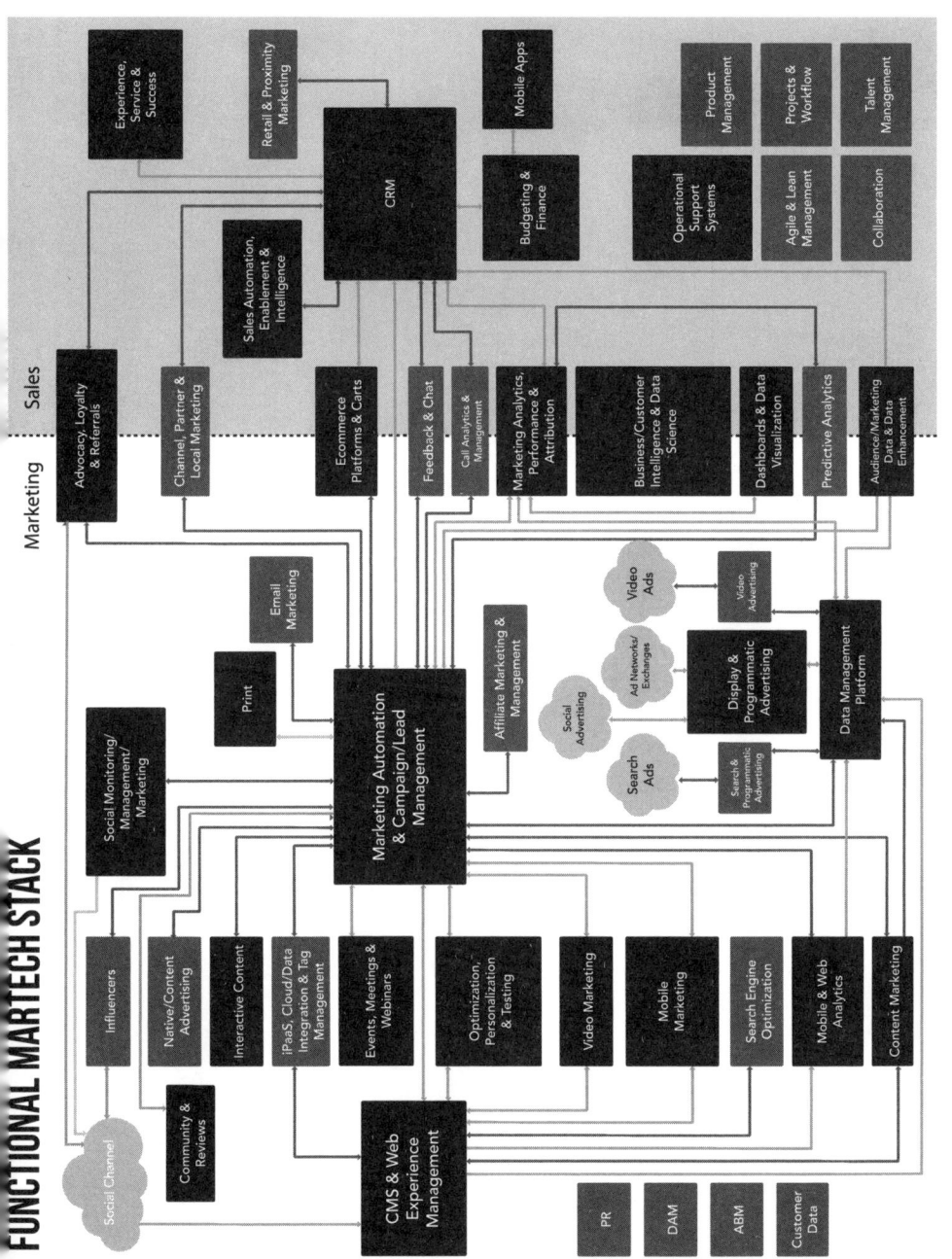

APPENDIX

FIGURE 4.3

THE REVENUE MANAGEMENT FRAMEWORK

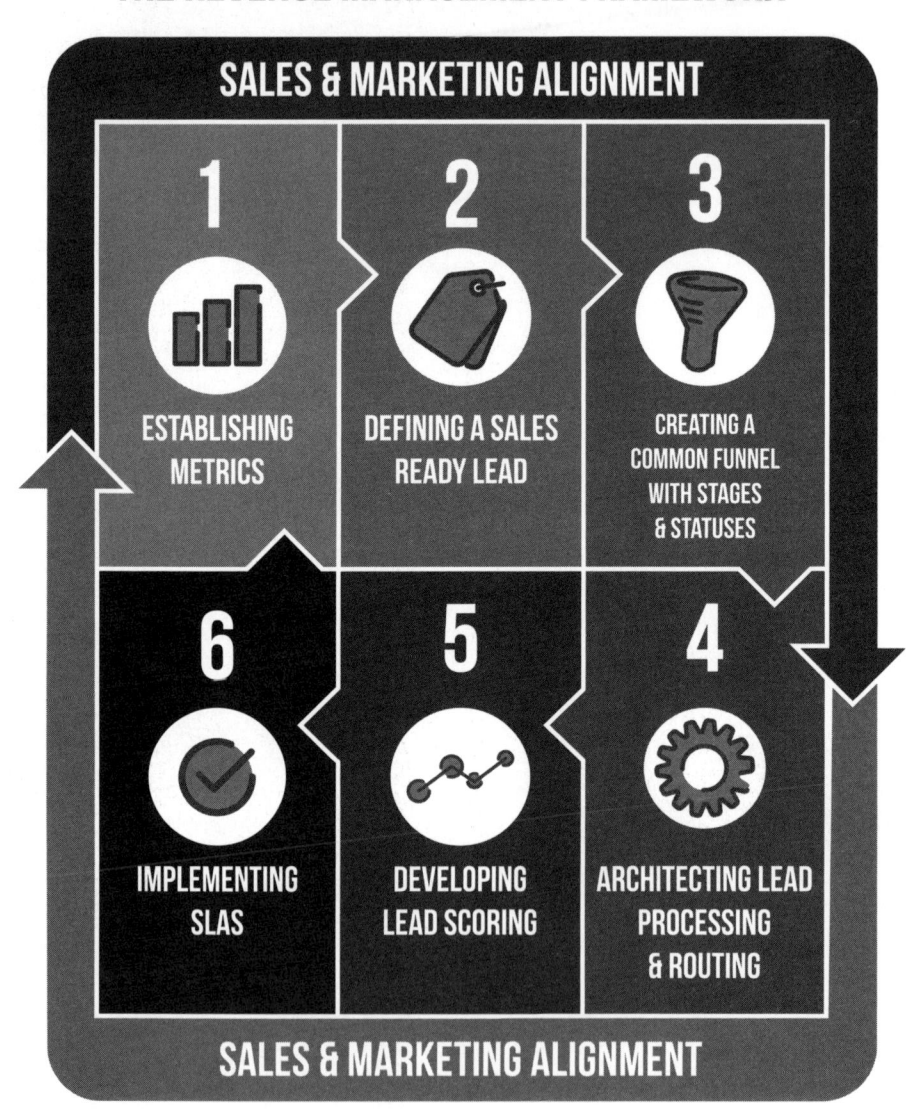

SALES & MARKETING ALIGNMENT

1. ESTABLISHING METRICS
2. DEFINING A SALES READY LEAD
3. CREATING A COMMON FUNNEL WITH STAGES & STATUSES
4. ARCHITECTING LEAD PROCESSING & ROUTING
5. DEVELOPING LEAD SCORING
6. IMPLEMENTING SLAS

SALES & MARKETING ALIGNMENT

FIGURE 5.1

THE CUSTOMER PYRAMID MODEL

CHANGE YOUR MINDSET

STEPPING UP: LEADING CUSTOMER CENTRICITY

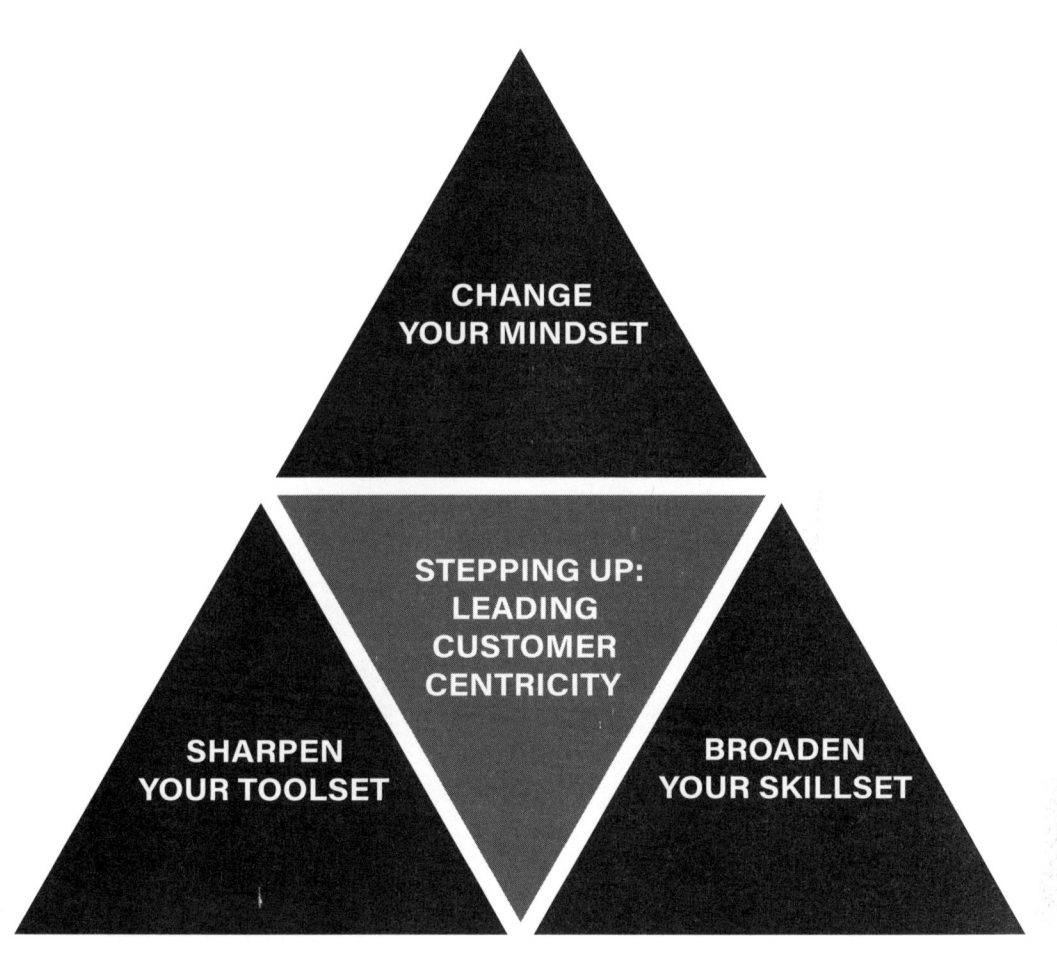

SHARPEN YOUR TOOLSET

BROADEN YOUR SKILLSET

FIGURE 6.1

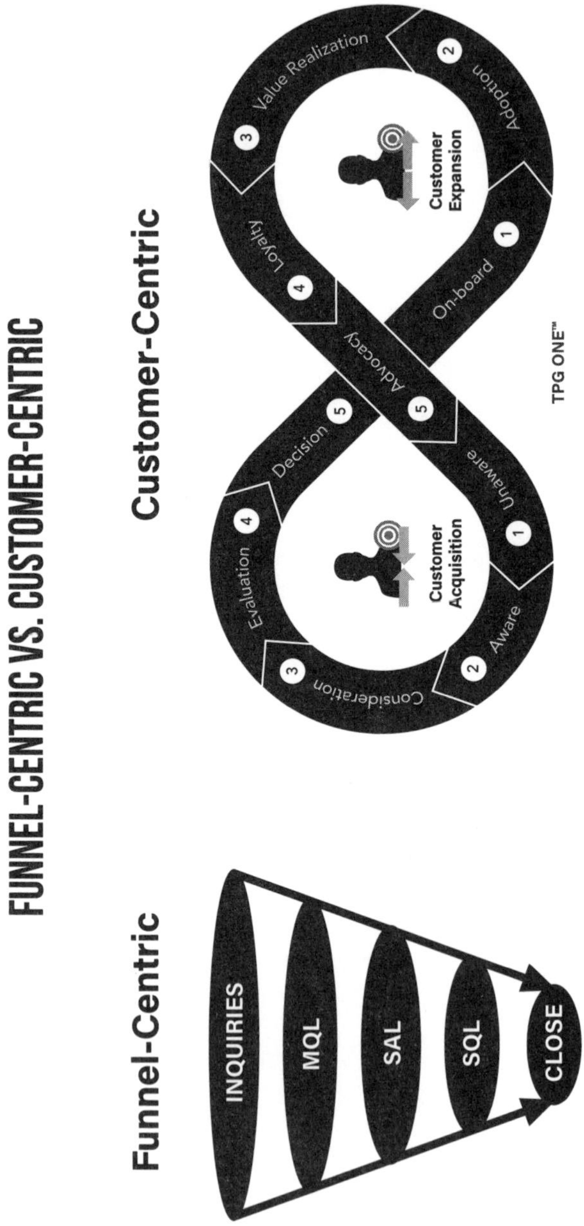

FROM BACKROOM TO BOARDROOM

FUNNEL-CENTRIC VS. CUSTOMER-CENTRIC

Customer-Centric

Customer Expansion
- 1 On-board
- 2 Adoption
- 3 Value Realization
- 4 Loyalty
- 5 Advocacy

Customer Acquisition
- 1 Unaware
- 2 Aware
- 3 Consideration
- 4 Evaluation
- 5 Decision

TPG ONE™

Funnel-Centric

- INQUIRIES
- MQL
- SAL
- SQL
- CLOSE

FIGURE 6.2

APPENDIX

CUSTOMER-CENTRIC MARTECH STACK

FIGURE 6.3

CREATE A MARTECH CATALOG

SYSTEMS 101:

What systems do you have?

Who is using each one, why, and how?

Who else could be using a system (anywhere in the company, not just in marketing)—for what and why?

How aware is everyone of all the tools available in the stack?

PLAYING NICELY TOGETHER:

What is the state of integrations?

What is the state of optimization for each system used?

What is the state of relevance (do you have the right tool for the job)?

DECISION-MAKING:

How are martech purchase decisions made?

DATA:

What is the state of your data?

How is data used, by whom and for what?

Where are the gaps?

COST STRUCTURE:

What are the martech costs?

Where are there system redundancies?

How effectively are the martech contracts managed?

How effectively are martech vendors managed?

ALIGNMENT TO GOALS:

How aligned is the martech ecosystem to goal and initiative attainment?

FIGURE 10.1

APPENDIX

INTERVIEWEES WITH ADVANCED DEGREES

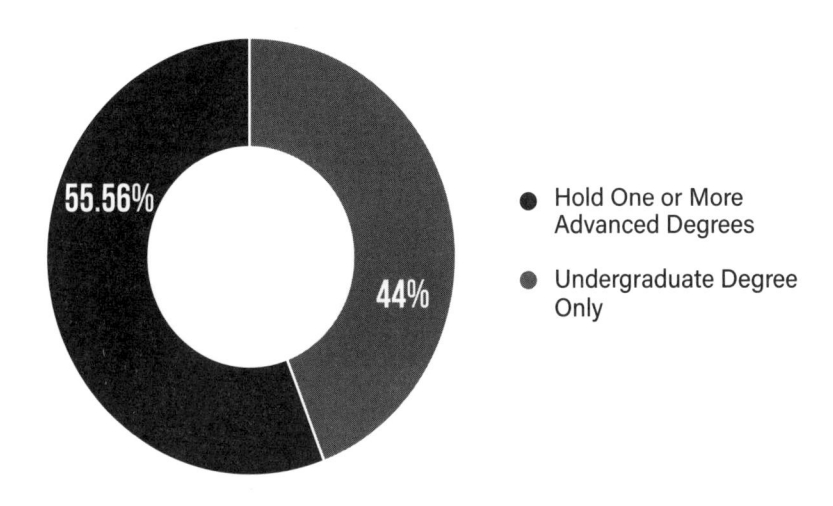

55.56% — Hold One or More Advanced Degrees
44% — Undergraduate Degree Only

FIGURE 11.1

DEGREES HELD BY INTERVIEWEES

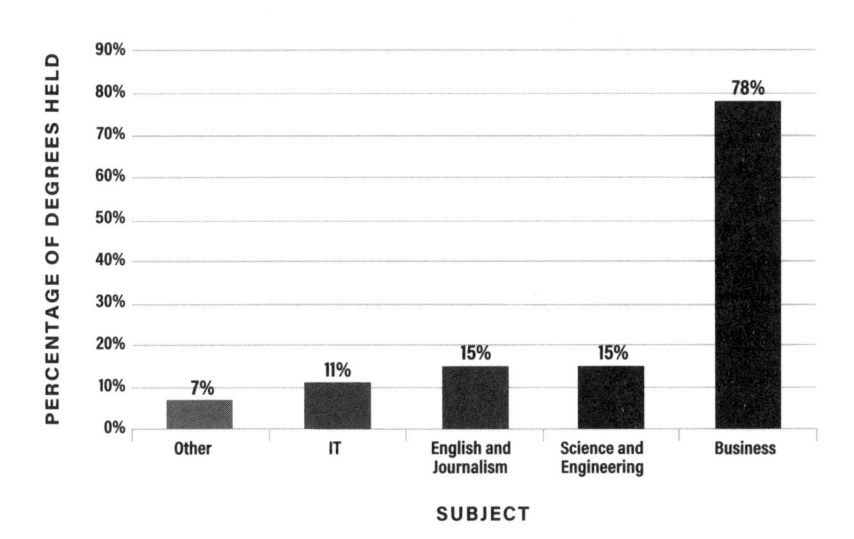

Subject	Percentage
Other	7%
IT	11%
English and Journalism	15%
Science and Engineering	15%
Business	78%

FIGURE 11.2

281

BUSINESS EXPERTISE, BY DEGREE

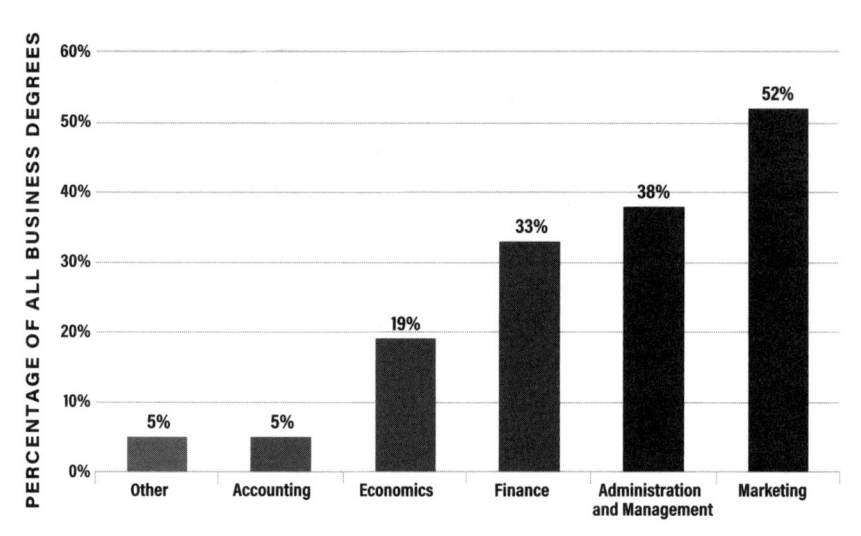

Subject	Percentage of All Business Degrees
Other	5%
Accounting	5%
Economics	19%
Finance	33%
Administration and Management	38%
Marketing	52%

FIGURE 11.3

AREAS OF WORK EXPERIENCE

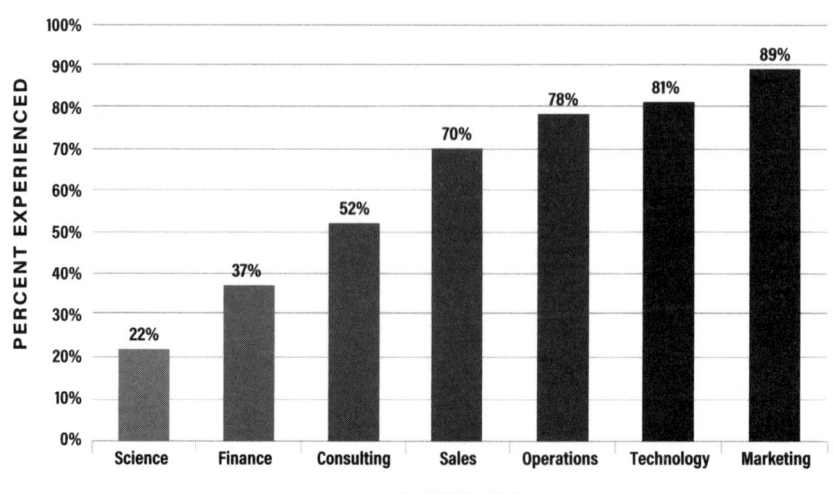

Discipline	Percent Experienced
Science	22%
Finance	37%
Consulting	52%
Sales	70%
Operations	78%
Technology	81%
Marketing	89%

FIGURE 11.4

APPENDIX

THE REVENUE MARKETING™ JOURNEY

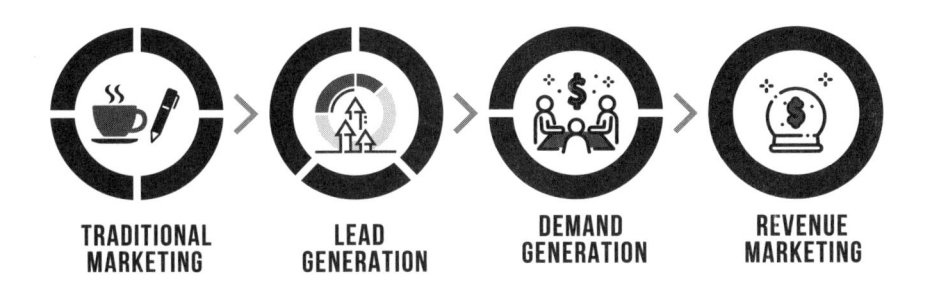

TRADITIONAL MARKETING > LEAD GENERATION > DEMAND GENERATION > REVENUE MARKETING

FIGURE 11.5

MOM MODEL CHARACTERISTICS BY STAGE

This model is additive. Each next stage adds new characteristics and retains all the prior positive characteristics.

MOM Stages of Maturity	1. Unaware	2a. Efficient—Doing things well	2b. Effective—Doing the right things	3. Get Revenue	4. Customer	5. Next Gen
Charter	No charter	To begin digitally transforming marketing by selecting, implementing, integrating and optimizing various marketing technologies. It is also important at this stage to introduce an analytics and data capability into the marketing organization.	To digitally transform marketing by marrying process and technology to improve the efficiency and effectiveness of marketing operations. Essential to this part of digital transformation is reengineering core marketing processes that enable marketing to obtain stated goals.	With digital transformation as the baseline, to enable marketing to hit the revenue number through process, technology and analytics.	With digital transformation as the foundation, to enable marketing to hit the revenue number by adding a strong customer capability requiring focus, understanding, customer data, customer metrics and customer analytics.	With digital transformation as the foundation, to build a unified operational capability that improves revenue performance through one line of sight to the customer.
Strategy	Marketing is a cost center. Reactive to marketing needs.	Marketing is a cost center. Reactive to marketing needs.	Marketing is a cost center. Reactive to marketing needs.	Marketing is a revenue center. Proactive to marketing driving revenue and needs of the business.	Marketing knows the customer better than anyone. Owns the customer journey. Proactive in understanding the customer and applying to needs of the business.	Everything is consolidated. One line of sight to revenue and customer. Owns a number and the customer journey. Proactive
Focus	Focus on marketing (internal)	Focus on marketing (internal)	Focus on marketing (internal)	Cross-functional focus (internal and external)	Cross-functional focus (internal and external)	Cross-functional focus (internal and external)
Structure	Traditional marketing structure	Dedicated structure for MO	Dedicated structure for MO	Dedicated structure for MO in marketing, collaborative cross-functional structure	Dedicated structure in marketing, collaborative cross functional structure	New consolidated operational org structure, new executive reporting structure. Beginning of Revenue Operations
Reporting	Reports to traditional CMO	Reports to Operational CMO	Reports to Operational CMO	Reports to CMO with a quota	Reports to CMO who may also be the CCO	Reports to head of operations or sales

	Traditional marketers	Adding analytical & technical folks to the team	Adding process folks to the team that can marry process and technology	Adding revenue marketers to the team	Adding customer czars to the team	Combining all with heavy analytics and insights
People						
Process	Poor	Tech processes	Marketing processes	Revenue processes, mostly for new acquisition	Customer processes across the entire customer life cycle	All processes with a focus on revenue processes (precursor to revenue operations)
Tech	ad hoc	Build foundation	Marry marketing processes and technology	Marry tech and revenue processes, across sales and marketing	Marry tech and customer processes, across customer facing functions	Consolidated stack under one owner
		Do things well				
Data	ad hoc	Begin to use data in using tech	Begin using data for improving marketing processes and performance	Revenue decisions	Customer journey data	One view of data
			Begin to make data-driven decisions	Data-driven decision making		
				Some actionable customer intelligence for sales and marketing	Actionable customer intelligence for sales and marketing	Actionable customer intelligence for all parts of the company
Customer - *Company Approach*	Company is product focused	Company is product focused	Company is product focused	Company is product or customer focused	Company is customer focused	Company is customer focused
Marketing Knowledge	Marketing does not know the customer	Marketing does not know the customer	Marketing does not know the customer	Marketing beginning to know the customer, uses data to learn and improvise campaigns to drive revenue	Marketing knows the customer better than anyone, uses and provides actionable customer insights to all functions	Org knows the customer better than anyone, uses and provides actionable customer insights to all functions
Measures	Activity based	Operational	Operational	Revenue	Customer	All: operational, revenue and customer
		Bits and bytes	Process improvement	Demand generation	Customer journey	A growth engine

FIGURE 11.6

ENDNOTES

1 "COVID-19 Digital Engagement Report." Twillio, accessed October 6, 2020. https://pages.twilio.com/rs/294-TKB-300/images/Twilios-Covid-19-Digital_Engagement_Report_4832.pdf.

2 "COVID-19 Digital Engagement Report."

3 Qaqish, Debbie. "A Modified Delphi Study: Forward-Looking Strategies for Chief Marketing Officer Accountability in a Digital Environment." PhD diss., University of Phoenix, 2018.

4 Moorman, Christine. "CMO Survey Report: Highlights and Insights." CMOsurvey.org, 2016. https://faculty.fuqua.duke.edu/cmosurveyresults/The_CMO_Survey-Highlights_and_Insights-Feb-2016.pdf. p. 34.

5 Qaqish, Debbie. "A Modified Delphi Study."

6 Abramovich, Giselle. "15 Mind-Blowing Stats about Digital Transformation." CMO by Adobe, March 23, 2015. https://www.cmo.com/features/articles/2015/3/23/mind-blowing-stats-digital-transformation.html#gs.RHD5n2A. p. 36.

7 Abramovich, Giselle. "15 Mind-Blowing Stats about Digital Transformation."

8 "COVID-19 Digital Engagement Report."

9 "COVID-19 Digital Engagement Report."

10 Moorman, Christine. "CMO Survey Report: Highlights and Insights."

11 Genesys. 3 Strategies to Improve the Customer *Experience*. Daly City, CA: Genesys, 2014. https://genbin.genesys.com/old/resources/3Strategies_improve_CX_EB06022014_screen_(1).pdf. p. 37.

12 "Covid-19 and the State of Marketing." The CMO Survey, June 2020. Accessed October 13, 2020, https://cmosurvey.org/wp-content/uploads/2020/06/The_CMO_Survey-Highlights-and_Insights_Report-June-2020.pdf

13 "Covid-19 and the State of Marketing."

14 Qaqish, Debbie. "A Modified Delphi Study."

15 Qaqish, Debbie. "A Modified Delphi Study."

16 Qaqish, Debbie. "A Modified Delphi Study."

17 Qaqish, Debbie. "A Modified Delphi Study."

18 Qaqish, Debbie. "A Modified Delphi Study."

19 Qaqish, Debbie. "A Modified Delphi Study."

20 Qaqish, Debbie. "A Modified Delphi Study."

21 Qaqish, Debbie. "A Modified Delphi Study."

22 Qaqish, Debbie. "A Modified Delphi Study."

23 Soforman, Jake. "Yes, CMOs Will Likely Spend More than CIOs by 2017." Gartner, 2016. Accessed October 27, 2020. https://blogs.gartner.com/jake-sorofman/yes-cmos-will-likely-spend-more-on-technology-than-cios-by-2017/.

ENDNOTES

24 Blum, Kelly. "Gartner Says Marketers Utilize Only 58% of Their Martech Stack's Potential." Gartner, November 18, 2019. https://www.gartner.com/en/newsroom/press-releases/2019-11-18-gartner-says-marketers-utilize-only-58--of-their-mart#:~:text=Marketing%20leaders

25 Qaqish, Debbie. "A Modified Delphi Study," 191. p. 71.

26 Zoominfo. "20 Sales and Marketing Alignment Statistics." Zoominfo blog. May 19, 2017. Accessed November 4, 2020. https://blog.zoominfo.com/sales-and-marketing-alignment-statistics/.

27 DMI Blog. "Missing the Mark: The Digital Marketing Skills Gap." Digital Marketing Institute, accessed September 30, 2020. https://digitalmarketinginstitute.com/blog/missing-the-mark-the-digital-marketing-skills-gap-in-the-usa-uk-ireland.

28 DMI Blog. "Missing the Mark: The Digital Marketing Skills Gap."

29 "The Ultimate List of Millennial Characteristics." Lucky Attitude, updated May 11, 2018. http://luckyattitude.co.uk/millennial-characteristics/#. p. 195.

30 PwC Global People and Organization. "Workforce of the Future." PwC Network, accessed June 9, 2020. https://www.pwc.com/gx/en/services/people-organisation/publications/workforce-of-the-future.html. p. 195.

31 DMI Blog, "Missing the Mark: The Digital Marketing Skills Gap."

32 Blum, Kelly. "Gartner Says Marketers Utilize Only 58% of Their Martech Stack's Potential." p. 191.

33 Panetta, Kasey. "How to Create an Effective Customer Journey Map." Gartner, June 10, 2019. https://www.gartner.com/en/marketing/insights/articles/how-to-create-an-effective-customer-Journey-map. p. 191.

34 NewsCred. "The Impact of COVID-19 on Marketing Teams." NewsCred Insights, accessed September 25, 2020. https://insights.newscred.com/impact-of-coronavirus-on-marketing-teams/.

35 "Covid-19 and the State of Marketing."

36 Skripak, Stephen J. "Preface: Teamwork in Business." From *Fundamentals of Business*. Pamplin College of Business and Virginia Tech Libraries. July 2016. p. 200.

37 Kleiman, Jessica. "How Multitasking Hurts Your Brain (and Your Effectiveness at Work)." *Forbes*, January 15, 2013. https://www.forbes.com/sites/work-in-progress/2013/01/15/how-multitasking-hurts-your-brain-and-your-effectiveness-at-work/#491862851013. p. 202.

38 Allocadia, 2017. "Marketing Performance Management Maturity Study: Original Research Benchmarking How Companies Run the Business of Marketing." https://www.allocadia.com/wp-content/uploads/2019/04/All-MarketingMaturityReport-2019.pdf?x29788. p. 226.

39 SMARP, "Change Management: Definition, Best Practices & Examples." April 16, 2020. https://blog.smarp.com/change-management-definition-best-practices-examples.